To Peter,

A very Happy _n Birthday

With much love,

Nikki & Bongy . X .

Classic Car Profiles

Volume 1

First published 1987

© Anthony Bird, James Leech, George A.
Oliver, Walter Wright, William Boddy,
Gordon C. Davies, John Appleton, A.S.
Murray, Kenneth Rush, T.R. Nicholson, J.
Dunscombe, Denis Jenkinson, Charles L.
Betts Jr., Godfrey Eaton, Keith Davey, A
Pritchard, Queens Park Villa Ltd, J.H.
Haynes & Co Ltd.

A FOULIS Book

Published by:
Haynes Publishing Group
Sparkford, Nr Yeovil, Somerset BA22 7JJ.
England

Haynes Publications Inc.
861 Lawrence Drive, Newbury Park.
California 91320 USA

British Library Cataloguing in publication data
Classic car profile.
  Vol. 1
   1. Automobiles—History
  629.2'222.09   TL15
  ISBN 0-85429-650-6

Library of Congress catalog card number 87-80608

Printed in England by:
J.H. Haynes & Co. Ltd.

Contents

Foreword

I was particularly pleased to hear that G T Foulis & Co had decided to publish a set of volumes comprising the 108 car profiles originally produced by Profile Publications Ltd. When first published many years ago they soon became extremely popular and nowadays are much sought after as rare collector's items.

The subject of each profile was selected for any number of reasons, it could be the fastest or the most flamboyant, the most complicated or the most rare, the most conventional or just because it was a milestone in the history of the motor car.

Each is written by a recognised authority and provides a comprehensive cameo of the history and development and much other detail. There are rare or unique black and white illustrations supported by specially commissioned scale drawings giving end views and side elevations in full colour.

Welcome back to this collection which will provide a wealth of information on such a wide range of memorable motor vehicles.

Kenneth Ball
Ditchling
Sussex

The G.P. 1908 & 1914 Mercedes

1

Mercedes

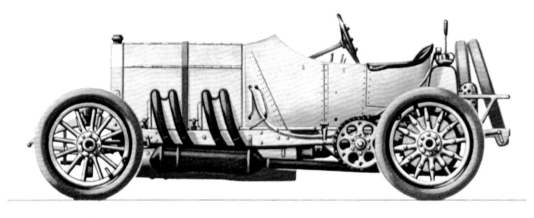

MERCEDES—as painted on the scuttle of Willy Poege's car, No. 2, for the 1908 Grand Prix.

THE 12·8-LITRE MERCEDES, winner of the 1908 Grand Prix at Dieppe. Average speed: 69 m.p.h. for 477 miles. Driver: Christian Lautenschlager.

0   5'

The 1908 & 1914 G.P. Mercedes

by Anthony Bird

1914 French Grand Prix at Lyons: Otto Salzer's car.

In the first years of the century racing car engines were composed of air and optimism encased in the least possible thickness of metal; that is, their designers were concerned primarily with making very large engines of the least possible weight rather than with increasing specific output. From this it has been argued that these designers were at best lazy and at worst inept, and that the ingenuity (possibly misplaced) of the engineer who could make a car of 13½ litres capacity (70 h.p. Panhard, 1902) fit into the 1,000 kg. weight limit was equalled only by the temerity of the man who could conduct such a monster over the roads of the period at speeds up to 90 m.p.h.

In fairness, however, it must be said, in view of the manufacturing techniques and materials available, that the designers were justified at first in concentrating on sheer size and weight-saving rather than in breaking new ground and increasing volumetric efficiency by raising crankshaft speeds and compression ratios. Indeed, on the evidence of their performances the 'monster' racing cars must have been considerably more efficient and less lethal than they appear, and as the designs permitted the use of relatively 'soft' springs neither the drivers nor the machinery suffered so much from rough surfaces as one might suppose.

By virtue of their lower build and the neat appearance of their honeycomb radiators, the earliest Mercedes cars looked much less clumsy and monstrous than their contemporaries. It has been an article of faith for many years that the first Mercedes of 1901 was completely new and revolutionary, but this is not so. In meeting Emile Jellinek's demand for a more docile and manageable successor to the 1899 24 h.p. Cannstatt-Daimler racing car, Wilhelm Maybach's particular genius was directed to refining and improving the old car without sacrificing its most successful features. Thus, many of the 'new' features of the Mercedes such as the steel frame, the selective

Photographs: Courtesy Daimler-Benz A.G.

(or 'gate-change') gear control, the low-tension magneto ignition and the famous honeycomb radiator were not new at all but had already been proved on the earlier models. In subsequent designs the Daimler Motoren Gesellschaft made numerous innovations, but never just for the sake of doing so and in some respects they were unduly reluctant to break away from the past: the retention of the scroll clutch is a case in point. In their 1908 and 1914 Grand Prix cars the policy of keeping certain fundamental and well-tried features was followed.

The 1907 Grand Prix was run under a fuel consumption formula which, sound though it was, did not please the competing firms, and for 1908 it was stipulated that the cars should have a *minimum* weight of 1,150 kg. and a *maximum* piston area of 117 sq. in. This limited cylinder bores to 155 mm. for 4-cylinder engines or 127 mm. for those with six cylinders. For the first time emphasis was put upon specific efficiency in terms of power developed per square inch of piston area; also for the first time, as a result, output exceeded 1 b.h.p. per sq. in. or 10 h.p. per litre.

By the standards of 1966 engines of 12 litres or so, which the bore limitation imposed, still seem pretty monstrous, but the new formula, particularly the

Salzer in the Paddock: note double-armed shock absorbers cased in leather.

The three 1908 Mercedes cars before leaving for the course: Lautenschlager No. 35; Poege No. 2; Salzer No. 19.

minimum weight limit, gave designers an opportunity to improve chassis rigidity as they no longer had to skimp the margin of safety in order to save a few ounces here or there.

Wilhelm Maybach left the Daimler Motoren Gesellschaft in 1907, and Paul Daimler returned from the Austrian branch of the concern to take his place, but it is at once apparent that Maybach's influence was still dominant in the 1908 Grand Prix cars, the design of which followed established Mercedes practice throughout.

With the bores (for 4-cylinder engines) limited to 155 mm. most of the competing firms sought to increase output by increasing the stroke without reducing rotational speeds; in other words, piston speeds were considerably increased by comparison with 1907—remarkably so when one considers the size and weight of the reciprocating parts. Clément-Bayard was the most daring with a stroke of 185 mm. and a maximum crankshaft speed of 1,560 r.p.m. to give a piston speed of 1,900 ft. per minute. Even this was notably less venturesome than Sizaire-Naudin who won the *Coupe des Voiturettes* (run immediately before the Grand Prix on the Dieppe circuit) with a single-cylinder engine of 250 mm. stroke which could run up to 2,400 r.p.m. giving a piston speed of 3,937 ft. per minute. By contrast the Mercedes dimensions were slightly more conservative with a stroke of 180 mm. According to Gerald Rose (*A Record of Motor Racing*, 1894–1908) and one other contemporary English source only car No. 2, driven by Willy Poege, had the 180 mm stroke, whilst Christian Lautenschlager (No. 35) and Otto Salzer (No. 19) had cars with 170 mm. stroke engines. The historical expert

Apparently only Willy Poege's car had 'Mercedes' painted on the scuttle.

at Daimler-Benz A.G. denies this and states that all three engines were of 180 mm. stroke. The bore was the maximum permitted—155 mm.—and the engines were rated at 120 PS or 135 DIN horsepower. It is certainly true that the solitary 1908 Grand Prix Mercedes, which survives in America, has a stroke of 180 mm., but it is also fair to point out that where it has been possible to verify them beyond question, the figures quoted by Gerald Rose in his monumental work are almost invariably accurate.

The engine had two camshafts, one either side, level with the bottom of the cylinder blocks and driven in the usual Mercedes fashion (though now somewhat old-fashioned) by exposed spur gears from the back of the crankshaft. The off-side camshaft gave motion directly to the tappets of the exhaust valves which were in pockets at the side of the combustion chambers with the inlet valves inverted above them; in present day language therefore the engine was of F-head formation. The inlet valves were opened by exposed push rods and rockers worked from the off-side camshaft and they were of the 'annular' form introduced on the 60 h.p. Mercedes of 1903. These annular, or concentric, valves were possibly influenced by Napier practice and certainly similar to a type of safety valve which had been familiar in the steam engine world for nearly a century, and the object was to increase the unrestricted port area for a given

Lautenschlager en route *to the start followed by Courtadi's Motobloc, Dimitri's Renault and Minoia's De Dietrich.*

The Dieppe circuit, 1908; Lautenschlager in action.

diameter and lift of valve. For low- and moderate-speed engines the annular valve gave satisfactory results, but probably required more frequent grinding to maintain an effective gas-seal than the ordinary mushroom valve with its conical sealing faces.

The single high tension magneto was driven by spur gears from the near side camshaft, and other well-tried Mercedes features included the scroll clutch—the *federbandkupplung*—which was as ecstatically praised by the motoring press of 1901 as it was vehemently slated by a later generation of writers who, most probably, never had first-hand experience of its alleged vagaries. The brake system was quite conventional for the period; that is the foot brake worked two contracting shoe brakes upon the countershaft, thereby imposing reverse loads upon the chains and sprockets, whilst the handbrake acted directly upon the back

wheels. The earlier Mercedes system of having two separate footbrake systems, each with its own pedal, had been given up together with the use of a water-drip arrangement to cool the brake drums; better friction materials made these refinements unnecessary.

The final drive by chain, the four-speed gear box, with all four ratios more or less equally spaced, and (inevitably) the selective 'gate' change which Mercedes had made famous, were all inherited from earlier practice. In order to avoid frictional losses arising from inaccurate pitching the driving and driven sprockets were of equal diameter, and the final drive reduction was made in the bevel gearing of the countershaft. It does not seem possible to ascertain the indirect ratios, but final drive ratio was 1·6 : 1 giving approximately 60 m.p.h. at 1,000 r.p.m. in the direct drive fourth gear.

By 1908 chain drive was beginning to be thought old fashioned for touring cars and several makers, Renault and Itala in particular, had already shown conclusively that the live-axle could stand up to the rigours of racing. The disadvantages of noise, and the rapid wear of exposed chains and sprockets, were of no consequence in racing and the positive advantages of less unsprung weight and the ease of altering final-drive ratios during preparation or practice were not to be gainsaid. Mercedes were not alone: Brasier, De Dietrich, F.I.A.T., Germain, Mors, Motobloc and Panhard-Levassor were still faithful to chain drive in the 1908 Grand Prix.

This race was notable for seeing the first appearance of 'pits'. They were just that—shallow emplacements dug by the side of the track, lined with timber revettments and stocked with the necessary spares and tools. The other outstanding feature of the affair was the prodigious consumption of tyres. Since racing began cars had been too fast for their tyres, but the greater speed of the 1908 cars over those of the previous year and the rough state of the track, which had been cut about by the Voiturette Race, showed up the inadequacies of tyre design. The Rudge-Whitworth

Pit work: not merely the inner tube but the air itself is almost visible in the off-side front tyre.

Down the straight.

centre-lock wire wheel had already won favour in England, but the Automobile Club de France barred it from the Grand Prix, apparently for no better reason than that the French makers had not got round to using it. Detachable rims were, however, permitted, and the Mercedes pit-staff worked wonders with the six nuts securing each rim to its felloe.

Had it not been for his nineteen tyre failures there is little doubt that Victor Rigal on the Clément-Bayard would have won; his average speed of 63·6 m.p.h. brought him to fourth place and represents an astonishing performance in view of his difficulties. The Mercedes were not so destructive (perhaps because of their lighter axles), but there were no spare tyres left at the pit during the last two laps. Fortunately neither Lautenschlager nor Poege needed more tyres and the former was able to hold first place which he had attained in the fifth lap, with the Benzs of Victor Hémery and Richard Hanriot next in succession. The order remained unchanged for the rest of the race and the final result was:

(10 laps = 477 miles)

Place	No.	Make	Driver	Average speed
1	35	Mercedes	Lautenschlager	69 m.p.h.
2	6	Benz	Hémery	67·5
3	23	Benz	Hanriot	67·4
4	11	Clement-Bayard	Rigal	63·6
5	2	Mercedes	Poege	63·3

The third Mercedes, driven by Salzer (No. 19) had broken the lap record in a time of 36 min. 31 sec. on the first lap; ignition trouble then set in, the car fell back to thirty-fifth place on the second lap and retired on the third. That the two leading German firms took first three places was a sad blow to French pride, but the great cost of Grand Prix racing made all the leading firms quite happy to agree to the suspension of Grand Prix events during 1909 and 1910.

1908 gearbox and counter shaft footbrakes with cover removed.

1914 Grand Prix: Louis Wagner en route to the course.

1914 GRAND PRIX MERCEDES

The 1914 Grand Prix, of twenty laps of the 23·3 miles Lyons circuit, was run on a capacity limit formula which fixed engine size at 4½ litres and maximum weight at 21 cwt. A look at some of the technical details destroys three of the sacred cows of motoring history:

Firstly—that aero engine practice did not influence car engine design until after the war. Both the 1913 and 1914 Mercedes racing engines had much in common with the firm's well-known aero engines. (And the 1906 'Adams Eight' had been powered by a modified Antoinette airship engine).

Secondly—that 'Hotchkiss drive', i.e. using the back springs to transmit driving thrust to the frame and to absorb braking torque, was superior to other contemporary systems as it avoided 'rear wheel steering'. This theoretical truth should have been amply disproved by the G.P. Mercedes, and many thousands of production cars of different makes, which handled excellently despite the use of a torque tube or some other form of torque-reaction linkage.

Thirdly—that rotational speeds much above 3,500 r.p.m. were not attainable because the virtue of opening inlet valves before top dead centre had not been realised. This puts the cart before the horse, and it was because metallurgy, sparking plug and valve spring weaknesses held back the practical application of high speed working that some 3,000 r.p.m. was regarded as a reasonably safe limit; at this speed there is no advantage to be gained by early inlet valve opening.

Paul Daimler was responsible for the 1914 racing Mercedes; although the firm's traditions were in no sense violated, the Maybach influence, which had been so clear in the 1908 cars, was no longer dominant.

Lautenschlager cornering, while his riding mechanic inspects the near-side rear tyre.

At the hairpin, Kenelm Lee Guinness (Sunbeam) swallows Lautenschlager's dust.

The photographs say all that needs to be said of the way racing cars had changed externally in six years. It must be remembered, however, that the high build and sit-up-and-beg driving positions of 1908 had not been retained purely by conservative adherence to touring car fashions. The very large engines had very large flywheels, and to give 6 or 7 inches clearance beneath a flywheel nearly two feet in diameter dictated a high chassis and floor level; this and other factors brought the driver's eye level some five feet or more from the ground in 1908. On the 1914 Mercedes this dimension had been reduced by some 10 or 12 inches, and the very narrow body (37 in. at the widest point) and *coupe vent* radiator helped reduce drag.

Though Mercedes still raced with 2-wheel brakes in 1914 (foot operated transmission brake and hand brake acting directly on the rear wheels in accordance with conventional practice), the hand brake mechanism showed novelty in the use of toggle mechanism, in place of cams, to expand the shoes which were flexible; the drums were also designed to 'give' a little and the greatest possible area of lining thus made contact with each drum. These brakes were probably as good as 2-wheel-only brakes could be, and a similar

Exhaust manifolding: priming cocks and one set of sparking plugs also visible.

arrangement is to be found on some of the Panhard-Levassors of the 1920s.

The cut-away drawing shows the 1914 4,483 c.c. Mercedes G.P. engine: the apparently old fashioned exposed valve springs and stems were retained to aid cooling and make for easy adjustment, but the crankshaft dimensions and combustion chamber and valve ports would have passed as up to date until quite recently. In accordance with the aircraft practice of the firm the ports and water jackets of the individual cylinders (93×165 mm.) were separate structures welded into place. This very costly form of construction allowed rigid control of the thickness of metal in all the vital areas and abolished the menace of distortion. Four inclined valves per cylinder allowed good breathing at the relatively low speeds used, and the single overhead camshaft was driven, by bevels and vertical shaft, from the back of the crankshaft to avoid torsional disturbances. The engine was designed to take four sparking plugs per cylinder, fed from two magnetos, though only three were used. This prodigality of sparks not only provided good flame-spread but was a safeguard against misfiring at high speed; sparking plugs were still apt to be unreliable in 1914. The engine was, in consequence, an extremely reliable one and developed 115 b.h.p. at 2,800 r.p.m.

The drawing also shows the plunger-pump system of pressure lubrication (the 1908 engines had still relied upon drip-feed-and-splash basically). One of the triple pump barrels drew in a small quantity of fresh oil from an external tank and added it to that already being circulated by the scavenge and feed pumps. In addition a foot-operated pump allowed the mechanic to feed fresh oil to cylinder walls and crankcase.

There were no departures from conventional practice in chassis, steering, or suspension, though the Mercedes face-cam and coil spring rebound dampers were noteworthy and the chassis was rather more rigidly braced than was then usual, with an X member in the centre of the frame. The old scroll

Lautenschlager takes a fast corner on his last lap. (Photo: Cyril Posthumus)

clutch had disappeared in favour of a double cone affair and the 4-speed gearbox gave motion to a propellor shaft and live axle. The shaft was enclosed in a tube and driving thrust and torque reaction were delivered to a ball trunnion joint mounted on the X member. Despite the pundits who assure us this arrangement promotes oversteer, the cars steered beautifully.

An uncommon feature of the rear axle was that the pinion shaft carried two driving pinions with the differential mechanism between them; each pinion meshed with a separate crown wheel—one to each half-shaft. This unusual arrangement had been done before and was to be done again; it had the merits of allowing great rigidity in the pinion shaft; the thrust of one driving pinion was counterbalanced by the opposite thrust of its fellow (thrust race bearings were not always as free from trouble as designers would have liked); above all it abolished the tendency to induce wheelspin by transverse torque reaction which, for racing cars particularly, was the most serious drawback of the conventional bevel-geared live axle.

The Daimler Motoren Gesellschaft entered five of these cars (the maximum allowed) for the event, and the preparation, testing and practising were done with a degree of thoroughness not previously seen in motor racing. It was this, and the reliability of the cars, rather than any outstanding novelty or merit of design which gave Mercedes a triple victory. Each car became, as it were, tailored to its driver and to the exigencies of the course. A sufficiency of crown wheels, half-shafts and driving pinions, for example, was provided to allow six different final drive ratios to be tried on each car during preparation. These ratios varied only between the narrow limits of 2·2 : 1 and 2·7 : 1. Maximum speed claimed was 112 m.p.h. and with the 2·5 : 1 ratio this was reached at 2,900 r.p.m. and a piston speed of 3,050 feet per minute.

In addition to their painstaking pre-race work, which was soon seen to pay dividends, the Mercedes team introduced a new element into racing—the absolute control of individual cars by signal from the pit. This robbed the driver of some of his individuality, and, in the opinion of many, took from motor racing its claim to be a sport, but there is no doubt it was an inevitable move and one which some other concern would have made if Mercedes had not.

Toughest opposition to the Mercedes came from Peugeot whose cars were faster round the corners by virtue of their 4-wheel brakes. At least one of the G.P. Mercedes was fitted with front brakes at one stage but at the time of the race all five relied on rear wheel braking only. Max Sailer was given the task of opening up the race and his Mercedes led for the first five laps and had by then gained a $2\frac{3}{4}$-minute lead over Georges Boillot's Peugeot; but this pace could not be maintained and Sailer went out on the sixth lap with a broken crankshaft. The need to make full use of their cornering and braking ability was already causing tyre trouble on the Peugeots.

Racing cars still carried (and needed) spare wheels in 1914; Wagner's car at the pits.

13

The conquering heroes: three of the team cars outside the Daimler-Benz works at Stuttgart-Untertürkheim.

From laps five to fifteen Peugeot seemed to be dominant, and when curiously slow pit work lost Lautenschlager two minutes on the eleventh lap the cautious punter might have baulked at putting any money on the Mercedes. On orders from the pit Christian Lautenschlager, Louis Wagner and Otto Salzer now began to close up and harry the opposition. On the eighteenth lap, which he covered at 68·7 m.p.h., Lautenschlager took a 23-second lead over Boillot who had, by then, little chance of winning and none at all when he broke a valve on the last lap. His was a magnificent attempt; particularly as he had to make eight tyre changes against Lautenschlager's four.

Mercedes had the satisfaction of taking first three places; Lautenschlager at an average of 65·83 m.p.h., Wagner at 65·3 and Salzer at 64·8. The race remained extremely close to the end; fourth place was taken by Jules Goux (Peugeot) at 63·94, and Dario Resta (Sunbeam) was fifth at 62·46.

Allowing for the vastly more difficult circuit it is seen that the 4½-litre cars of 1914 were notably superior to their 1908 predecessors whose engines were nearly three times as big.

Although the 1908 type of car continued to appear in competitive events for some while, and, indeed, Mercedes and Benz chassis of this period were still favoured in the 'twenties as suitable foundations on which to build 'specials' for record attempts or particular events (by the simple old-fashioned expedient of cramming in the largest engine the work could stand), the 1908 Grand Prix cars represent the last magnificent specimens of a dying breed. By contrast, the 1914 cars were very much in advance of their time in almost all respects but their brakes.

It has been said that no cheer was raised and no hands clapped as the three Mercedes crossed the finishing line in 1914, and this has been attributed to the tense feelings brought about by the imminence of war. It seems unlikely that the spectators at the Lyons circuit were particularly aware of the terrible doom then preparing, but that the rigid system of control imposed on the Mercedes team left the spectators puzzled and disapproving. The future pattern of racing procedure was drawn and public approval was at first withheld.

Four weeks later the pistol shot which started the war was fired. A macabre twist to the tale is provided by the fact that the chauffeur at Sarajevo who was wounded in the attempt to drive the murdered Archduke out of range was Otto Merz, a Mercedes apprentice, one time riding mechanic to Poege and himself a famous racing driver in the 'twenties.

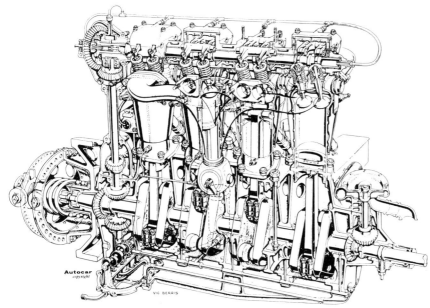

The 1914 Grand Prix Mercedes engine.

© JAMES LEECH

Mercedes radiator emblem
as carried by the 1914 Grand
Prix cars.

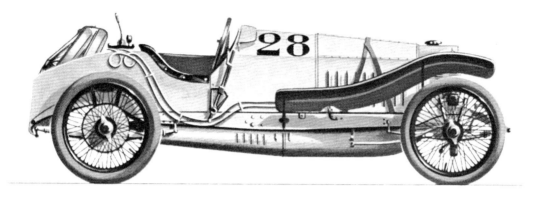

THE 4½-LITRE MERCEDES, winner of
the 1914 Grand Prix at Lyons. Average
speed: 65·83 m.p.h. for 466 miles.
Driver: Christian Lautenschlager.

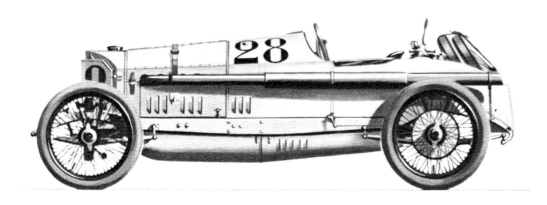

0   5'

1914 G.P. Mercedes with front-wheel brakes: Otto Salzer's car in the 1922 Targa Florio. (Photo: Radio Times, Hulton Picture Library)

SPECIFICATION 1908 GRAND PRIX MERCEDES

12·8 litres capacity. Designer, nominally Paul Daimler but most details of design basically similar to those already established by Wilhelm Maybach.

ENGINE: 4-cylinders, cast iron, in two blocks of two. Integral cylinder heads, inlet valves in detachable cages, exhaust valves accessible through screwed caps. Bore 155 mm.; stroke 170 mm. except for car No. 2, which is stated by Gerald Rose (*A Record of Motor Racing 1894–1908*), to have had a stroke of 180 mm. (See Text.)

Camshafts: One either side of engine at upper crankcase level driven by spur gears from rear of crankshaft.

Valves: Two to each cylinder, situated in valve chests at the near sides of the blocks. The exhaust valves directly operated by tappets from near side camshaft, and the inlet valves inverted over them and operated by push rods and rockers from off side camshaft. Inlet valves of Maybach annular form.

Ignition: Single Bosch high-tension magneto driven by spur gears from near side camshaft; one sparking plug to each cylinder.

Carburettor: Single, Mercedes.

Lubrication: Essentially 'drip and splash'. Oil lifted by quadruple plunger pumps to sight feeds on dash, thence by gravity to main bearings, supplemented by hand pump to feed to cylinder walls and to maintain crankcase level. Big ends fitted with dippers.

CHASSIS: Channel section.

Clutch: Mercedes 'scroll'.

Gearbox: Separate; 4-speeds and reverse.

Final drive: Bevel geared differential countershaft integral with gear box and final drive by side chains to 'dead' axle. Ratio of drive bevels: 1·6 : 1.
Ratio of chain wheels: 1 : 1.
(The chainwheel ratio was, of course, easily altered to suit different conditions. As raced in 1908, the ratios used allowed approximately 60 m.p.h. at 1,000 r.p.m. on direct drive.)

Suspension: Nearly flat laminated plate springs (leafsprings) front and back damped by friction shock absorbers.

Brakes: Footbrake: Contracting brakes acting on countershaft imposing reverse loading on chains and sprockets. *Handbrake:* Expanding shoes acting on drums integral with final drive sprockets on rear wheels.

Wheels: Wooden, artillery pattern, twelve spokes front and rear. Fixed hubs and detachable rims. The wheels were obviously not standardised; some photographs show six nut fixing of detachable rim, others show eight; one photograph shows rear wheels without detachable rims.

Tyres: 880 × 120 front; 895 × 135 rear.

Weight: Unladen, approx. 1,340 kg.

Claimed output: Approximately 120 h.p. at 1,400 r.p.m.

Maximum speed: Approximately 100 m.p.h.

SPECIFICATION 1914 GRAND PRIX MERCEDES

4½ litres capacity. Designed by Paul Daimler. In addition to winning the event for which it was designed the Mercedes also won the 1915 Indianapolis 500 Mile race and, with front brakes added, the 1922 Targa Florio. A supercharged 1914 Grand Prix car won its last event in 1926.

ENGINE: 4-cylinders 93 mm. bore and 165 mm. stroke (4,483 c.c.). Separate steel cylinders, mounted on aluminium base, with integral heads and welded-on valve ports and water jackets.

Camshaft: Single, overhead, driven by bevel gears and vertical shaft from rear end of crankshaft.

Valves: Four to each cylinder inclined at 60 degrees. Three cams per cylinder one working inlet valves by a forked rocker, the other two working the exhaust valves by separate rockers.

Ignition: Two Bosch high tension magnetos, driven by skew gears from vertical valve motion shaft and supplying three sparking plugs per cylinder; the latter horizontally placed two on inlet side and the third on exhaust side of each cylinder head.

Carburettor: Single Mercedes.

Lubrication: Wet sump and full pressure system by plunger pumps with automatic provision for maintaining sump level. Supplementary oiling by foot pump at mechanic's option.

CHASSIS: Channel section with double drop and X-bracing.

Clutch: Double cone.

Gearbox: Separate; 4-speeds and reverse. Indirect ratios: 4·8 : 1, 7·4 : 1, 11·1 : 1 at the final drive ratio of 2·7 : 1. Variations of final drive between 2·2 : 1 and 2·7 : 1 naturally affected the above ratios slightly.

Final drive: Propellor shaft and torque tube to bevel geared live axle with two driving pinions, crown wheel to each half shaft and differential mechanism acting between the driving pinions.

Suspension: Flat laminated plate springs ('leaf' springs) front and back damped by Mercedes face-cam dampers.

Brakes: Single footbrake, acting by contracting shoes on drum behind gearbox. Hand-brake expanding shoes by toggle action in drums on rear wheels.

Wheelbase: 9 ft. 4 in.

Track: Front, 4 ft. 4½ in. Rear 4 ft. 5 in.

Wheels: Rudge-Whitworth triple row tangent wire wheels, demountable by centre-lock nut.

Tyres: Front, 820 × 120. Rear 895 × 135.

Weight: Unladen 21½ cwt. Starting-line weight 26½ cwt.

Claimed output: 115 b.h.p. at 2,900 r.p.m. Piston speed 3,050 ft./min.

Maximum speed: Approximately 112 m.p.h. (Probable slight variations according to final drive ratio.)

© Anthony Bird, 1966

The Rolls-Royce Phantom I

2

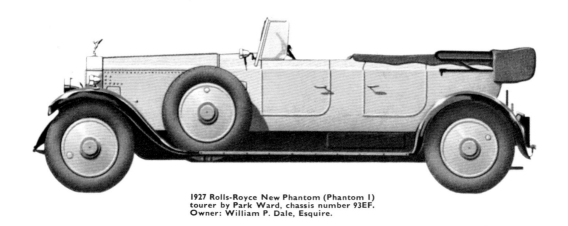

1927 Rolls-Royce New Phantom (Phantom I)
tourer by Park Ward, chassis number 93EF.
Owner: William P. Dale, Esquire.

ROLLS-ROYCE

ROLLS

RR

ROYCE

0   6′

© **WALTER WRIGHT, 1966.**

The Rolls-Royce radiator badge was red until 1933.

The Rolls-Royce Phantom I

by George A. Oliver

J. Pierpont Morgan, the American banker, was the original owner of this 1929 car. It is seen at Loch Clunie, Scotland, during a short tour of that country in 1958.
(Photo: Montagu Motor Museum)

The New Phantom Rolls-Royce was introduced during the 23rd year of its designer's career as a manufacturer of motor-cars and although it was by then his eighth major design project it was only the third new model to reach the production stage in the 20 years between 1906 and 1925.

All but two of these designs were created between 1903 and 1906, during a period of highly concentrated effort that began, modestly, with the development of the neat little 10 h.p. two-cylinder model and ended, magnificently, with the introduction of the splendid 40/50 h.p., six-cylinder 'Silver Ghost' car.

The latter was the only Rolls-Royce then made until the introduction of the Twenty in 1922, and despite the fact that its design was in certain respects behind the times when production was resumed in 1919 demand continued at a high level well into the 'twenties. Between 1920 and 1924, indeed, yearly output ran at a higher level than that of the best pre-war year and fell sharply in the opening months of 1925 only because of the forthcoming change-over to the new 40/50 model. It was in production at Derby until the early summer of 1925 and until 1926 at the Springfield, Massachusetts, plant of Rolls-Royce of America, Inc.

Under the conditions then prevailing Rolls-Royce were quite right to concentrate on production of their existing car until the time was opportune to introduce a successor. The years of grace allowed them to design the Twenty and get it into production, to develop their mechanical-servo four-wheel brake system and to make a final decision on the kind of engine most suitable for the new 40/50.

Several different types had been tried.
". . . a twelve-cylinder engine of the "V" type, an engine with eight cylinders in line, and a six-cylinder engine with overhead-camshaft, were all designed,

made, and tested. The supercharger was also tried and rejected on account of its noise, its complication, and its extravagance.

After seven years of experiment and test . . . the 40/50 h.p. six-cylinder Phantom chassis emerged, and is offered to the public as the most suitable type possible for a mechanically propelled carriage under present-day conditions."

So said the company in the catalogue for the new car.

What was not said was that Packard had marketed an excellent V-12-engined car—the Twin Six—from 1915 until 1921 and had followed it with an even more successful straight-eight. No reference was made to the fact that Cadillac had been using a V-8 engine since 1915: nor was there any mention of rival cars that were powered by overhead-camshaft engines, among them the 40/50 Napier, the Lanchester 40 and the 37·2 h.p. Hispano-Suiza.

While the extra power of engines of the latter type was obtained at the expense of utmost quietness and smoothness these qualities, which had more to do with the post-war sales success of the 'old-fashioned' Ghost than is yet appreciated, could be retained, and useful extra power provided by making the new engine of the overhead-valve type. It was very much like the one that Royce and his designers had created for the Twenty but more complicated and more than twice as large in terms of cubic capacity and developed power.

At 2,250 r.p.m. (the maximum of the Ghost) it gave off:

". . . 33 % greater horsepower, this being due to improvements in the form of the cylinder head, to a better disposition of the ignition plugs, etc."

On neither side of the Atlantic was there any mention of the actual developed power which was, in

16 EX, one of the surviving Phantom I 'Continental' models. H. I. F. Evernden, a member of Royce's design team, was principally responsible for the design and development of this high-performance car. (Photo: Ian Graham)

fact, about 100 b.h.p. Rolls-Royce reticence on this subject has been inconsistent over the years, figures for the Ghost, the Twenty, the Phantom III and the Silver Wraith having been officially quoted at different times.

In any case the New Phantom had sufficient power to provide the increase in acceleration and top speed necessary to establish it in the leading rank of the world's high-performance luxury cars. After all not so many were capable of really high speeds in 1925 and the 75–80 m.p.h. maximum of the standard Phantom I was exceeded by few other cars of its day.

In Britain such a speed was of little value, legally speaking, because of the universal 20 m.p.h. speed limit, but its advantages for long-distance touring abroad were immediately appreciated. It was just as well that bodybuilders were then coming round to overdue acceptance of the fact that there was nothing basically indecent either in collaborating more closely

than before with the chassis builder or in saving weight; the general introduction of four wheel brakes and balloon tyres was making cars heavier and weight-saving had become increasingly important.

The chassis of the Phantom, complete with tyres, battery, petrol, oil, and water, but excluding spare wheel, lamps and other accessories, was about 4,000 lb., or 37 cwt. The total weight allowed under guarantee including '. . . chassis, body, passengers and all else therein or thereon' was 58 cwt. In 1936 the 165 b.h.p. Phantom III was limited to 59 cwt.

Small wonder then that these large cars had to have large-capacity engines. Early Ghosts were square, both bore and stroke being $4\frac{1}{2}$ in. From 1909

A prototype Phantom I 'Continental' at Brooklands Race Track during development testing there in 1927. (Photo: Old Motor)

In the late 'thirties the English enthusiast, Douglas Fitzpatrick, supercharged his Phantom I with great success. He contrived an extremely tidy arrangement of the blower and non-standard carburettors. (Photo: Douglas Fitzpatrick)

Sir Henry Royce (right), his friend Sir James Percy, and an early New Phantom at Le Canadel, Southern France, where Sir Henry spent most of his time from 1911 onwards. (Photo: Rolls-Royce Ltd.)

the stroke was lengthened to $4\frac{3}{4}$ in., capacity rose from 7,036 c.c. to 7,428 c.c. and the rated horsepower, by R.A.C. formula, was 48·6. The Phantom engine had a longer stroke—$5\frac{1}{2}$ in. and a narrower bore—$4\frac{1}{4}$ in., a swept volume of 7,668 c.c. (468·14 cu. in.) and an R.A.C. rating of 43·3 h.p.

Although its six cylinders were grouped together in two blocks of three (as were those of the Ghost) they shared a common, detachable head. In general appearance the new engine had the up-to-date look of its smaller sister, with a 'colour' scheme of black and white—mainly stove enamel and aluminium. Finishes somewhat easier to maintain replaced the copper and brass so noticeable a feature of the Ghost engine and the result was a decided aesthetic success.

The outlines of all later Rolls-Royce and Bentley six-cylinder engines may be traced back to those of the Twenty. In its turn the latter inherited its general layout from the Ghost, and it is because of this continuity of design thinking that in any examination of a particular model one has to refer constantly, back-

wards and forwards, to other designs from Derby or Crewe.

The engine of the Ghost was set low in the frame. Because of its longer stroke and the fact that its valves had gone upstairs, so to speak, that of the Phantom was taller and narrower. The Ghost was Edwardian—and early Edwardian at that—whereas the Twenty was truly a Vintage car, the engine and chassis of which, little changed except in details, remained up-to-date looking well into the 'thirties. From the beginning its suspension and road-holding were excellent and remained adequate for all subsequent increases of power and speed.

Visitors to the Science Museum, South Kensington, London, may see this impressive part-sectioned Phantom I engine.

During the 1931 Schneider Trophy air races a Phantom I, with truck body, was used to carry Rolls-Royce aero-engines between Derby and Calshot at high—and certainly illegal—speeds.
(Photo: Rolls-Royce Ltd.)

According to Mr. Douglas Tubbs and to Mr. Anthony Bird, by far the most reliable writers on Rolls-Royce cars today, the Phantom was not, at first, altogether satisfactory as far as its springing and road-holding were concerned. Although the writer has a large experience of this model on the road he cannot say that he has ever been aware of any shortcomings of this kind.

To be fair, however, it should be said that the cars known best to him are of 1927 vintage and by that year modifications had been made to the steering and suspension. Early in 1927 the front axle was lightened, a short time after hydraulic shock absorbers were substituted for the friction devices previously fitted at the front, and later that year the big Hartford

friction dampers at the rear were also replaced by Rolls-Royce hydraulics, the restraining influence of which was much more consistent.

The main fault of the Phantom I, in all probability, was the fact that it retained the Ghost chassis, with cantilever springs at the rear. Under certain conditions these can allow the back of a car so fitted to float in a rather sickly manner unless they are extremely well controlled—as in the Lanchester system, for example. Wide-section, low-pressure tyres did not help either, and their effect on steering was not a good one. It is rather surprising that Royce did not scale-up the chassis of the Twenty when he was planning the Phantom—but it was not until 1929 that the larger Rolls-Royce got a chassis to match the quality of its engine.

All the same it had very light steering, in spite of its directness and the small-diameter wheel inherited from the Ghost.

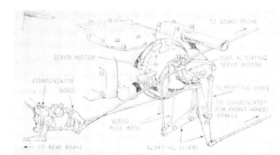

The Rolls-Royce mechanical servo brake system, seen here in the form used for early New Phantom chassis, featured a quite elaborate arrangement of rods and levers.
(Photo: Rolls-Royce Ltd.)

The majority of American-built Phantom I chassis carried bodies built by Brewster, an old-established New York coach builder taken over by Rolls-Royce of America Inc. in 1926. This 1928 phaeton is a fine example of Brewster skills.
(Photo: Pettit's Museum of Motoring Memories)

Perhaps the most richly decorated interior of any automobile ever made was that of the 1927 New Phantom, now owned by Mr. Stanley Sears. Although its exterior appearance is impressive enough it gives no hint of the Regency richness within. Clark of Wolverhampton built this unique body. Below: *Interior of the Sears New Phantom.* (Photos: Thomas–Photos)

Another striking feature was the effectiveness of its braking system. Royce's adaptation of the mechanical-servo operation used so effectively by Hispano-Suiza since 1919 was carried out with typical thoroughness, so that the worrying problem of arresting the onward rush of a three-ton motor-car from any speed within its range was most satisfactorily solved. Such a good job was made that the layout was used, with detail changes only, until 1939, and in modified form is still being used on certain current Rolls-Royce models.

The servo-motor itself, a quite small disc-clutch carried at the side of the gearbox, rotates slowly all the time the car is moving, its drive, in effect, being provided by the rear wheels. Initial movement of the pedal begins direct application of the rear brake shoes and at the same time draws together the friction discs of the servo. Through a system of most carefully proportioned levers fixed to the back-plate of the latter the momentum of the still-moving car is then used to engage both front and rear brakes, the driver's effort being considerably amplified as far as the rear shoe engagement is concerned. To allow for weight transfer under these conditions the overall effort is distributed front and rear in a one-third to two-thirds ratio.

One is inclined to think that both Royce and Birkigt (his opposite number in Hispano-Suiza) appreciated the irony of a situation that saw the former paying royalties to his principal rival for the use of an idea. The mechanical servo, as used by Hispano, was somewhat less highly-developed than that of the Rolls-Royce (for example, it did not operate in reverse) but it was effective enough in use and was one of the many features that enabled this make to take such a commanding position in its class throughout the 'twenties. The combination of a vigorous overhead-camshaft engine, for which an output of more than 130 b.h.p was claimed, splendid steering, brakes and road-holding, impressive appearance—even its inspired name—gave it near-irresistible attraction for sophisticated, wealthy motorists of its time.

Like all other cars in its class except the 40/50 Rolls, however, it has not survived in significant numbers, despite its undoubted quality. As far as Britain is concerned the only serious rival in the late 'twenties, the 6½-litre Bentley, has been preserved in reasonable numbers—but, in the main, in its more sporting forms. Of the excellent Lanchester 40, a strong challenger, scarcely any examples are left, and another 'native' rival, the 40/50 Napier, is represented now by one or two cars only.

One cannot speak from first-hand knowledge of the position elsewhere, though in the United States, for example, one knows that many of the fine luxury cars of the 'twenties are cherished still—the Twin-Six Packard, the straight-eight of the same make, the V-8 Cadillac, the Duesenberg and some others. One knows also that the number of Springfield Rolls-Royces that have survived there is considerable . . . from all of which it is tempting to deduce that the appeal of the Phantom is still significant.

Over 2,200 Phantom chassis were built at Derby between 1925 and 1929, and between 1926 and 1931 1,240 left the Springfield plant. It was a considerable achievement to produce and sell almost 3,500 ex-

Hooper and Co. built few more handsome and impressive bodies than this 1926 Sedanca-de-Ville. Its link with the elegant carriages of the 18th and early 19th centuries is an obvious one. (Photo: Rolls-Royce Ltd.)

pensive automobiles during a period of ever-growing financial difficulties on both sides of the Atlantic.

In Britain the price of the 12-ft. chassis was £1,850, the long-wheelbase (12 ft. 6 in.) car costing £50 more. Neither of these prices included such essentials as the lamps, speedometer, clock, spare tyre, 'side wheel carrier', windscreen wiper or mascot—but they were part of the equipment of a complete car, however, and included in its cost. This was never low: in 1928 the least expensive car catalogued, a striking open tourer on the long chassis, cost £2,602, or £650 10s. per seat, and the most expensive, an impressive Cabriolet de Ville, was priced at £2,932.

With the multiplication of approximately five that had to be made at that time to convert from pounds, English, to dollars, American, it is hardly surprising that price tended to be left out of Springfield publicity.

Each car had a three-year guarantee and it was suggested that it should be returned to the makers every 50,000 miles for dismantling and examination. This was more than twice the distance laid down for the Ghost and the same as that recommended for the later Phantom II and III.

Hand-oiling points were still a feature of the Derby chassis, but the Springfield cars had a centralised

lubrication system from the start. As long as this was regularly inspected, to ensure that there were no blockages, it was of the greatest value in preventing wear. The American-built chassis differed in many other ways despite the fact that they were generally supposed to be mechanically identical with the home product.

The Derby chassis had dual ignition, by coil and magneto, and a 12-volt electrical system, whereas the Springfield cars had two independent but synchronised coils, and a 6-volt battery. They also had the carburettor on the offside of the engine, the ignition and dynamo, or generator, on the near-side (the opposite of the Derby layout), and a three-speed, centre-change gearbox.

Flexibility of running was, of course, to be expected from a Rolls-Royce and in spite of its extra vigour the engine of the Phantom had quite remarkable 'elasticity.' Sheer cubic capacity was a factor, as it always is in this respect, but quality of design and construction played the more important part. The nickel-chrome steel crankshaft which, like the camshaft, ran in seven bearings, was fully machined all over to extremely fine limits and carried a vibration damper at its front end. The engine itself was mounted

One of the most attractive cars illustrated in the 1928 Phantom I catalogue was this tourer on the long chassis. It cost £2,602 complete. (Photo: Rolls-Royce Ltd.)

Note the typical drum-shaped lamps and front bumper (or fender) of the first American-built New Phantom, chassis number S-400-FL. (Photo: Rolls-Royce Club of America, Inc.)

In 1927 the engineer Amherst Villiers supercharged a Phantom I, using an Austin 7 engine to drive the blower. Not surprisingly, perhaps, nothing came of this unique 10-cylinder machine.
(Photo: Autocar)

at three points in the frame, with a patented friction-damping device—'to eliminate vibrations otherwise unavoidable due to a vigorous engine at low speeds'—as the catalogue put it.

The carburettor was the twin-jet instrument that Royce had designed for the Silver Ghost and which, in combination with a superb ignition system, had had so much to do with the steam-engine-like flexibility of running of that unique car. The revised induction system incorporated a throttling device that diverted hot exhaust gases to the intake branch just above the carburettor on depression of the accelerator pedal, thereby providing extra heat for the ingoing charge on acceleration. Like the exhaust cut-out also fitted this device was a source of potential trouble after some time.

Automatic advance and retard was a new feature of the dual ignition but it had an over-riding control by lever, set in the quadrant at the steering-wheel centre. This also carried the governor lever and the mixture control, and because of the mechanically-perfect linkages used any movement of these levers had an immediate effect on the running of the engine.

By a most ingenious and splendidly-made, hydraulically-operated mechanism both coil and magneto ignition systems were automatically controlled according to the speed of the engine. Because of their different characteristics they had to be advanced or retarded at differing rates, whilst remaining in synchronisation, and this operation, requiring considerable, consistent effort, applied via a fascinating arrangement of linkages, was powered by oil drawn-off under pressure from the engine lubricating system.

The latter distributed oil at three different rates—at 25 lb. per sq. in. to the crankshaft and connecting-rod bearings and to the gudgeon pins, and through relief valves, at about $3\frac{1}{2}$ lb. pressure, to the overhead-valve rocker-shaft, and, at about $1\frac{1}{2}$ lb. pressure, to the timing gears. Throughout the engine and, indeed, the whole car ample bearing surfaces, properly lubricated, ensured extremely long life for all components.

Royce did not normally favour the use of chains (which he regarded as an admission of inability to produce gears that would remain silent) but the starter motor of the Phantom drove the gearbox layshaft by chain, through a jaw-clutch and an epicyclic reduction gear. The result of this quite unconventional arrangement (first seen on post-war Ghost chassis) was really silent starting.

Silence of operation was a feature, also, of the overhead-valve gear, and it gave rise to much favourable comment from those who tried the new model shortly after its introduction. Tappet adjustment was unusual, being effected by turning the rocker bushes (the bores of which were eccentric with their outer diameters) the required amount and locking them by a nut positioned at one end of each half of the split rocker shaft.

The Duke of Windsor (then Prince of Wales) used this Phantom I during a visit to Thanet, England, in 1926. The body is a convertible.
(Photo: Radio Times Hulton Picture Library)

Elegance was not a feature of this 1926 three-quarter Cabriolet-de-Ville, on chassis number 101-SC. Its body panels and wheels had a simulated wood-grain finish.
(Photo: Montagu Motor Museum)

Yet another special feature, this time inherited from the Ghost, was the governor-controlled throttle, which held engine speed constant at any chosen setting, uphill, downhill, or on the level. Its principle and its *modus operandi* are a little too complicated, taken together, to describe in detail here, but the degree of fine control possible is altogether remarkable. The governor lever can be set up the quadrant to give, let us say, 30 m.p.h. on the level and this speed will be maintained uphill or down, without intervention on the part of the driver unless an unusually steep gradient is encountered

With the aid of the governor an experienced driver could do extraordinary things, not only in getting away on the steepest of hills, with the heaviest of loads, without slipping back (or even touching the accelerator pedal), but in changing gear without apparent effort. The gear-lever of the Phantom was shorter than that of the Ghost but it controlled a change every bit as tricky for the inexperienced or mechanically insensitive driver, and any outside help was welcome. To hold the car in each gear Royce relied on retaining notches in the gear-lever gate instead of springs inside the gearbox and in times of stress it was easily possible to forget their existence....

In other respects the car was built on straightforward lines—front suspension by long, flat, flexible semi-elliptic springs, with long cantilevers at the rear: final drive by a propeller shaft enclosed in a massive torque tube, and spiral-bevel gears; fully-floating half-shafts; pressed-steel frame, with tubular cross-members; rear-mounted fuel tank with Autovac feed; dry, single-plate clutch and so on.

But everything was designed with the greatest of care and consideration: the standards of workmanship and assembly were of the highest, and the best available materials were used, test-pieces from each batch being rigorously inspected whenever possible. The springs were not only polished all over before assembly—they were matched to the known weight of the completed car; the frame side-members were individually paired and all bolts passing through them were fitted to their holes; the radiator shutters could be opened or closed from the dashboard: closed, and in combination with the solid-sided, heavy-gauge aluminium bonnet and engine under-shield, they helped to conserve engine heat for hours

on end while the car was standing and by so doing reduced bore wear considerably.

The number of individual features of this kind was very great. Apart from affording interested examining parties considerable satisfaction when the car was at rest they each contributed in a rather special way to the balance of qualities it possessed when under way.

It is not too far-fetched to say that getting into a Phantom I is rather like boarding a small motor-launch, for the car gives on its springs and the length of bonnet ahead of the driver is impressive. His position is high and commanding and the levers on his right are not unlike those once found on self-propelled water vessels....

Once the car is on the move, its smooth progression over all but the roughest surfaces and its quietness (notable, even by present-day standards) again remind one of motion over water rather than over land. Gear noise is faint and all controls surprise by their lightness and precision. A full range of instruments is laid out for the driver's inspection and re-assurance that all is well, and it is unlikely that a single one will not be clearly seen from the driving

Although the cylinders of the New Phantom engine were arranged in two blocks of three they shared a common cylinder head, as this drawing shows. (Rolls-Royce Ltd.)

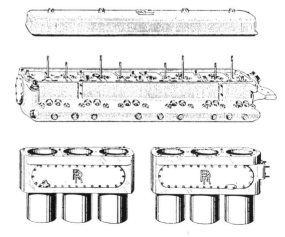

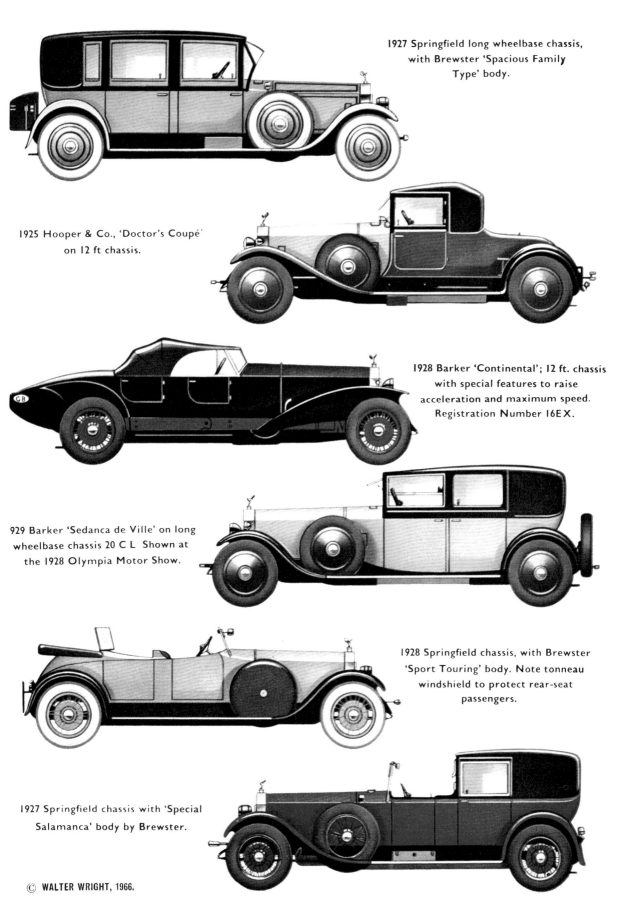

1927 Springfield long wheelbase chassis, with Brewster 'Spacious Family Type' body.

1925 Hooper & Co., 'Doctor's Coupé' on 12 ft chassis.

1928 Barker 'Continental'; 12 ft. chassis with special features to raise acceleration and maximum speed. Registration Number 16EX.

929 Barker 'Sedanca de Ville' on long wheelbase chassis 20 C L Shown at the 1928 Olympia Motor Show.

1928 Springfield chassis, with Brewster 'Sport Touring' body. Note tonneau windshield to protect rear-seat passengers.

1927 Springfield chassis with 'Special Salamanca' body by Brewster.

Towards the end of the 'twenties cars became lower and sleeker in appearance, this 1928 Olympia Show model Sedanca-de-Ville by Barker being typical of its period.
(Photo: Rolls-Royce Ltd.)

seat. Needless to say both front wings are in view, Rolls-Royce making sure of this down the years by supplying bonnet and scuttle with their chassis. . . .

By present-day standards the Phantom is large, no doubt, but with its easy cruising speed of 60 or more miles per hour, its effective brakes and light controls, and its quietness and comfort of ride it is still a worthy long-distance touring car. While it would be realistic to expect an all-year-round fuel consumption of 10–12 m.p.g., upwards of 14 m.p.g. is possible on long runs.

Even higher performance was available from the later cars, which had an aluminium head (with the plugs arranged six-a-side) and the compression ratio raised from 4 to 4·2 to 1. There was also available a short-chassis, 'Continental' model that could exceed 90 m.p.h. if fitted with a specially designed body. The New Phantom may not have been quite so outstanding in its day as some other Rolls-Royce models have been in theirs but its success, commercially-speaking at least, was no less impressive.

© George A. Oliver, 1966

This 1927 Park Ward tourer has much of the traditional elegance of line and proportion associated with the leading English coachbuilders.
(Photo: George A. Oliver)

ENGINE: 6 cyl. in line: $4\frac{1}{4}$ in. bore, $5\frac{1}{2}$ in. stroke, 7,668 c.c. R.A.C. rating 43·3 h.p.
overhead-valves, push-rod operated.
seven-bearing crankshaft, with vibration damper at front end.
3-stage pressure lubrication system with gear-type pump.
Rolls-Royce twin-jet carburettor with separate starting carburettor on top of induction manifold. Autovac feed from rear tank.
dual-ignition, with coil and magneto: automatic advance and retard with over-riding hand control; full synchronisation of both systems.
12-volt lighting and starting: 75–80 amp. hour battery; Rolls-Royce dynamo and starter-motor.
cooling system by water-pump and thermo-syphon: radiator shutters hand-controlled from instrument panel.

TRANSMISSION: single dry-plate clutch in unit with engine: clutch-stop fitted.
separate four-speed and reverse gearbox, with right-hand gate change: three-point mounting in frame.
propeller shaft enclosed in torque tube: spiral-bevel final drive with fully-floating half-shafts: spur gear type differential.

BRAKES: Rolls-Royce mechanical servo-operated brakes on all four wheels, pedal operated, independent set of shoes fitted to rear wheels and operated by hand lever.

STEERING: worm and nut.

WHEELS: centre-lock Dunlop wire wheels (steel artillery type also available).

SUSPENSION: semi-elliptic front: cantilevers at rear: adjustable friction-type shock absorbers until 1926, when hydraulic dampers were fitted at front: in 1927 hydraulics also fitted at rear.

CHASSIS DETAILS: Wheelbase: normal, 144 in.; long, $150\frac{1}{2}$ in.; track: normal, front, 57 in., rear, 56 in.; long, front, $58\frac{1}{2}$ in., rear, $57\frac{1}{2}$ in.; frame width: 36 in.; overall length: normal, $190\frac{1}{2}$ in., long, $196\frac{3}{4}$ in.
Tyres: 33 in. × 5 in. straight-side: 33 in. × 6·75 in. (7 in. × 21 in.).
Turning circles: normal: 53 ft., right-hand, 46 ft., left-hand; long: 55 ft., right-hand, 48 ft., left-hand.
Fuel tank capacity: 18 or 20 gallons, 3 gallon reserve from 1927.
Final drive ratio: 3·47 or 3·25 to 1.
Chassis price: normal, £1,850; long, £1,900.

The V-12 Hispano-Suiza

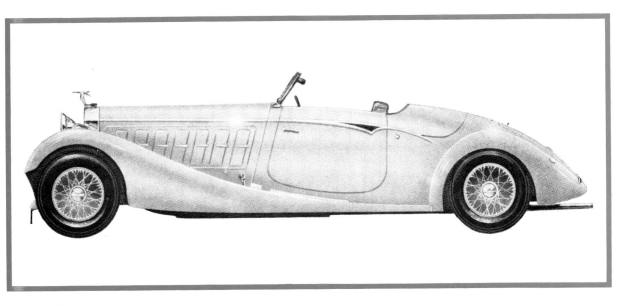

Stork mascot

HISPANO SUIZA

THE V12, 11·3-LITRE HISPANO-SUIZA
TYPE 68-BIS, with 2-seater drophead coupé
coachwork by Saoutchik.
Owner: C. W. P. Hampton, Esquire.

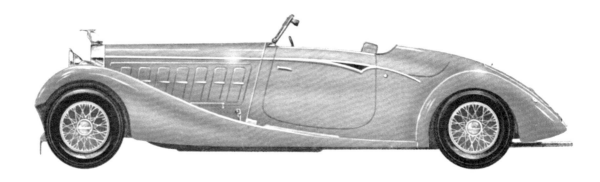

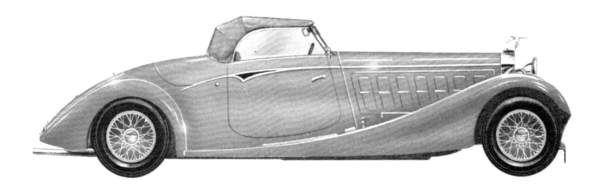

Radiator badge

3

The V-12 Hispano-Suiza
by William Boddy

A typical example of the V12 Hispano-Suiza, one of the last great luxury cars of its era; coachwork by Saoutchik.
(Photo: Mr. V. F. Mashek)

The Hispano-Suiza, first made in Spain at Barcelona but later a French car in its own right, was one of the great makes, a *grand marque*, during what is now called the Edwardian period of motoring history and it carried on this acclaim throughout the Vintage years, 1919–1930.

Before the First World War the 15·9 h.p. Hispano-Suiza 'Alphonso' with its long-stroke T-head four-cylinder engine was one the pioneer sporting cars, and fast for its size. After the Armistice of 1918 the famous 37·2 h.p. six-cylinder overhead camshaft Hispano-Suiza made its auspicious appearance, a luxury car beautifully finished and endowed with mechanical-servo-assisted four-wheel brakes at a time when most of the world's cars, no matter what you paid for them, had but back-wheel anchors and Rolls-Royce were not provoked into fitting the new-fangled front brakes until late in 1924.

Through fine road performance and enough racing successes to endorse its fame, the Hispano-Suiza (which had appeared first in Barcelona in the year 1906, as a 20/24 h.p. 3·7-litre chassis and also in 40 h.p. 7½-litre form, pioneering the afterwards-popular unit construction of engine and gearbox) sold in admittedly small numbers to discerning motorists who appreciated high-speed, good brakes and an excellent gear change, even if the gearbox provided only three forward speeds.

With its reputation made and a Paris factory turning it out, the Hispano-Suiza was nevertheless in a difficult position as the Vintage years ran out. The financial slump of 1930 seriously restricted the demand for expensive, hand-made motor-cars. If sales were to be made of such vehicles, they had to be of top quality.

Having built gentlemen's motor carriages since 1919,

the old Spanish firm decided that survival depended upon making something which would once again be a motor-car out of the ordinary, an automobile to out Rolls Royce.

Marc Birkigt, the talented designer of the Vintage 37·2 and 45 h.p. six-cylinder Hispano-Suizas had, during the First World War, used the basic design of these later car power units to build a very well-known vee-eight aeroplane motor. This V8 Hispano-Suiza aero engine, although afflicted with teething troubles, was built by fourteen firms in its native France, not to mention seven others in America, England and Italy. Wolseley were one of the English companies to build these Hispano-Suiza engines and the Wolseley Viper was flown in SE5 and other aeroplanes and won

Marc Birkigt, 1878–1953. (Photo Boissonnas)

This 9½-litre Kellner-bodied version of the V12 54/220 Hispano-Suiza was owned by André Dubonnet in 1933.
(Photo: Mr. C. W. P. Hampton)

fame at Brooklands track in Sir Alastair Miller's 11-litre Wolseley Viper racing giant.

So when Birkigt decided that by 1929 his fine six-cylinder cars were just about obsolete, he was conversant with vee engines. Thus it should not have occasioned too much surprise that the Hispano-Suiza which was to cause as much comment and excite as much praise during what we in England now call the post-vintage-thoroughbred period (1931–1940) as the Vintage Hispanos before it, had a vee twelve cylinder power unit.

The connection with the 1914–18 war is even closer than the foregoing may suggest, because, although Birkigt's production aero motors were V8s, before the end of hostilities he had on the drawing board, if not on the test bed, a V12 engine of the same bore and stroke, using a shaft-driven o.h. camshaft above each cylinder bank, and it was half this engine, in effect, which he had taken for his sensational 37·2 h.p. or 32 c.v. car engine.

The bore and stroke of this war-time aero motor were 100 × 140 mm. and in designing the great V12 car engine Birkigt used the same cylinder-bore size but also used a stroke of 100 mm., to give a 'square'

power unit with a swept volume of no less than 9,424 c.c. There was, however, one vital difference. Whereas up to that time, Birkigt had been a keen exponent of the single overhead camshaft operating directly on the vertical overhead valves, in his new V12 car engine he went over to push-rod and rocker valve gear. It may have been that the aim was quieter running. At all events, with the cylinder blocks at an angle of 60 deg. it was convenient to have the camshaft in the crankcase between them, and the comparatively short cylinder-stroke meant that the push-rods need not be very long and so were of decently light weight.

Let us examine the great V12 Hispano-Suiza in detail.

The Type 68 V12 Hispano-Suiza has been described by one authority as the most magnificent motor car ever to be built in series production, this writer adding that under the prevailing changed economy it is unlikely that anything like it will ever be catalogued again.

The engine had integral cylinder blocks and heads of aluminium alloy, finished in the old Hispano-Suiza tradition by enamelling under pressure. In these cylinder blocks the screwed-in liners were of hardened

Off-side view of the 11·3-litre V12 engine. Note the downdraught carburettors between the cylinder blocks and the dual exhaust system. (Photo: Mr. Ronald Barker)

Near-side view of the V12 engine. Note the water pump at the front of the crankcase and the traditional stove-enamel finish. (Photo: Mr. Ronald Barker)

These illustrations emphasise the enormous wheelbase length of the 54/220 model. In fact, four chassis lengths were available.
(Photos: Mr. C. W. P. Hampton)

nitralloy steel. Within the vee formed by the cylinder blocks the two-choke Hispano-Suiza carburettors were accommodated, while ignition was by two sets of sparking plugs in each cylinder fired independently by twin Scintilla magnetos.

The exhaust manifolding comprised two manifolds for each cylinder bank, these being vitreous enamelled. Lubrication and cooling were conventional, the latter system employing two circulatory pumps, one for each block, and a fan to stir water through the enormous radiator. The connecting rods were tubular. A power output of 220 b.h.p. at the modest peak crankshaft revolutions of 3,000 per minute was claimed for the original 9½-litre power unit, which had a compression-ratio of 6·0 to 1.

Chassis design was along the accepted lines of the late Vintage period. In other words, the frame was sprung on half-elliptic leaf springs, the whole chassis very rigid and well-suited to such a heavy fast motor-car. The drive from the engine went through a multi-plate clutch to the usual three-speed-and-reverse gearbox, which had gear ratios of 5·44, 4·10 and 2·72 to 1, although a lower set of ratios was available for cars carrying excessively heavy coachwork.

Final drive was by means of a torque-tube-enclosed propeller shaft and, visualising a considerable variety of body styles on the new car, Hispano-Suiza contrived no fewer than four different lengths of chassis, respectively with wheelbases measuring 11 ft. 3 in., 12 ft. 2 in., 12 ft. 6 in., and 13 ft. 2 in. It must be remembered that individual coachbuilders still plied their trade in those times, and they were nicely accommodated by these four chassis varieties and by the lower gear ratios, which stemmed from a choice of four different back axle ratios, 2·72, 2·89, 3·0 and 3·3 to 1.

It was late in 1931 that the great V12 Hispano-Suiza made its appearance and at once it was hailed by those who could still afford such extravagant luxuries as one of the world's finest motor-cars. It was a car which possessed performance of an order which put it in the top flight, an automobile which was endowed with that impeccable Hispano-Suiza steering that contrives to make such huge cars feel much smaller than in fact they are to the person behind the steering wheel; although the new V12 turned the weighbridge at in the region of 2½ tons and was capable of very appreciably exceeding 100 m.p.h., the gearbox-driven mechanical brake servo, in conjunction with enormous ribbed brake drums on each wheel, a legacy from the 37·2 h.p. Hispano-Suiza of 1919, provided adequate means of arresting the Type 68.

It was indeed a fine production and one entirely fitted to carry on the tradition of cars which had featured in novels in both England and France ('The Green Hat' by Michael Arlen and 'L'Homme à l'Hispano' by Pierre Frondaie) and which had in their time been the favoured motor-cars of the King of Spain and of the multi-millionaire Woolf Barnato, who afterwards bought the Bentley Motor Company.

Many people thought the horse-power estimate for the Type 68 of 220 b.h.p. conservative and certainly the V12 possessed very impressive acceleration from any pace up to about 80 m.p.h. in spite of its great weight. The new car made its début at the Paris Salon of 1931, a show where so many famous cars have had their first showing to the motor critics and where, in those days, the most remarkably optimistic confections were exhibited side by side with vehicles intended for serious production. The big Hispano-

Driving compartment of C. W. P. Hampton's Type 68-bis. Note central tachometer, neatly grouped instruments and rear-view mirror incorporating altimeter and internal temperature thermometer. (Photo: Mr. Ronald Barker)

Suiza with its traditional radiator shape and winged badge was the proudest offering at this just-post-Vintage show.

To introduce the new model the late Charles Faroux, father of motoring journalists, drove one as fast as he could from Paris to Nice and back and straight into the Hispano-Suiza showrooms during the period of the Paris Salon, where it was alleged a large sheet of white paper was waiting to receive it. Over this sheet of paper the still-hot car was brought to rest, and it is said that for the period of the Exhibition not a drop of oil fell from it, proof of the most careful assembly and inspection of what was a very complicated piece of engineering.

It was some time before the V12 Hispano-Suiza came to England, but early in 1934 one of these cars was the subject of a road-test report in the pages of *The Autocar*. They tried a car fitted with a Vanvooren drophead-coupé body, the weight of which was no less than 39 cwt. Using the highest of the available axle ratios, 2·7 to 1, the car lapped Brooklands track at 95 m.p.h. and was timed over the flying half-mile at fractionally over 100 m.p.h. As to acceleration, a mile-a-minute was accomplished from rest in 12 seconds, 80 m.p.h. was reached in a matter of 19 seconds and the top gear pick-up was truly astonishing, a steady 30 m.p.h. to 50 m.p.h. occupying only six seconds. Dropping into the middle speed, the time for this performance was reduced to a mere four seconds.

This ability to accelerate from a crawl to 80 or 90 m.p.h. very rapidly indeed and the ability of the 54/220 Hispano-Suiza to cruise effortlessly at any speed up to its maximum to a great extent undermined the arguments of those critics who maintained that the gear ratios of the three-speed gearbox were too widely spaced. Indeed, without dropping out of top gear, the closed V12 Hispano-Suiza was able to increase speed from 10 to 70 m.p.h. in a matter of 21 seconds, and would come down to walking pace in this same gear. Although *The Autocar* obtained only 100 m.p.h. from a coupé version on Brooklands

The ex-Dubonnet Hispano-Suiza as modernised by C. W. P. Hampton in 1955.

Below: A V12 coupé of the mid-'thirties. Note the unusually styled front bumper.

No chassis lent itself better to spacious, elegant coachwork than the V12 Hispano-Suiza. This Type 68 long-chassis version carries a limousine body by Henry Binder of Paris.

(Photos: Mr. C. W. P. Hampton)

1933/34 9½-litre V12, thought to have been owned by Lord Rothschild. The exotic coachwork is probably by Figoni et Falaschi.
(Photo: Mr. C. W. P. Hampton)

track, other examples were able to show a top speed of around 105–108 m.p.h. With such performance petrol consumption might have been anticipated in single figures; in fact, the big Hispano-Suiza returned 11 m.p.g.

By the time the car had become established in England the makers had decided to gild the lily and it is to the Type 68-bis that the foregoing performance figures refer. The difference was that the cylinder stroke had been increased by 20 mm. to 120 mm., so that the swept volume had gone up to the impressive capacity, for a post-Vintage or indeed, for a post-Edwardian production motor-car, of 11,310 c.c. This produced a maximum power output of 250 b.h.p. without taking the crankshaft speed beyond the previous modest 3,000 r.p.m.

By 1934 the chassis price in England of the V12 was £2,750 and the Vanvooren coupé which the concessionaires used as the Press car and demonstrator was listed at a cool £3,500.

The V12 Hispano-Suiza remained in production until the Munich crisis in 1938. It needed very few modifications during its production run of eight years.

Later models had ignition by twin Scintilla Vertex magnetos instead of using the four coils of the earliest Type 68 cars. Incidentally, the sump held as much as 3¼ gallons of lubricant and the valve timing differed from that adopted by Birkigt for the 37·2 h.p. Hispano-Suiza only in much earlier opening of the exhaust valves. The exhaust valves, which were on the outside of the heads, opened 60 deg. before b.d.c. and closed 5 deg. after t.d.c., while the inlet valves, conveniently situated to be fed by the carburettors within the engine's vee, opened at 7 deg. after t.d.c. and closed 45 deg. before b.d.c. The tappet clearances (hot) for the V12 engine were 14-thou. inlet and 18-thou. for the exhaust.

There was nothing unique about a vee-twelve engine for use in an automobile when the Type 68 Hispano-Suiza made its début in 1931, but it is worth remembering that it was not until 1936 that Rolls-Royce replaced their six-cylinder in-line engine with the V12 Phantom III. This was perhaps the most silky and silent automobile ever built, but its 7·3-litre engine was deliberately intended to give these results, whereas the Hispano-Suiza V12, while extremely flexible and

David Scott-Moncrieff's Type 68 Chapron-bodied car, originally built for Marcel Boussac, which effectively portrays the large radiator area and famous stork mascot of the late pre-war Hispano-Suiza.
(Photo: Mr. Ronald Barker)

A stately Berline-de-Ville, with carriage auxiliary lamps, on the 1933 Type 68 chassis. (Photo: Col. J. R. Buckley)

quiet, delivered its performance with a trace of arrogance, so that whereas the English car was luxury personified, the car from France was of more sporting aspect. And, of course, Rolls-Royce never disclose the power developed by their automobile engines, so that there is no direct comparison to be made with the 250 b.h.p. so easily produced by the Type 68-bis Hispano-Suiza. In 1937 the Rolls-Royce Phantom III chassis cost £1,900.

In England the V12 with the winged-badge became sought after by wealthy collectors and Peter Hampton managed to maintain two immaculate specimens in captivity at his home and motor house in Sussex (the latter reputed to be larger than the former!): a Type 68 12 ft. 2 in. two-door coupé registered OXU 91 and a Type 68-bis two-seater registered AYU 899. And at the Royal Aircraft Establishment, Farnborough, they have a nicely-preserved SE5 in flying trim, with a Viper V8 engine, forerunner of the V12 Hispano-Suiza aero engine on which the automobile V12 power unit of 1931 may be said to have been based.

The V12 was not the only model produced by the famous French company in the post-vintage period, although it was by far the most impressive.

The 6½- and 8-litre six-cylinder models persisted up to 1933, but they rightly belong to the Vintage era. By 1931 Hispano-Suiza had absorbed the Ballot concern, which had originally built engines for Delage and other French car manufacturers and later made some very nice cars of its own, notably the 2-litre range. To tie in with this allegiance a 4½-litre Hispano-Suiza power unit was installed in a Ballot chassis (the gearbox had a central change-speed lever, which offended the purists almost as much as the similar gear change on the first vintage Rolls-Royce Twenty chassis!). This model was called the Junior.

After a few years this lesser-Hispano was replaced by the 30/120 h.p. car. This had a bore and stroke for

In their day, these cars won many top awards in Beauty Contests, graced by elegant women. This 1933/34 Type 68-bis is said to be owned today by Charles A. Chayne, Vice-President of General Motors Inc. (Photo: Mr. C. W. P. Hampton)

Above and below: Almost as elegant as the V12, the long chassis 30/120 lent itself to specialised coachwork like this Sedanca-de-Ville.
(Photos: Mr. Morin Scott)

its six-cylinder engine of 100 × 110 mm., giving a capacity of 5·2 litres. Alas, the central gear lever persisted, as indeed it did on the V12 cars, which had synchromesh on top and second gears. This 30/120 h.p. Hispano-Suiza had push-rod-operated overhead valves and ignition by twin coils, and the valve timing was closely related to that which Birkigt had worked out for the overhead camshaft 6½-litre car. A demonstrator 30/120 h.p. model came to England, with a pillarless Vanvooren saloon body, which turned the scales at 35 cwt. This was late in 1934, the car giving performance figures of 0–50 m.p.h. in 12·2 seconds, 0–60 m.p.h. in 19·6 seconds, and a top speed over a timed ¼-mile of just below 83 m.p.h. This was achieved with the long-wheelbase chassis pulling a top gear of 3·65 to 1. Needless to say, the gearbox contained but three forward speeds; 30–50 m.p.h. occupied 8·6 seconds in top, but the time was reduced to 5·8 seconds if the 5·4 to 1 middle gear was used. The price of this saloon model was £1,895 in England in 1934; a short-chassis version of the 30/120 h.p. car was available with an axle-ratio of 3·4 to 1, which would perhaps have reached 90 m.p.h.

In whatever guise it was made, the Hispano-Suiza was a car beautifully finished beneath the bonnet and possessed of good performance and a high degree of

A Saoutchik three-seater body, with 'dickey' behind the hood, on the 1938 30/120 chassis. (Photo: Dr. L. B. Paling)

refinement. During the hey-day of the 6½-litre model a similar overhead camshaft 27 h.p. version had been offered to those discerning enough to crave an Hispano, but not sufficiently wealthy to run one of the 6½-litre or 8-litre models. This was made at the Barcelona factory but in the mid-nineteen-thirties this became uneconomical to produce and its 85 × 110 mm. overhead camshaft engine was replaced by a push-rod overhead valve 80 × 100 mm. 3-litre power unit rated at 20 h.p.

It is happier, however, to regard the great V12 as the swan-song of the Hispano-Suiza. By 1939 the Paris factory was given over to aero-engine manufacture. The post-war Hispano was a front-wheel-drive V8 of between 3- and 4-litres and it was shown at the Geneva Motor Show in 1946. The suspension was of new conception.

The car remained afterwards at the Paris factory until about November 1958, when it was broken up without the knowledge of Maurice Heurteux, the President of Hispano-Suiza, who, six months later, offered it as a gift to Morin Scott, the President of 'Les Hommes à l'Hispano'. Too late, alas!

The 30/120 Hispano-Suiza in drophead coupé form.

It was the very exciting Pegaso which I saw being made when I was conducted round the old Barcelona home of Hispano-Suiza after the war. Even that did not last very long, and soon Pegaso were back to concentrating on building their very fine heavy trucks.

© *William Boddy, 1966.*

SPECIFICATION: HISPANO-SUIZA V12

ENGINE: Twelve cylinders in two banks of six, forming a 60 deg. vee. *Tipo 68:* 100 × 100 mm. bore and stroke, 9,424 c.c. *Tipo 68-bis:* 100 × 120 mm., 11,310 c.c. Overhead valves operated by push-rods and rockers. Aluminium cylinder blocks and integral fixed alloy cylinder heads. Steel cylinder liners. Tubular connecting rods; light-alloy pistons. Pressure lubrication. Cooling by a water pump for each cylinder block, and fan. 5·0 to 1 or 6·0 to 1 compression-ratio. *Ignition:* dual Scintilla magnetos firing two sets of sparking plugs on later engines, battery and four coils on early Tipo 68 engines. Two twin-choke Hispano-Suiza carburettors. Main jets 160, pilot jets 70. *Firing order:* 1R, 6L, 5R, 2L, 3R, 4L, 6R, 1L, 2R, 5L, 4R, 3L. *Valve timing:* Inlet opens 7 deg. a.t.d.c., inlet closes 45 deg. a.b.d.c., exhaust opens 60 deg. b.b.d.c., exhaust closes 5 deg. a.t.d.c. *Tappet clearances:* Inlet 0·014 in., exhaust 0·018 in., engine hot. *Power output:* 190 b.h.p. at 3,000 r.p.m. on 5·0 to 1 compression ratio, 220 b.h.p. at 3,000 r.p.m. on 6·0 to 1 compression ratio from Tipo 68 engine. 250 b.h.p. at 3,000 r.p.m. from Tipo 68-bis engine.

(Photo: Mr. C. W. P. Hampton)

Sports Saloon by Vanvooren on light chassis.

Coupé de Ville by Kellner
on normal chassis.

Drophead Coupé by Saoutchik
on light chassis.

'Aerodynamique' Sports Saloon
by Franay on light chassis.

Cabriolet three-seater by
Million Guiet on short chassis.

Sedanca Limousine-de-Ville by
Letourneur et Marchand on long chassis.

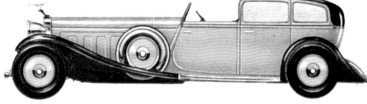

Coupé Limousine-de-Ville by
Binder on normal chassis.

© GORDON C. DAVIES, 1966.

A very rare Hispano-Suiza model—the Hispano-Ballot Type 26. This is probably the sole example to be imported into Britain. Now owned by Lord Doune, it is a 1934 example with coachwork by Lancefield of London. (Photo: Norval Ltd.)

GEARBOX: Three forward speeds and reverse controlled by central lever. Ratios (with 2·7 to 1 axle ratio), 2·7, 4·1 and 5·44 to 1.
AXLE RATIOS: 2·7, 2·89, 3·0 or 3·3 to 1.
WHEELBASE: 11 ft. 3 in., 12 ft. 2 in., 12 ft. 6 in. or 13 ft. 2 in.
WEIGHT: (coupé body), 4,880 lb.
CHASSIS PRICE: £2,750.

PERFORMANCE: Tipo 68-bis with coupé body and 2·7 to 1 axle ratio: 0–50 m.p.h. in 9·4 sec., 0–60 m.p.h. in 12·0 sec., 0–70 m.p.h. in 15·0 sec., 0–80 m.p.h. in 19·0 sec. Maximum speed, 108 m.p.h. Fuel consumption, 10–11 m.p.g.

SPECIFICATION: HISPANO-SUIZA 30/120

ENGINE: Six cylinders in-line, detachable cylinder head. 100 × 110 mm. bore and stroke, 4,900 c.c. Overhead valves operated by push-rods and rockers. Dual battery and coil ignition.
GEARBOX: Three forward speeds and reverse, controlled by central lever. Ratios 3·65, 5·40 and 7·25 to 1.
AXLE RATIOS: 3·4 to 1 or 3·65 to 1.
WHEELBASE: 11 ft. 3 in. *Track:* 4 ft. 9 in.
WEIGHT: (Saloon body), 35 cwt.
PRICE: (in 1935 with saloon body), £1,895.
PERFORMANCE: 0–50 m.p.h. in 12·2 sec., 0-60 m.p.h. in 19·6 sec., 30–50 m.p.h. in 8·6 sec. in top gear, 5·8 sec. in second gear. Speed over timed quarter-mile, 82·95 m.p.h.
PETROL TANK CAPACITY: 22 gallons.
FUEL CONSUMPTION: 14–17 m.p.g.
TURNING CIRCLE: 46 ft.

SPECIFICATION: BALLOT HISPANO-SUIZA TYPE 26

ENGINE: Six cylinders in line, 90 × 120 mm. (4,560 c.c.). Maximum engine speed, 2,800 r.p.m. Aluminium monobloc cylinders. Overhead valves operated by shaft-driven overhead camshaft. Pump cooling. Thermostat control. Water in circulation, 22 litres. Scintilla dynamo driven from nose of camshaft. Tubular connecting-rods.
CHASSIS: Half-elliptic suspension. Hispano-Suiza mechanical-servo four wheel brakes. Multi-plate clutch. Three-speed and reverse gearbox. Final drive by torque tube. Fuel feed by Autoflux fuel pump from 95-litre petrol tank.
DIMENSIONS: Wheelbase, 11 ft. 6½ in. Track, (front), 4 ft. 6½ in. (rear), 4 ft. 8 in. Overall length, 15 ft.
MAKERS: Establissements Ballot, 27 and 39, Boulevard Brune, Paris.

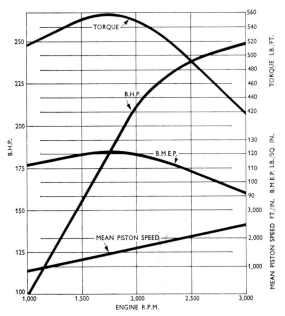

Power curves for the 11.3-litre Hispano-Suiza

The Jaguar XK Series

4

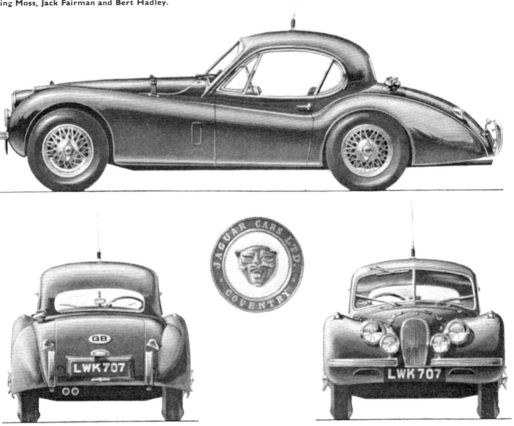

LESLIE JOHNSON'S XK 120 fixed head coupé
which averaged 100·31 m.p.h. for seven days at
Linas-Montlhery in August, 1952. Co-drivers:
Stirling Moss, Jack Fairman and Bert Hadley.

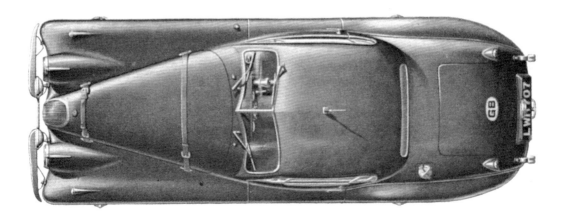

0   5′

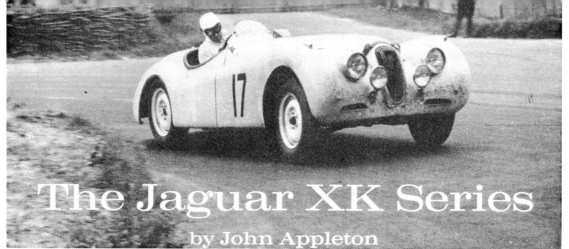

The Jaguar XK Series

by John Appleton

Leslie Johnson and his travel-stained XK 120 at Le Mans, 1950.

Jaguar's 'XK' series of motor cars was produced from 1948 to 1961, in three basic forms—the XK 120, XK 140, and XK 150—each type being offered in a choice of three body styles. Most famous of them all was, of course, the XK 120 which remained in production until 1954 when it was succeeded by the XK 140; this, in turn, was replaced in 1957 by the XK 150.

The term 'XK' was evolved from the name of an engine. The '120' of XK 120 represented the car's maximum speed, and the figure was in fact a conservative one. Development of the series was not confined to increases in performance, however, and the subsequent '140'/'150' suffix must be regarded purely as the type number, without any special meaning.

In order to set out this brief profile chronologically it is necessary to look back first of all to 1935, when Jaguars were not Jaguars at all, but SSs.

The SS—a *marque* in its own right since 1931—had always been powered by very 'standard Standard' engines. 1935 was the year in which the 'Jaguar' suffix was added, and it was then that the *marque* began to acquire some mechanical individuality of its own. William Lyons, who had founded his 'Swallow' side-car shop in Blackpool back in 1922, was now controlling one of Coventry's major motor manufacturing plants, and decided it was high time that his company should control its own future from the engineering standpoint. One of his first actions, then, was to acquire from Humber the services of William Heynes, and to appoint him chief engineer.

1935 was also the year in which the SS 90—the company's first genuine sports two-seater—was introduced. Apart from a new design of cylinder head undertaken by Harry Weslake, the elegant SS had until then made few pretensions to really high performance, although a team of SS I tourers had won an award in the 1934 International Alpine Trial. In the remaining pre-war years, however, Heynes developed the two-seater (which, in 1936, became the SS Jaguar 100) into a machine that was highly successful both in competitions and on the road. Today the SS Jaguar 100 is regarded as one of the truly classic sports cars. One $3\frac{1}{2}$-litre example was coaxed into producing 160 b.h.p. for short periods using special fuel and an incredible 15 to 1 compression ratio. This b.h.p. figure became the yardstick for Jaguar's post-war engine project.

War brought car production to a standstill, and SS Cars Ltd., in common with its contemporaries, set to work in other directions—mainly on sidecar, trailer and aircraft work. This did not prevent Lyons from looking with customary astuteness to the future. Shortly before hostilities ended the team of Lyons, Heynes, and Claude Baily (chief designer) was further strengthened by the return of Walter Hassan who had been working for several years on Bristol aero engines. By 1945, when the company became Jaguar Cars Ltd., several new engine sketches had already been drawn—mainly, so it is said, during 'fire-watching' at the company's Foleshill, Coventry, factory.

The aim of the Jaguar team was to build a robust,

Leslie Johnson winning at an average speed of 82.19 m.p.h. at Silverstone in 1949—the XK 120's first race and its first victory.
(Photo: Louis Klemantaski)

smooth, flexible engine capable of high power output and continuous development. Designs were code-named 'X'.

Jaguar's first double overhead camshaft engine to reach construction stage was the XF, a four-cylinder of 1,360 c.c. (66·5 × 98 mm.). Its main purpose was to prove the new cylinder head and valve-gear; this it did satisfactorily, but the crankshaft was inadequate for the high revolutions envisaged. The XG, another 'four', was a more conventional pushrod design based on the existing 1¾-litre cylinder block originated by Standard, and on the BMW 328 head.

A final basis for the production unit was found in design XJ. This was built both as a four-cylinder (2 litres, 80·5 × 98 mm.) and as a six-cylinder (3·2 litres, 83 × 98 mm.). Most of the important experiments were carried out on the 'four', which consequently underwent many alterations and led to an XK version of similar dimensions. The 3·2-litre XJ would undoubtedly have replaced the then-still-current 2·7- and 3·5-litre pushrod engines but for its inadequate low-speed torque. Its stroke was therefore increased, and thus it became the 3,442 c.c. seven-bearing production six-cylinder XK unit.

Earl's Court, 1948, saw the first appearance of the XK, and public acclaim was immediate. Whilst Heynes and his colleagues had been working on the new engines and chassis, Lyons's flair for 'line', so evident in previous SS and Jaguar designs, had resulted in an inspired body style which in many ways created a revolution in the whole concept of the sporting two-seater.

The enthusiasts who came in droves to the Jaguar stand had, in fact, already been given a hint of what to expect—in terms of power unit at least—when, in the summer of 1948, that indefatigable record-breaker Goldie Gardner had borrowed one of the works' experimental four-cylinder 2-o.h.c. 2-litre engines. Fitted with this unit, Gardner's almost venerable streamlined record car had broken three international Class E records on the Ostend-Brussels *autoroute*. The engine developed 146 b.h.p. at 6,000 r.p.m., with a safe maximum of 6,500 r.p.m.; it had a 12 to 1 compression ratio, and gave the car a two-way average of 176·694 m.p.h. for the 'flying kilometre'.

When the XK 100 was announced at Earl's Court that autumn, its power output rating was 105 b.h.p. at 5,000 r.p.m., with a compression ratio of 7 to 1—a compact and efficient engine working well within its limits. But, although listed by the factory for some time, the XK 100 never actually went into production. The attraction of its larger brother was too great, and

Mr. Lyons (who became Sir William Lyons in 1956) with Tazio Nuvolari at Silverstone, 1950. Nuvolari enjoyed his practice session with the XK 120, but was too ill to drive in the actual race.

the 2-litre, 4-cylinder, 3-bearing XK project was eventually shelved during 1949. The beefy 6-cylinder had won the day; the XK 120 had arrived.

Lack of choice of power unit did not deter would-be XK 120 customers. There were many other reasons why William Lyons's new car should be coveted. Its box-section chassis was orthodox yet immensely rigid. The independent front suspension was by low-stress torsion bars and wide-base wishbones—a result of exhaustive tests combined with Heynes's admiration for Citroën practice. Rear suspension was by semi-elliptic springs. The car had re-circulating ball steering, and its hydraulic brakes operated on 12-in. drums. (These two items were the only chassis features to alter drastically during the life of the XK series —and not without reason, for the original brakes in particular were not really up to the performance of the car when driven hard.) Above all, it was clothed in that beautiful flowing body.

Strange though it may now seem, it was initially intended to construct only 200 XK sports cars, in order that the engine could be tried out by the public as a prelude to being placed in a new saloon car of wider appeal. (This was to be the Mk. VII, introduced late in 1950.) Floods of orders, however, forced Lyons to lay down a full production programme for the XK 120.

The first examples—just over the 200—were fitted with aluminium bodywork mounted on a wooden frame. The new programme changed all this, and arrangements were made with the Pressed Steel Company to provide steel body pressings. This alteration in production planning, together with the inevitable

Stirling Moss drives Tom Wisdom's XK 120 to victory in the 1950 Tourist Trophy, held in pouring rain at Dundrod, N. Ireland.

Bob Berry, now Jaguar's P.R.O., at Pardon hairpin, Prescottt, in his XK 120, early 1950s. The aero screen and metal 'tonneau' cover were amongst the many optional extras. (Photo: T. C. March)

and innumerable problems of launching any brand-new model, created a delay. The first export models were delivered to the United States of America in 1949, but it was not until the following year that a steady flow began—and, even then, home customers were fed in very small helpings.

Public interest in the XK 120 was, nevertheless, maintained without difficulty. Jaguar's chief tester, Ron Sutton, took a car to 'Gardner's strip' on the Belgian motorway near Jabbeke in May 1949 and, with hood and sidescreens in place, averaged 126·448 m.p.h. over the measured mile using low-octane pump fuel. With aero screen, streamlined undershield, and a metal cover over the passenger's seat, a speed of 132·596 m.p.h. was accomplished.

In August three XK 120s, painted red, white, and blue, were entered for the first-ever international Silverstone one-hour production car race. They came home first and second, driven by Leslie Johnson and Peter Walker respectively. 'Bira' spun the other car whilst leading, due to a puncture, and could not regain the circuit.

Jaguar did not set up a competition department until the C-type—Jaguar's first car to be built specifically for racing—was being prepared for the 1951 Le Mans 24-hour race. In any case, the XK 120 was as

much a touring car as a sports car. This was borne out by the luxurious manner in which it was equipped, but belied by its performance which many racing drivers were naturally anxious to exploit. In 1950 and succeeding years the company did in fact prepare a number of production-type cars for competition, and several XK 120 drivers were given works support. For 1950 six drivers were allocated specially-prepared cars differing from the standard specification only in detail. During their 'term of office', however, these aluminium-bodied cars had various modifications carried out upon them. In a sense they were development cars, and the list of optional extras increased rapidly. In summer 1951, for example, performance equipment available to the public included: lightened flywheel, 9 to 1 pistons, high-lift ($\frac{3}{8}$ in.) cams, stiffer torsion bars and springs, special brake linings, special clutch, twin exhausts, wire wheels, bucket seats, 24-gallon fuel tank, and other modifications. The cost of completely equipping a car in this fashion was in the region of £160. This was the beginning of the constant development which has been pursued steadily to this day.

The six works-prepared XK 120s of 1950 were allocated to Leslie Johnson, L. H. ('Nick') Haines, Peter Walker, Clemente Biondetti, Ian Appleyard, and

Left: *The Marathon de la Route (or Liège) has only once been won without loss of time, by Johnny Claes and Jacques Ickx of Belgium in 1951, driving the XK 120 seen arriving back in Liège, followed by the XK 120 of Laroche and Radix, who finished fifth. Note the straight-sided windscreen (a feature of the early aluminium-bodied cars) of the winner, compared with the curved-edge type (Laroche's car).* Right: *This Ferrari-like Oblin-bodied XK 120 was second, driven by Herzet and Baudoin. Claes, Herzet and Laroche also took the Team Prize for Jaguar.*

Tom Wisdom. Between them they achieved some outstanding and often unexpected victories. The most important international wins of their first season were gained by Ian Appleyard in the Alpine Rally and by Stirling Moss (driving Wisdom's car) in the Tourist Trophy race.

Ian Appleyard's name was to become linked inseparably with the 'Alpine'. In 1948 he had won a *Coupe des Alpes* and put up Best Performance overall with an SS Jaguar 100 in heroic circumstances, after an epic drive following a delay to assist an injured competitor. His 1950 Alpine sortie brought similar success—Best Performance and a *Coupe* once again—and this was only the beginning.

Tom Wisdom's T.T. entry was driven by Stirling Moss, as Wisdom had fixed himself up with a drive for the Jowett team. It was this race that 'made' Moss. Undeterred by a downpour that set the Dundrod circuit awash, he extended his lead throughout the race and won it with the outward calm that was later to create a World Champion in all but name.

These were by no means the XK's only successes in its first full season. Besides many more victories in Europe, Phil Hill and others were bringing prestige to the *marque* in Jaguar's major money-spinning export country—America. (Hill was, incidentally, probably the first man to convert an XK engine to 3·8 litres.) It is particularly interesting to note, too, that three XK 120s made an exploratory trip to Le Mans, and acquitted themselves quite well. Leslie Johnson and 'Bert' Hadley were actually lying third—

and lapping faster than the leading Talbot—when, after approximately twenty-one hours of racing, the clutch gave up; but the car had travelled in remarkable silence, putting in a lap at nearly 97 m.p.h. before retiring. The other XKs finished 12th (Clark and Haines) and 15th (Whitehead and Marshall).

Jaguar's premises at Foleshill were bursting at the seams and, with the announcement of the Mark VII saloon towards the end of 1950, there began a gradual move to a larger factory several miles away in the Allesley district of Coventry. This transfer was completed in 1952 with little effect on the ever-increasing volume of production.

The XK 120 roadster was joined in 1951 by a fixed-head coupé version of equally attractive proportions and similar mechanical specification.

The XK's competition achievements reached their highest pinnacle in 1951. Ian Appleyard put up best performance in the Tulip, R.A.C., and Alpine Rallies;

One of the most successful rally cars of all time, Ian Appleyard's XK 120, leads a similar car during a test forming part of the 1951 R.A.C. Rally, in which Appleyard put up a Best Performance. Later modifications included the fitting of wire wheels, and the car is seen (below) as it is today in the Montagu Motor Museum, wearing the plates from its 1952 Coupe des Alpes—its third in a row.

Fastest speed ever recorded by an XK Jaguar was 172 m.p.h. by Norman Dewis on the Belgian autoroute in 1953.

Johnny Claes scored the only 'clean sheet' ever accomplished in the notoriously tough Liège-Rome-Liège marathon and won the Spa production car race; and Stirling Moss was first at Silverstone. The XK 120's international successes for that year are almost endless. Somewhat naturally, however, such a docile, quiet, and fully road-equipped sports car could not continue to hold off the more specialised opposition with such regularity; and, after all, Jaguar was building and racing full-blown competition cars by now. The future of the XK range was to be its continued refinement and modernisation as *road* transport.

In 1952 a more powerful special equipment version was announced; and in 1953 came a third body style, the drophead coupé.

Whilst development plans went ahead in Coventry, the XK 120 was still performing with great credit, particularly in rallies. Appleyard continued his winning streak in the Alpine by taking home a *Coupe* in 1952, and another in 1953 to bring his total to five. He was, in fact, the first man to win an Alpine Gold Cup for penalty-free drives on three consecutive occasions. (Much-coveted *Coupes des Alpes* were won by XK 120 drivers on eight occasions altogether—Appleyard four times; Habisreutinger, Gatsonides, Gendebien and Mansbridge once each.) In its early days David Murray's *Ecurie Ecosse* team of XK 120s gained victory in innumerable races. Private owners lightened and modified their own XKs, amongst the most successful at different times being Hugh Howorth, Dick Protheroe and Bob Berry, to mention only a few.

It is not possible to mention more than several of the XK 120's achievements here. One particular event which must be recalled, however, is the high-speed demonstration that took place at Linas-Montlhéry in August 1952. Leslie Johnson had previously used the bumpy, banked French circuit to average 107 m.p.h. for 24 hours (with Stirling Moss) and later to cover over 130 m.p.h. for an hour. Now he returned, not with his familiar white roadster, but with a bronze fixed-head coupé—and with a much bigger goal in view. His goal was to average over 100 m.p.h. for a week and (with a team of co-drivers comprising Moss, Fairman and Hadley) that is exactly what he accomplished—and four World records into the bargain. This more than compensated for the failure of the works C-types to finish, let alone repeat their 1951 win, at Le Mans that year—and Jaguar's sales soared higher than ever.

As if proof of the XK 120's performance were needed, Norman Dewis (who had succeeded Ron Sutton as Jaguar's chief test driver) took a modified and stripped roadster to Jabbeke in 1953 and, crouched beneath a perspex 'bubble', covered a mile at a mean 172·412 m.p.h.—the highest speed ever recorded by an XK Jaguar.

The XK 140 was announced in autumn 1954, by which time more than 12,000 XK 120s had been constructed—rather more than had been the original intention! The new car was offered with the same three body alternatives, but whereas the drophead and roadster models were similar in appearance to their predecessor (apart from heftier bumpers and a new grille), the fixed-head coupé had a much larger cockpit with room for extra luggage—even the occasional passenger—behind the seats. The standard engine developed 190 b.h.p. and the special equipment version (with C-type cylinder head) 210 b.h.p.

The car had rack-and-pinion steering, and larger-

Left: Leslie Johnson brings the XK 120 coupé across the line at Linas-Montlhéry after it had averaged over 100 m.p.h. for a week in 1952 (16,851 miles in 168 hours) (Photo: P. A.- Reuter). *Right: The XK 120 coupé, perhaps the most beautiful of all the XK models, competing in the 1954 Alpine Rally and driven by Reg Mansbridge.*

47

Ian Appleyard parted with NUB 120 at the end of 1952 and acquired another XK 120 (RUB 120), with which he won his last Coupe des Alpes in 1952. Thereafter he reduced his activities but competed with success from time to time. His XK 140 coupé (VUB 140) during the 1956 R.A.C. Rally, was second overall to the Aston Martin of Lyndon Sims. (Photo: Charles Dunn)

diameter torsion bars of the type fitted to special equipment XK 120s. Overdrive was now listed among the optional extras. Weight distribution was improved by moving the engine further forward, and placing the battery (previously behind the seats) forward of the bulkhead. Although handling and braking were better than before, the XK 140 was very definitely a high-speed touring car. Nevertheless it was raced and rallied with some success by privateers. One of the more interesting versions to be seen around the circuits (long after the model was obsolete, incidentally), was David Hobbs' XK 140 drophead coupé fitted with the efficient Hobbs Mechamatic gearbox; this car went very quickly indeed, proving beyond doubt that automatic transmission—which is now becoming almost commonplace in sports-racing cars—could be adapted successfully for motor-racing. It was the Borg Warner box, however, that became optional on production models late in 1956.

Jaguar's long-term plans had, in 1957, come to a state of major change. The company had just announced its withdrawal from official participation in motor-racing, leaving *Ecurie Ecosse* in Europe and Briggs Cunningham in America to continue to bring home most of the D-type's laurels. Unit construction was 'in', disc brakes were 'in', fully independent suspension was 'in'. We know the result—the E-type. First introduced in 1961, it bears a very close affinity in design to the D-type racing car whose superb stability, reliability and braking power brought three successive Le Mans victories.

It would not be fair to say that the XK series came in like a lion and went out like a lamb. All the same,

it must be stated that its final manifestation represented a point approaching the zenith of this particular basic design. The XK 150 was more refined than ever; interior space was increased still further, and modernised. Like the 120 and 140 before it, it came in three body styles with the option of pressed-steel or wire wheels—although only a few were made with the former. Like all Jaguars, it provided remarkable value for money.

First, in May 1957, came the fixed-head and drophead coupé models; the open model, the first Jaguar roadster to have wind-up windows, did not appear until early 1958. The trusty, military four-speed gearbox (which was robust but very slow, yet which Jaguar did not improve upon until 1964) was still fitted as standard, with or without overdrive; the Borg Warner fully automatic transmission was also available, as on the later XK 140s. Power ratings remained at 190 and 210 b.h.p., although the latter engine (fitted to most of the XK 150 models built) gave its maximum power at slightly lower r.p.m. than the 'C-head' XK 140. The excellent rack-and-pinion steering was retained, as were the basic suspension design, the separate chassis, and the 'live' rear axle.

Even those who were openly rude about the rather 'podgy' lines, the high scuttle, and some of the XK 150's other now-slightly-dated features, were full of praise for the car's most important new item of specification. After more than five years of racing and of co-operative experiment with Dunlop, Jaguar had at last fitted disc brakes to a production car—and to all four wheels at that. (A standard XK 150 with the old Lockheed two-leading-shoe drum brakes was still offered, but the writer has never seen one.) All Jaguars have featured disc brakes for more than six years now, but in 1957, although overdue, they were still a novelty and the XK 150 got a fine recep-

XK 140 in roadster form. On all XKs the rear wheel spat was omitted when wire wheels were fitted. Note the protective bumpers and the one-piece grille.

Testing... *the XK 150 drophead coupé at the Motor Industries Research Association's Nuneaton proving ground during tests of the Dunlop disc brakes introduced on production Jaguars in 1957.*

tion. In this department, where the XK 120 had been somewhat lacking, the XK 150 excelled.

In 1958, the XK 150 'S' was announced. Initial examples of this 250 b.h.p. model were for export only. The straight-port cylinder head with its three 2-in. SU carburetters was basically the same as that incorporated on today's Mark Ten and E-type. A larger-bore engine (3,781 c.c., 87 × 106 mm.) became available in 1959—the first change in XK dimensions for over ten years. This, like the '3½', was offered in two- or three-carburetter versions—thus creating four engine specifications for the XK series. Both XK 150 'S' models featured lead-bronze bearings, stronger clutch, lightened flywheel, quick-change disc brake pads, and twin fuel pumps.

Performance of the XK 150 'S', whether 3·4 or 3·8 litres, was quite exceptional. Its fade-free braking, predictable handling, and effortlessness at all speeds were fully 'up to the minute'—successfully belying the fact that the basic design was really more than twelve years old. At Geneva in March 1961, however, the inevitable occurred. Once again concepts changed overnight just as they had done at Earl's Court, 1948. The E-type had arrived.

NOTES ON ROAD TESTS

The first major independent road-test of the XK 120 was published by *The Motor* in November 1949. Using one of the aluminium-bodied roadsters, a mean maximum speed of 124·6 m.p.h. was achieved over four half-mile runs in opposite directions. The overall fuel consumption for 174 miles at 'moderately high speeds' worked out at a praiseworthy 19·8 m.p.g. The car accelerated from 0 to 100 m.p.h. in 27·3 seconds and covered the standing ¼-mile in 17·0

seconds. Later, however, *The Autocar* tested one of the first steel-bodied examples which, although only slightly heavier, could not approach *The Motor's* performance and fuel consumption figures. Both journals were full of praise for the car in practically all respects, although *The Motor* did openly criticise the weak head lamps. The two magazines were delighted with the powerful braking, although this was to become something of an Achilles heel when the XK 120 was entered for competitions.

It was a rare pleasure to drive such a car as the XK 120 in the early 1950s. Its exceptional speed and acceleration were way beyond those of most other cars on the road, and at that time its rarity was such as to render the mere driving of the XK 120 a piece of utmost Jonesmanship. Road-testers would therefore include mild warnings in those days, such as: '... it is the driver and the road that are the limiting factors, and not the car.' In that particular test of a 180 b.h.p. fixed head coupé in 1953, *The Autocar* achieved a mean speed of 120·5 m.p.h., but pointed out that traffic on the Jabbeke road had prevented the ultimate speed from being attained.

When *The Autocar* tested the special equipment (210 b.h.p.) XK 140 in fixed head form three years later, they went to the Continent again and managed a resounding mean maximum of 129·25 m.p.h. in overdrive. This represented little more than 5,000 r.p.m. and the academic nature of the maximum speed is further indicated by the fact that *Autosport*

Touring... *note the XK 150's return to a 'slatted' type grille, as opposed to the XK 140's one-piece grille.*

tested the same car in this country and could reach only 121·6 m.p.h. *The Motor's* original XK 120 had weighed 25½ cwt. (29 cwt. in test trim), whereas *The Autocar's* XK 140 tipped the scales at 28 cwt. (31 cwt. as tested). The two cars, however, covered the standing ¼-mile in almost identical times. *The Autocar* and *Autosport* both found that the improvements to weight distribution, steering, and suspension had turned the 'XK' into a much more pleasant car to handle.

With the XK 150 came a further increase in weight, and *The Autocar's* fixed-head coupé weighed 32½ cwt. as tested. With the same overdrive ratio (3·19) as the XK 140, its mean average speed was 123·7 m.p.h. Acceleration, however (probably due to the 'B' type head replacing the 'C' type head) was better than that of the XK 140, and the standing ¼-mile was covered in 16·9 seconds.

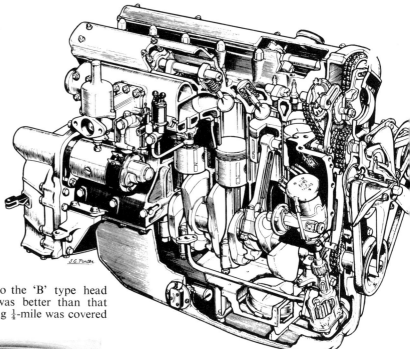

The 3½-litre, twin overhead camshaft Jaguar XK 120 engine. (*Motor* drawing)

Few bodybuilders attempted to emulate the 'Lyons Line'. A successful design, however, was this one-off XK 150 by Bertone which did not try to be anything other than typically Italian—although there is a 'Jaguar air' about the radiator grille, and the wheels and headlamps look familiar.

The Autocar, The Motor and *Autosport* all tested the same 3·4-litre 250 b.h.p. XK 150 'S' coupé soon after it was announced. Its straight-port head with three 2-in. carburettors brought its performance well beyond that of any previous 'XK'. Obtaining representative road test figures had by now become a more specialised occupation, and the comparison between the three journals' figures is noteworthy. For example:

	The Autocar	The Motor	Autosport
Overall m.p.g.	17·0	18·6	18·0
Maximum m.p.h.	134·0	132·0	132·3
0–100 m.p.h. (seconds)	22·4	20·3	20·0
Standing ¼-mile (seconds)	16·2	16·2	15·8

Surely the best 'XK' performance ever recorded by a motoring paper was *Autosport's* 136·3 m.p.h. from a 3·8-litre 265 b.h.p. XK 150 'S' in 1960. The 0 to 100 figure of 19 seconds is not so very far short of today's E-type times!

Illustrations not acknowledged are reproduced by courtesy of Jaguar Cars Ltd.

Robust: *the XK 150 overdrive model chassis.*

XK 120 Roadster, introduced in 1948.

XK 120 Drophead Coupé, introduced in 1953.

XK 140 Fixed-head Coupé, introduced in 1954.

XK 140 Drophead Coupé, introduced in 1954.

XK 140 tail-badge reading:
Winner Le Mans 1951-3.

XK 150 Fixed-head Coupé, introduced in 1957.

XK 150 'S' Roadster, introduced in 1958.

XK 150 tail-badge reading:
Winner Le Mans 1951-3,
1955, 1956, 1957.

© A. S. MURRAY, 1966.

XKs are travelling faster today than ever. Leading this duel at the 1964 National Jaguar Club Crystal Palace meeting is Robin Beck's immensely powerful 3·8-litre XK 120 'Special', which develops 290 b.h.p. Following, with Jackie Stewart at the wheel, is Eric Brown's XK 120 drophead which is very 'D-type' in its mechanical make-up. Note re-positioned headlamps of both cars.

BRIEF SPECIFICATION COVERING THE WHOLE XK SERIES

ENGINE: Six cylinder Jaguar XK engine; 70° twin overhead camshafts driven by two-stage roller chain; high-tensile aluminium alloy cylinder head with hemispherical combustion chambers; chrome-iron cylinder block; aluminium alloy pistons; steel connecting rods; $2\frac{3}{4}$ in. diameter counterweighted crankshaft carried on seven large steel-backed bearings; forced lubrication by submerged pump with full-flow filter.

CHASSIS: Straight plane steel box-section frame of great strength; torsional rigidity ensured by large box-section cross-members; independent front suspension incorporating transverse wishbones and torsion bars controlled by telescopic dampers; rear suspension by long silico-manganese steel semi-elliptic springs controlled by telescopic dampers (piston-type rear dampers on **XK 120**).

ELECTRICAL: Lucas 12 volt system; 64 amp.-hours at 10-hour rate with current voltage control; ventilated dynamo.

TRANSMISSION: Borg and Beck 10 in. s.d.p. clutch. Synchromesh single helical gearbox four speeds and reverse. Laycock de Normanville overdrive standard on **XK 150 'S'**, and optional on **XK 140** and **XK 150**. Borg Warner fully automatic transmission optional on late **XK 140** and all **XK 150** models except the **XK 150 'S'**. Hardy Spicer open propeller shaft. Hypoid bevel final drive.

BRAKES: Lockheed 12-in. diameter drums on **XK 120** and **XK 140** (friction lining area = 208 sq. in.). Dunlop 12-in. diameter discs on **XK 150** (rubbed area = 540 sq. in.).

STEERING: Burman recirculating ball on **XK 120**. Alford and Alder rack-and-pinion on **XK 140** and **XK 150**.

WHEELS: 6·00 × 16 pressed steel or wire. (Wire wheels only on **XK 150 'S'**.)

FUEL CAPACITY: 14 gallons.

The XK 150 roadster introduced at the 1958 New York Show. Note the one-piece windscreen and wind-up windows. (XK 150S models were identified externally by a small 'S' motif on the door.)

INTRODUCTION OF MODELS

Year	Model	Body Type	Engine
1948	XK 120	Open two-seater	3·4 litre
1951	XK 120	Fixed-head coupé	3·4 litre
1953	XK 120	Drophead coupé	3·4 litre
1954	XK 140	All three styles	3·4 litre
1957	XK 150	Fixed and drophead	3·4 litre
1958	XK 150	Open two-seater	3·4 litre
1958	XK 150 'S'	All three styles	3·4 litre
1959	XK 150	All three styles	3·8 litre
1959	XK 150 'S'	All three styles	3·8 litre

Principal Dimensions

	XK 120	XK 140	XK 150
Wheelbase	8' 6"	8' 6"	8' 6"
Track—front	4' 3"	4' 3½"	4' 3⅜"
Track—rear	4' 2"	4' 2½"	4' 3⅜"
Length	14' 5"	14' 8"	14' 9"
Width	5' 1½"	5' 4½"	5' 4½"

XK SERIES
Production Engine Specifications

	XK 120			XK 140		XK 150			
	Standard Models	Standard with Modifications	Special Equipment *	Standard	Special Equipment *	Special Equipment		'S' Models	
c.c.	3,442	3,442	3,442	3,442	3,442	3,442	3,781	3,442	3,781
Bore	83 mm.	83 mm.	83 mm.	83 mm.	83 mm.	83 mm.	87 mm.	83 mm.	87 mm.
Stroke	106 mm.	106 mm.	106 mm.	106 mm.	106 mm.	106 mm.		106 mm.	
Carbs. (S.U.)	2 × 1¾"	2 × 1¾"	2 × 1¾"	2 × 1¾"	2 × 1¾"	2 × 1¾"		3 × 2"	
C.R.	7 : 1 / 8 : 1	8 : 1 / 9 : 1	8 : 1	8 : 1	8 : 1	8 : 1	8 : 1	9 : 1	9 : 1
B.H.P.	150 / 160	180 / 190	180	190	210	210	220	250	265
(at) R.P.M.	5,000 / 5,200	5,300 / 5,400	5,750	5,500	5,750	5,500	5,500	5,500	5,500
Year	1948/9	1951	1952	1954	1954	1957	1959	1958	1959

* The Special Equipment XK 120 was known as the 'XK 120 M' in America. Similarly, the Special Equipment XK 140 was known as the 'XK 140 MC'.

The Lanchester 38 & 40 H.P.

5

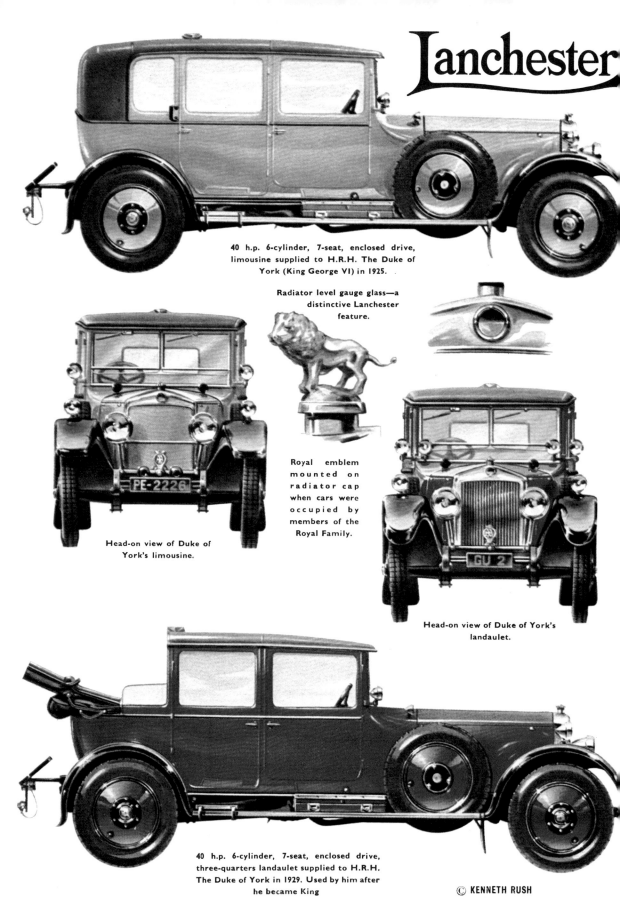

Lanchester

40 h.p. 6-cylinder, 7-seat, enclosed drive, limousine supplied to H.R.H. The Duke of York (King George VI) in 1925.

Radiator level gauge glass—a distinctive Lanchester feature.

Royal emblem mounted on radiator cap when cars were occupied by members of the Royal Family.

Head-on view of Duke of York's limousine.

PE-2226

GU 2

Head-on view of Duke of York's landaulet.

40 h.p. 6-cylinder, 7-seat, enclosed drive, three-quarters landaulet supplied to H.R.H. The Duke of York in 1929. Used by him after he became King

© KENNETH RUSH

The Lanchester 38 & 40 H.P.

by Anthony Bird

All weather: rigid side screens, generally attributed to Standard, c. 1924, on 1922 long chassis Lanchester Forty. (Photo: Daimler Co. Ltd.)

The better to appreciate the Lanchester Forty it is necessary to take a quick look at its immediate predecessors, the Lanchester Thirty-eight of 1910–14 and the 'Sporting Forty' which appeared just before the war stopped production.

From 1895 to 1909 Frederick Lanchester was solely responsible for design, not only of the cars themselves but of the smallest details of bodywork, fittings, components, tool-trays and so forth; his youngest brother, George, was his right-hand man in the execution of his designs. With the coming of the 38 h.p. 6-cylinder car, and its smaller sister the 25 h.p. 4-cylinder model in 1910–11, the roles were reversed with George as chief designer and Frederick as his consultant.

Nobody would claim that 'Dr Fred' could suffer fools gladly, but there is good reason to symphathise with him in seeing much of folly in the directorial interference and penny-pinching mismanagement which hampered the company which bore his name. Frederick once said of his Directors: "Well, they seem to change their minds pretty often—but if I had a mind like theirs I'd change it as soon as I could." The friction became unendurable, and Frederick Lanchester had only a consultative connection with his company from 1909 to 1913 and thereafter ceased to have any connection at all.

As, however, the 38 h.p. and 25 h.p. models were evolved from the 20 h.p. and 28 h.p. 4- and 6-cylinder cars of 1904–6 they may be said to have more of Fred than of George in them. In deference to the needs of 'the standardised chauffeur', as Frederick said, the side lever steering and pre-selector control had already been abolished in favour of wheel-steering in 1910, and the method of controlling the epicyclic gears had been disguised to resemble the conventional foot clutch and 'gate' gear lever; but one of George Lanchester's innovations was the use of pressed steel chassis girders in place of the square section tubes formerly used.

The horizontal overhead valves, ante-chamber combustion space and the famous wick carburettor were retained, but the flywheels were moved from the front to the back of the engines in order to take advantage of the torsional vibration damper, mounted on the front of the crankshaft, which Dr Fred had devised in 1909 in order to get the Daimler company out of trouble. The use of the damper allowed the stroke to be increased, with no loss of refinement, and the new engines were 'square' at 4 in. × 4 in. against the 4 in. × 3 in. 'over-square' dimensions of their predecessors. The manifolding was re-designed and the exhaust manifold was water-jacketed.

The output of these new engines was extremely good by the standard of the time. The 6-cylinder 4 in. × 4 in. unit was of 4·8 litres capacity and developed 48 b.h.p. at 1,400 r.p.m., and about 63 b.h.p. at a peak speed of 2,200 r.p.m. This represents approximately 15 b.h.p. per litre and compares very favourably with the contemporary 7·4 litre Rolls-Royce which reached an identical output of 48 h.p. at 1,250 r.p.m. The absolute maximum of the Rolls-Royce engine was also about 65 b.h.p. but was reached at a lower speed—about 1,750 r.p.m.

The Lanchester Thirty-eight would have been capable of considerable development. In the late 1920s Lord Ridley took a standard 1913 torpedo tourer, fitted it with high-lift cams and more powerful valve springs, together with a supercharger, thereby nearly doubling the output with no loss of reliability. The consternation of owners of 4½-litre Bentleys or 38/250 Mercedes, who found themselves being left behind by his ponderous and obsolete touring car, gave Lord Ridley many a pleasant moment.

The parallel-motion cantilever suspension front and back, and the Lanchester worm drive were unaltered except in detail. Also, the unique placing of the engine between the dashboard and the front seat, so that driver and front passenger sat on either side of it, was retained. This layout necessitated an engine much narrower and more compact than most designers of the time would have cared to attempt, but had the advan-

55

1912 Standard 'torpedo' 38 h.p. tourer with electric lighting and starting equipment—but the side-lights are still 'oil-cum-electric'.
(Photo: Mr F. W. Hutton-Stott)

tage of allowing the greatest possible passenger space, and very wide doors, upon a relatively short and very rigid chassis. It also allowed the back seat to be kept well ahead of the rear axle in the best modern manner. Using a different formula, made possible by new techniques and materials, better tyres and smaller wheels, Mr Issigonis has achieved a similar result with his transverse engined cars; but in general it has taken designers and the public more than sixty years to realise that there is no real merit in giving the machinery a more commanding view, and a better ride, than the cash customers.

The Lanchester Company had been amongst the first to make their own coachwork, and in the new models, particularly the 'torpedo' tourers, George Lanchester achieved a handsome and well-balanced line which was as successful, in its way, as the original twin-cylinder cars had been. Mr George recently told the writer that he always liked to see new designs 'in the round' before putting them in hand, and consequently carved scale models in Cheddar cheese direct from the drawing board. He would not confess to the mouse-power of the models.

In 1909 'Owen John', *The Autocar* columnist, had predicted that within five years the folly of wasting space on an unnecessarily long bonnet would be seen by the public and most leading manufacturers would copy the 'Lanchester engine position'. It was not to be; such Lanchester innovations as high-pressure lubrication, light steel pistons, and the famous worm gear (once so hotly attacked in the technical journals) were widely copied by 1913, but fashion decreed that motor cars must have bonnets, and the public decided that the longer the bonnet the better the car must be.

In 1913, therefore, the Lanchester Directors instructed their chief designer to bring out a car of conventional appearance to supplement, not to supplant, the existing models. It was a wise decision; there was no point in swimming against the tide but *The Automobile Engineer* regretted that:

> "a company such as the Lanchester have found it impossible to educate their potential customers to an appreciation of the correctness of Lanchester principles. . . . The new model may be regarded as a concession to the sporting, or owner-driver motorist, who wants a Lanchester car without the Lanchester peculiarities of appearance. . . ."

Having decided on a conventional-looking car, and having decided to call it the 'Sporting Forty' in an attempt to woo the owner-driver (a class of customer generally despised by the Company's chairman), the Board then went the whole hog, threw away the baby with the bath water, and instructed their designer to 'go conventional' throughout with a side valve engine, 'Hotchkiss drive', semi-elliptic springs front and back and a bevel geared live axle. George Lanchester was able to put up convincing arguments in favour of keeping the cantilever suspension at the back, and the worm geared axle, but had to give way on the use of conventional semi-elliptics and dumb-

Above: 1912 Lanchester 38 h.p. leaving Stockholm for the Swedish Winter Trial, 1913. Both the Lanchesters which entered finished and won Bronze Medals. (Photo: Autocar)

Francis Hutton-Stott in command of his 1913 38 h.p. At his left hand are starter lever, hand throttle, ignition advance/retard, mixture strength control, oil tell-tales for engine and gearbox and Bosch starter-coil and magneto switch.

Production type 'Sporting Forty', 1914: note modern treatment of streamlined wing lights.　　　　(Photo: Mr John Stanford)

irons in front. Nor could he get his Board to budge over the side-valve engine which they appear to have insisted upon for no better reason than that everybody else had one.

Consequently the 'Sporting Forty' was the first and only Lanchester car to have an L-head side-valve engine (4 in. × 4½ in.). The chassis had many points of merit and, in improved form, was used for the post-war Forties, but although *The Automobile Engineer* and other journals praised the car, the designer disliked it and gives thanks to this day that the war intervened to stop production after only six had been made.

The sporting bodywork George Lanchester designed for the car is as handsome as one could wish to see, and its performance was far from despicable. The designer, however, persists in regarding the car as an abortion and on being asked if he was not being unjust he wrote:

"... perhaps the term abortion *is* too strong. Bastard would be more appropriate. The engine was in my opinion a retrograde step: it was an L-head side-valve arrangement which, after the T-head, was about the worst form of combustion chamber conceivable, but one that was in vogue at that time. Fuel economy was poor, combustion tended to roughness and b.h.p. was poor for the dimensions. Otherwise the chassis was good—a forerunner of my 1919 40 h.p., but the latter was improved. . . .

"Although I had no illusions about the ... 1914 40 h.p. it was stated by one owner, in a letter, to

have averaged 50 m.p.h. from London to Liverpool."

The 'Sporting Forty' Lanchester would be of no consequence if it did not illustrate so clearly the all-too-common folly of non-technical managers having too much say in technical affairs. It was this failing which ultimately led to the collapse of the Lanchester Motor Company and its disastrous absorption by Daimler in 1931.

Well-informed motor historians have described the post-Kaiser-War Lanchester Forty as a splendid but old-fashioned motor car: this verdict misses the point that the only really old-fashioned feature of the car was its sheer quality. In *The Thoroughbred Motor Car, 1930–1940** David Scott-Moncrieff, the Purveyor of Horseless Carriages to the Nobility and Gentry, describes it as:

"... that lovable, lordly, ultra-luxurious carriage, utterly Edwardian in conception, the Lanchester 40 h.p. 6-cylinder. It was priced at £1,800 for the chassis alone and was jewelled in every hole ... this glorious anachronism ... was majestic progress *in excelsis*, but really rather deceptive, because, although at over 65 m.p.h. the 6¼-litre o.h.c. engine tended to lose interest, the speed and ease with which one did long ... journeys was surprising. ..."

This, though complimentary, is misleading. The 'glorious anachronism' was far from anachronistic; indeed, there can have been few Edwardian engines of only 6¼ litres capacity capable of propelling two and half tons of lordly motor carriage at the

George Lanchester and the prototype 'Sporting Forty'.　　　　(Photo: Montagu Motor Museum)

1919 London Show car on short chassis o.h.c. Lanchester Forty.   (Photo: Mr F. W. Hutton-Stott)

78 m.p.h. of which the Lanchester was capable, and many features of the design represented new departures in automobile engineering practice.

The chassis structure was, admittedly, based upon the pre-war 'Sporting Forty', but as all Lanchester chassis since the first production model had been of exceptional torsional and beam strength by comparison with their contemporaries, it cannot be thought particularly old-fashioned. Improvements on the 1914 pattern included making the centre section of box-girder form and an increase in the already generous dimensions of the side members. As the old Lanchester dodge of putting the petrol tank amidships (with the wick carburettor recessed into it) and using it as a torsional member had had to be abandoned on the 1914 car, because of the change of engine position, the Forty chassis were cross-braced with tubular members varying from $2\frac{1}{2}$ in. to 6 in. in diameter.

The engine was a totally new concept. The Lanchester Motor Company during the war, in addition to making shell-cases, paravanes and armoured cars on the Thirty-eight chassis, had been given contracts to build a number of the old Renault-designed R.A.F. L.A. aero engines, and these were followed by the more modern Sunbeam Arabs. When the war ended George Lanchester and his brother Frank, the sales manager, wanted to continue the aero engine work with the object, ultimately, of developing their own designs. Almost inevitably, the Directors could see no market for the flying machine in time of peace and the aero engine department was

disbanded as quickly as possible. George was, however, able to persuade the Board to forget the side-valve engine and to give him a free hand. Consequently the overhead camshaft unit designed for the new Forty was clearly influenced by aero engine practice; it was an advanced design by 1919 standards and still far from an anachronism ten years later.

The new engine had its six cylinders cast in two blocks of three which were mounted upon a sturdy and handsomely 'snailed' aluminium crankcase. The bore remained unaltered at 4 in., and the R.A.C. rating, in consequence, was still 38·6 h.p., but the stroke was increased to 5 in. and in standard form the engine delivered some 100 h.p. As always with a Lanchester design, great care and many experiments had gone into the design of induction and exhaust manifolds, and very little modification was needed on the racing Lanchesters to increase output by nearly one-half.

The inclined, overhead, hollow stem tulip valves (two per cylinder) were commanded by a single overhead camshaft centrally placed between them; this was driven by worm gearing from a vertical shaft at the front of the engine. From the vertical shaft a skew-geared cross shaft gave motion to the distributor for the coil ignition and to the water pump and magneto, and a short layshaft, parallel with the

Interior of 1919 Show car, showing marquetry work in burr walnut.   (Photo: Autocar)

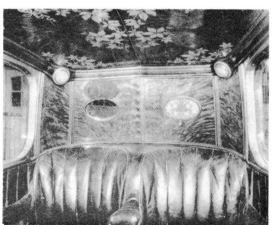

Duke and Duchess of York leaving for New Zealand in 40 h.p. Lanchester PE2226 (see page 2). In this car the present Queen Elizabeth II made her first public appearance at the age of six weeks.   (Photo: Radio Times Hulton Picture Library)

Archie Millership, chief demonstrator, testing a Forty in Charlecote Park, June 1920. (Photo: Mr F. W. Hutton-Stott)

Lanchester body frame of cast aluminium and ash, 1922. Later examples had aluminium centre pillars and rear quarter-framing. (Photo: Mr George H. Lanchester)

crankshaft, was driven by helical gearing from it. This short shaft carried two more worm wheels, one of which gave motion to the dynamo whilst the other received motion, via a free-wheel *escargot* clutch, from the starting motor. Both of these components, in consequence, stood vertically side by side on the near-side rear quarter of the engine.

This expensive arrangement of auxiliary drives could be condemned as unduly complex, but it made all the components completely accessible for routine servicing.

The cylinder heads were non-detachable—a desirable attribute in an engine where cost is of no consequence as better water passages round the vital areas may be provided without risk of leakage and failure. The objection of increased cost of servicing was largely met in the Lanchester, as the inlet valves were in detachable cages whilst the exhausts seated directly upon the cylinder head metal (thereby getting the best use of the cooling water), but could be dropped down upon the piston crowns and removed through the inlet ports. It was therefore possible to decarbonise and grind-in valves without completely dismantling the engine. This was in marked contrast to the Bentley and some other famous contemporaries.

One of the Lanchester features which had to be thrown away on the Sporting and post-war Forties was the famous, and highly satisfactory, wick carburettor. Not only was it sneered at as old-fashioned by all those who failed to appreciate how completely trouble-free it was, but its bulk was too great to accommodate inside a conventional bonnet. Now that the petrol tank was banished to the back of the car,

the old expedient of recessing the carburettor into the tank itself could no longer be used. A Smith 4-jet instrument, modified to Lanchester requirements, was used on the Forties, and one detects a wistful note in the first descriptive catalogue which said that this carburettor would be found to be *almost* as economical as the old wick vapouriser.

Another Lanchester feature which had to go was the cantilever and parallel-motion front suspension; this had gone in the interest of modernity on the 'Sporting Forty' and on the post-war cars, although the cantilever springs were retained at the back, the parallel-motion linkwork had to be abolished there also as it was too difficult to accommodate now that a conventional bonnet made it necessary to push the bodywork further back in relation to the wheelbase.

A torque tube and ball joint took over the functions of the linkwork; this was a slightly retrograde step as the back axle now rose and fell on its springs in the arc of a circle, whereas formerly the links had constrained it to a truly vertical path to the benefit of tyre life and road holding. In order to keep the circular movement as small as possible (it was, in any event, a trifling defect which many would have been content to ignore) George Lanchester made the torque tube as long as possible, by re-designing the gear, main clutch and transmission brake components in order to reduce their combined length by more than half.

The compounded, roller bearing, epicyclic gear trains remained little altered, but the long multi-disc clutch for the direct drive was moved from its place at the rear of the gear trains and replaced by a single-disc clutch conventionally placed in a recess in the

How odd that even Lanchester had not thought of a mechanical windscreen wiper by 1923. (Photo: Daimler Co. Ltd.)

J. G. Parry Thomas in the
'Rapson Lanchester'.
(Photo: Radio Times
Hulton Picture Library)

flywheel. Similarly the equally long, oil-cooled, multi-disc footbrake, which had been an extension of the direct-drive clutch on the pre-war models, was replaced by a normal expanding shoe brake acting on a ribbed drum outside the gearbox.

In the earlier arrangement the multi-disc clutch had only been concerned with the direct-drive top gear; the starting load had been taken on the contracting crab-brake clutches of the low, compound or reverse epicyclic trains. Now, the single-disc clutch not only looked after direct drive but took the starting load as on a conventional car, and the individual clutches of the epicyclic trains were relieved of this duty. There was some slight merit in this, but it was counterbalanced by the disadvantage that a characteristic 'epicyclic whine' was audible when a car was standing with the engine running.

The other distinctive Lanchester feature of a separate oil pump and high pressure lubricating system for the gear mechanism was retained. Although one may regret that the need to conform had obliged the Lanchester brothers to give up the fool-proof preselector control of their earliest models, the epicyclic box on the Forties gave the driver a swift and silent 'crash-proof' gear change equal to that of the best synchromesh system.

The Directors had long since given up worrying about the 'hour-glass' worm gearing and this item remained virtually unaltered, but in general the fully floating back axle was a new design as far as the shafts, casing and bearings were concerned. All the parts of the chassis and mechanism were superbly finished and, where a choice had to be made between reducing cost or providing for accessibility, durability or some other facet of quality, cost had to go by the board. The I-beam front axle, for example, was machined all over in order that any forging defects might be readily discovered in course of inspection.

Also for the new models, and probably for the first and only time in the history of motor manufacture, George Lanchester designed and set up his own plant for making road springs. He and his brother had never been really satisfied with the products of the established spring-smithing firms, finding in them too many departures from specification, and the better control over quality made possible by their own plant enabled the Lanchester Company to be sure that contact between the spring leaves was of the order of 85 per cent of the surface against the 15–20 per cent of the best 'professionally'—made leaf springs.

New methods were also introduced into the body building department; these included the use of cast light-alloy framing (with ash 'fillers' to provide anchorage for trimming), and duraluminium panelling with welded joints. These joints were not in general use for some ten years; they were better than the traditional coachbuilders' butt joints tacked to an ash frame and concealed by beading pinned through to the timber. Detachable plates allowed the cast framing to serve as a conduit for electric wiring, and the Lanchester bodies were erected upon light steel sub-frames which were then attached to the chassis with rubber mountings. When a customer specified bodywork by an 'outside' coachmaker (a practice the Lanchester Motor Company tried to discourage) a sub-frame would be sent to the chosen coachbuilder so that the Lanchester Company could be sure the completed body would drop into place on their chassis without any of the usual cutting, drilling, filing or other desperate expedients then so commonly needed. Bodywork provided by specialist firms was generally found to be considerably heavier than the Company's own, and necessitated stiffening the rear springs and spoiling the suspension characteristics.

By making a great effort the Lanchester Company had a Forty ready for the 1919 Motor Show. This car survives (see page 6), and the unusual, but not unattractive, two-door saloon body was designed to give the utmost comfort to four persons only, rather on the lines of the Rover 2,000, with each passenger, in effect, accommodated in a separate armchair. The inlaid marquetry roof and interior door panels, the silk blinds, the silver fittings and the luxurious black leather upholstery provoked King George V, who opened the Show, to remark: "Very fine, Mr Lanchester, but more suited to a prostitute than a prince, don't you think?"

With the Forty the Lanchester Motor Company

Tommy Hann's 1911 racing Lanchester saloon 'Hoieh-Wayereh-Gointoo': later altered to an open single-seater and re-named 'Softly-Catch-Monkey'.
(Photo: Radio Times Hulton Picture Library)

Archie Millership and Lanchester Forty at Shelsley Walsh, 1923.

(Photo:
Mr F. W. Hutton-Stott)

started a period of rivalry with Rolls-Royce for the cream of the 'carriage trade', and one of their first moves was to reduce the chassis price from £2,200 to £1,800 in 1921 in order to be £50 cheaper than the Silver Ghost. All press reports were extremely encouraging and many implied that the Best Car in the World was now made in Birmingham. Indeed, the Silver Ghost, superb though it was, was outstripped for fuel economy (by a small margin), performance and passenger comfort, whilst remaining superior only in mechanical silence. In outright speed, given bodies of equal weight and windage, there was little in it—3 m.p.h. to 5 m.p.h. perhaps. On 3rd March, 1920, *The Motor* reported the Lanchester as being able to accelerate smoothly in top gear from 3 m.p.h. to 85 m.p.h. George Lanchester regards this as an exaggeration, but says that 3 m.p.h. to 78 m.p.h. was well within the car's top-gear compass.

The modern critic might well think it odd that the Forty had no front wheel brakes at first. As the car's smaller stable mate, the 21 h.p. 'pup', had excellent 4-wheel brakes from 1923 onwards it seems odd that the Forty still relied on 2-wheel braking. The reason lies not in any lack of *nous* on the part of the design staff, but in that curious directorial attitude which so frustrated the Company's development. A valued customer, confirmed Lanchester owner for many years, tackled the Chairman and pointed out that with traffic growing denser, and speeds faster, it was illogical that the heavier, faster and more expensive model should have less effective brakes than its cheaper and lighter sister. Mr Hamilton Barnsley's memorable reply was to the effect that the Twenty-one was an owner-driver's car and owner-drivers often lacked skill—but the Forty was a gentleman's car and gentleman had chauffeurs who knew better than to go dashing about relying on their brakes to get them out of trouble.

In 1924, however, word got around the trade that Rolls-Royce were about to fit front brakes to the Silver Ghost. The prohibition was consequently lifted and for the 1925 season the Lanchester appeared with admirable 4-wheel brakes: the better to deal with torque reaction the beam front axle was replaced by a tubular axle such as the pre-war models had had. The new brake system was often described as hydraulic; in the sense that the brake shoes were not expanded by hydraulic rams, one to each wheel, this is incorrect. It was a mechanical system with servo assistance given by a hydraulic ram, served by a hydraulic accumulator, in which pressure was maintained by the lubricating pump in the gear box.

After this ingenious, but costly, device had been in use for a short while a representative of the Belgian Dewandre concern called to demonstrate their new vacuum servo mechanism. Mr George Lanchester liked this for its simplicity but disliked it for its lack of 'feel'. The salesman undertook to have the defect eradicated and Lanchester undertook to place an order once he was satisfied. The Dewandre mechanism was duly modified, and Lanchester duly fitted the Forty with vacuum servo in the interest of economy.

With the same object of reducing production costs the engines were slightly modified in 1925. The costly layshaft arrangement was superseded by a cheaper, but less attractive, layout with the dynamo driven from the magneto cross shaft, and a normal starter and Bendix drive in place of the silent free-wheel clutch. The dynamo now took the place of the coil-ignition distributor, and the latter was moved to the top of the rocker cover and driven by worm gearing from the camshaft. These were the only major modifications made to the Forty during its production life.

* * * *

The Forty may have been a 'gentleman's car', and as such worthy of its place in the affections of such customers as Sir John Ellerman (alleged to be the richest man in England), The Jam Sahib of Nawanagar ('Ranji' the cricketer), the Duke of York (King George VI) and the Maharajah of Alwar, whose splendid folly of a state landau on a special long-chassis Forty is shown on page 11, but to many enthusiasts of the time the Lanchesters were better known for their Brooklands exploits. The name was not unknown there by 1921 because of the successes, and consistent endurance, of Tommy Hann's famous streamlined 'Softly-Catch-Monkey' which started life as a 25 h.p. landaulet in 1911.

1921 2-seater 'Brooklands' Lanchester Forty. The name 'Winni Praps Praps' was onomatopoeic and derived from the car's exhaust note on over-run.

(Photo: Montagu Motor Museum)

In 1921 George Lanchester and Arthur Bird (Works Manager) fitted a narrow staggered-seat racing shell to a Forty and took it to Brooklands to investigate the phenomenon of high speed wheel wobble which plagued so many manufacturers at that time. The car attracted the attention of S. F. Edge who drove it and reported:

"... I worked the speed up to over 100 m.p.h. without the least discomfort. This is a very remarkable tribute to the Lanchester design of suspension ... the biggest bump on Brooklands was swallowed up by a gentle motion. ... It seems difficult to believe that a firm who specialises in luxurious private cars should be able to produce practically their normal car capable of such a wonderful performance. ..."

Though Edge's attempt in 1922 to break his own 12-Hour Record in the Lanchester was frustrated by the reappearance of slight wheel wobble, which he did not notice but which caused George Lanchester to order the car in; he did succeed in beating several of the Class G Records which he had captured a few weeks earlier in his Spyker (see Table A). As the Lanchester showed so remarkably little daylight between its wheels and the notoriously bumpy track Lionel Rapson transferred his allegiance from Rolls-Royce to Lanchester Forty as a trial horse for the 'unpuncturable' double tread tyres he was then trying to promote. In the intervals of running tyres to destruction at high speed during the next four years a special single-seat Lanchester together, occasionally, with the car Edge had driven and 'Softly-Catch-Monkey', took part in those races for which they were eligible. They invariably performed creditably and often successfully.

Amongst the few alterations made to the Rapson car were special rebound dampers, a new exhaust system and Brooklands silencer on the standard manifold, alteration of the final drive ratio from 9 : 35 to 10 : 33 and compression raised from 5·8 : 1 to 6·2 : 1. A new induction pipe with twin carburettors was also fitted.

As a racing car the Lanchester Forty was essentially ugly and purposeful, with great stamina. The Brooklands 'regulars' liked 'Old Softly' and the racing Forty, and J. G. Parry Thomas, who often drove for Rapson, found it admirable. In August 1924 Parry Thomas, with George Duller and Rapson as co-drivers, set off

Off side of 'Forty' engine showing advanced design of induction manifold. (Photo: Montagu Motor Museum)

in the Forty in an attempt on the World's Long Distance Records.

For the first one and a half hours Rapson's insistence on trying a new type of cover led to so many stops for wheel changing that average speed could not be raised above 80–85 m.p.h. Well-proven tyres were then fitted and the first record fell at 97·95 m.p.h. after five hours. Then the great car just went on and on for fifteen hours, breaking thirty records and

Armoured car chassis for the 11th Hussars. The Lanchester armoured Forties had six speeds forward and reverse and an emergency steering gear at the back.
(Photo: Mr George H. Lanchester)

SPECIFICATION: LANCHESTER THIRTY-EIGHT
1910 (for 1911 season) to 1914

ENGINE: 6-cyl., 4 in. × 4 in., 1910–12, cast singly, 1913–14 in pairs. 4,800 c.c.

VALVES: Overhead, horizontal, two per cylinder, operated by rocking levers and flat plate springs.

CAMSHAFTS: Two, in upper half of crankcase.

IGNITION: H.T. magneto and Bosch trembler coil for starting.

CARBURETTOR: Lanchester patent wick vapouriser.

ELECTRICAL SYSTEM (after 1912 only): Delco/Lanchester, 8/32 volt dynamotor-starter with series/parallel switchgear and automatic charging control.

COOLING: Honeycomb radiator, thermo-syphon, two fans.

CLUTCH: For direct drive, Lanchester multi-disc.

CLUTCHES: For indirect gears, contracting 'crab' brakes on epicyclic gear drums.

GEARBOX: Lanchester patent compound epicyclic, 3-speed and reverse with separate high pressure lubricating system.

TRANSMISSION: Open propeller shaft.

FINAL DRIVE: Lanchester patent enveloping worm gear.

BRAKES: Foot. Lanchester multi-disc (oil-cooled) on transmission.
Hand. Expanding shoes in drums on rear wheels.

SUSPENSION: Lanchester patent; cantilevered plate springs with parallel-motion radius and torque links at front and back.

CHASSIS DETAILS

WHEELS: Wire, centre lock. Tyres 895 × 135.

WHEELBASE: Short 10 ft. 7 in.
Long 11 ft. 7 in.

TRACK: 4 ft. 10 in.

WEIGHT: Long chassis with standard touring body, 35 cwt.

MAX. SPEED: Approximately 65 m.p.h.

Chassis price: Short £800, Long £825

LANCHESTER

Many Lanchester owners preferred not to display the radiator badge and considered the unique gauge glass (see page 2) sufficiently distinctive.

1923 7-seat, enclosed drive, three-quarters landaulet.

1926 short chassis, standard 5-seat tourer body (note front wheel brakes).

1924 3-seat coupé.

1920 long chassis, 7-seat tourer (New York Show model).

1927 7-seat, open front, limousine.

State Landau built for H.R.H. The Maharajah of Alwar in 1924.

© KENNETH RUSH

averaging 104 m.p.h. for the last 100 miles (Table B).

In effect the Forty was replaced by the Straight-eight, the last 'real' Lanchester, in 1929, but it remained available to order until 1931, in which year the Lanchester Motor Company succumbed to the financial panic. Their bank overdraft was called in and the B.S.A./Daimler Group (whose overdraft was too big to disturb) bought the assets of their old rivals and used the honoured name of Lanchester as a brand label for their second grade models.

Rear view of chassis: Lanchester Forty no. 1679.
(Photo: Montagu Motor Museum.)

TABLE A

August 1922   Class G. World Records over 4,998 c.c. and up to 7,784 c.c.

200 miles		77·77 m.p.h.	S. F. Edge
300 ,,		81·33 ,,	,,
400 ,,		80·37 ,,	,,
2 hours 191 miles, 1,610 yards		75·48 ,,	,,
3 ,, 273 ,, 1,213 ,,		75·72 ,,	,,
4 ,, 361 ,, 1,422 ,,		80·28 ,,	,,
5 ,, 442 ,, 1,415 ,,		80·40 ,,	,,

and corresponding kilometre records

TABLE B

August 1924

300 miles (standing start)	97·95 m.p.h.	Parry Thomas	
400 ,,	,,	98·32 ,,	,,
500 ,,	,,	96·18 ,,	,,
600 ,,	,,	95·87 ,,	Thomas/Duller
700 ,,	,,	94·54 ,,	,,
800 ,,	,,	94·66 ,,	Thomas/Duller/ Rapson
900 ,,	,,	94·82 ,,	,, ,, ,,
1,000 ,,	,,	95·27 ,,	,, ,, ,,
1,100 ,,	,,	95·72 ,,	,, ,, ,,
400 kilometres	,,	157·00 k.p.h.	Parry Thomas

and all kilometre records up to 900
and 1,000, 1,100 and 1,200 kilometre records

3 hours 293 miles, 1,272 yards	97·91 m.p.h.	Parry Thomas	
4 ,, 393 ,, 651 ,,	98·34 ,,	,,	
5 ,, 480 ,, 560 ,,	96·06 ,,	Thomas/ Duller/Rapson	

and all records up to 15 hours

15 hours 1,148 miles, 843 yards 76·56 m.p.h. Thomas/ Duller/Rapson

---

SPECIFICATION: LANCHESTER 'SPORTING FORTY'
Designed late 1913, six produced 1914–15

ENGINE: Six cylinders (two blocks of three), 4 in. × 4½ in. 5,561 c.c.

VALVES: Side valves (two per cylinder) in L-head.

CAMSHAFT: Single, in crankcase upper half.

IGNITION: As 38 h.p. model.

CARBURETTOR: Smith 5-jet.

ELECTRICAL SYSTEM: C.A.V., 12 volt.

COOLING: Honeycomb radiator, pump and fan.

CLUTCHES, gears, transmission, final drive and brakes: As on 38 h.p.

SUSPENSION: Rear, as on 38 h.p.
Front, semi-elliptic springs; not shackled at rear ends but sliding between trunnion rollers.

CHASSIS DETAILS

WHEELBASE: 11 ft. 8 in.

TRACK: 4 ft. 10 in.

WEIGHT: Not recorded.

MAX. SPEED: Approximately 70 m.p.h.

Chassis price £885, complete sports tourer £1,035.

SPECIFICATION: LANCHESTER FORTY
Model produced, 1919–29 and nominally available to order 1929–31

ENGINE: Six cylinders (two blocks of three), 4 in. × 5 in. 6,178 c.c.

VALVES: Overhead inclined, tulip shaped (two per cylinder).

CAMSHAFT: Single overhead.

IGNITION: H.T. magneto; and coil, battery and distributor.

CARBURETTOR: Smith 4-jet.

ELECTRICAL SYSTEM: C.A.V., 12 volt.

COOLING: Honeycomb radiator, pump and fan.

CLUTCH (main): Single dry plate.

CLUTCHES, for individual gear trains, by contracting 'crab' brakes on epicyclic gear drums.

GEARBOX: Lanchester patent compound epicyclic, 3-speed and reverse with separate high pressure lubricating system.

TRANSMISSION: Propeller shaft enclosed in torque tube.

FINAL DRIVE: Lanchester patent enveloping worm gear.

BRAKES, 1919–24: Foot. Expanding shoes in drum on transmission.
Hand. Expanding shoes in drums on rear wheels.
1924 onwards. Foot brake operating on all four wheels with servo assistance firstly by Lanchester hydraulic system, secondly by Dewandre vacuum.

SUSPENSION: Rear. Cantilevered plate springs—torque tube.
Front. Semi-elliptic.

CHASSIS DETAILS

WHEELS: Wire centre-lock, or bolt-on steel disc.

TYRES: 895 × 135 B.E. Later models 33″ × 6¾″ well-base.

WHEELBASE: Short, 11 ft. 9 in.
Long, 12 ft. 6 in.

TRACK: 4 ft. 10 in.

WEIGHT: 40 cwt.

MAX. SPEED:
Standard 7-seat tourer, approximately 78 m.p.h.
Single seat racing car, approximately 110 m.p.h.

Chassis Price: 1919 £2,200 reduced to £1,800 in 1921.

The Duesenberg J & SJ

Duesenberg

Script used in catalogues
and advertisements,
c. 1931/2.

Duesenberg insignia found on various parts
of the car.

0 ———— 5'

Model J, 1932, with touring body by Derham, on the
153½″ wheelbase chassis.

The Duesenberg J & SJ

by T. R. Nicholson

1935 JN Sedan by Rollston.   (Photo: William C. Kinsman)

In December 1928 the United States was riding the crest of a wave of unprecedented prosperity. Before another twelve months had passed, the Stock Market crash was going to herald its sudden end, but at the moment, such a prospect was inconceivable. Nothing epitomised the boom so well as the mushroom growth of the American motor industry since the war, so it was entirely appropriate that the New York Salon at the end of the year should see the unveiling of the ultimate in American motoring, regardless of expense —the Model J Duesenberg.

The Salon was the natural place for such a revelation. It was, in the words of a contemporary, 'for people of long-established culture and wealth, possessing the inevitable good taste which accompanies these two characteristics, and the inclination to cater to it'. It was also, needless to say, for the rich who did not give a damn for culture or taste. Until now, the aristocrats of the Salon had always been the imported luxury cars: Rolls-Royce, Isotta-Fraschini, Minerva, Mercedes-Benz and the rest. Americans who sought the best without qualification chose these. The new Duesenberg aimed to change this, and to some degree succeeded. The implication of its advertising copy, which showed it in juxtaposition with the foreigners, was clear: the latter, until now given best, had been displaced. The Duesenberg's slogan was, quite simply, 'The World's Finest Motor Car'.

It was a vehicle quite outside the experience of anyone familiar only with American cars (though for that matter, virtually nothing like it existed in Europe, either). Its 'foreignness' to the native scene was so compulsive that years after its introduction, careless writers, additionally misled by its name, were still referring to it as a German car. Claimed power output—265 b.h.p.—and performance, 89 m.p.h. in second gear and 116 m.p.h. in top with an open four-passenger phaeton body—were beyond the experience even of a nation more familiar than the rest with big,

fast cars. The new Chrysler Imperial 80, with 112 b.h.p., was announced as 'America's Most Powerful Motor Car'. Then the Duesenberg Model J arrived. Top gear acceleration was of the order of 10–80 m.p.h. in 22 seconds. The Model J was enormous, yet usually managed to combine elegance with its impression of overbearing dimensions. The chassis price was $8,500 in 1929; then about £1,700. Other American luxury cars were cheap in comparison with those of Europe; not so the new Duesenberg. It also differed from its competitors everywhere, with the exception of the Type 41 Bugatti Royale, in that it combined technical characteristics and the performance of a racing car with the smoothness, if not silence, of the most sophisticated luxury car, and in that (for this very reason) it attracted the enthusiastic owner-driver and was usually seen with bodies that opened.

Such was the impression that the Model J made. The men behind it were a fascinating pair. The Duesenberg Motors Company of Indianapolis had been run by Frederick Samuel Duesenberg and his younger brother August. Fred was a self-taught engineer who combined the qualities of an imaginative dreamer, a man of driving action and a fine craftsman. His first passenger car, the Model A of 1921, had been built to the highest mechanical standards, regardless of cost, and had been the first American production car to have a straight-eight engine and hydraulic brakes. His racing cars, the basis of his passenger vehicles, had brought him still greater fame. However, the latter had been cloaked in very ordinary, dull bodies, and were usually unexceptional performers. The wealthy expected more than this for their money, and Duesenberg Motors went into receivership in 1926.

The man who acquired the majority stockholding was Eric Lobban Cord, President of the Auburn Automobile Company. He was a dynamic, far-sighted businessman with revolutionary styling ideas who had already transformed the old, dull Auburn

A masterpiece and its creator: Fred Duesenberg at the wheel of one of the first SJs, a 1932 La Grande phaeton.
(Photo: William C. Kinsman)

into a fashion leader. When he gained control of Duesenberg Motors, he also took over Lycoming Motors of Williamsport, Pennsylvania, a large-scale constructor of proprietary engines for the makers of assembled cars. Cord allowed his acquisitions full autonomy. Fred Duesenberg was appointed Engineering Vice-President of the new company of Duesenberg, Inc., while his loyal satellite August was made Assistant Chief Engineer. Cord, however, insisted on the new Duesenberg being the altogether extraordinary vehicle it was, in terms of performance, size and looks. Fred had wanted a smaller car.

THE CHASSIS

All bodies were custom-built; that is to say, they were made by outside body-builders. Duesenberg Inc. supplied only the chassis, together with the long, sweeping wings, the bumpers, six wheels, and the instrument panel, so let us look at that first. From first to last, over a production period of nearly ten years, the Model J changed little. The engine, made by Lycoming, was remarkable not only for its power output, but also for its design. At a time when most American engines were simple, low-stressed, side-valve units whose cheapness and reliability were more important than their efficiency, that of the Model J was of undisguisedly racing type, which was not surprising considering the make's illustrious competition

history. The eight cylinders, disposed in line, had a bore and stroke of 95 mm. × 121 mm. (3¾ in. × 4¾ in.), giving a cubic capacity of 6,882 c.c. (420 cu. in.). This was normal enough, but two chain-driven overhead camshafts operated four overhead valves, two inlet and two exhaust, per cylinder. The valves were inclined at 70 degrees, allowing hemispherical combustion chambers, which were fully machined. Valve seats and sparking plugs were surrounded by ample water jackets. The standard compression ratio of 5·2 : 1 was low, but domed pistons could be had as an extra.

The cylinder head was detachable, and the cylinder block and crankcase were an integral casting, in accordance with standard American practice. The pistons, which were of aluminium, were fitted with three compression rings and one oil ring. The connecting rods, too, were of aluminium, and the gudgeon pins were of the fully-floating type. The whole assembly weighed 3¾ lb. The massive five-bearing crankshaft was of heat-treated chrome-nickel steel, statically and dynamically balanced, and weighed 150 lb. It was fitted with a torsional vibration damper consisting of two copper-lined cartridges each filled with mercury and bolted to opposite sides of the crankshaft between numbers one and two cylinders. Peak revolutions were 4,250 r.p.m. The sump held 1½ gallons of oil. The 6-volt electrical system was by

Left: Power house: Offside of the SJ engine; Right: Nearside of the SJ engine.
(Photos: William C. Kinsman)

J chassis awaiting test at the Indianapolis Speedway. (Photo: William C. Kinsman)

Delco-Rémy, incorporating dual coil ignition. A twin-choke updraught Schebler carburettor looked after induction. From November 1932 a downdraught manifold, optional earlier, was supplied, mostly with a Stromberg carburettor. There was both an electrically-driven and a mechanical fuel pump, feeding from a 26-gallon tank at the rear. This large engine was rubber-mounted on the chassis at four points.

The gearbox was a normal sliding-pinion affair, with three widely-spaced forward speeds, as was normal in America. Second-gear reduction was by constant-mesh gears, in the interests of silence. Power was transmitted through an unusual, specially-made double dry-plate clutch, made by Long, via a propeller shaft enclosed in a torque tube to a silent hypoid spiral bevel final drive. This was available in a variety of ratios: 3·78, 4, 4·3, or 4·7 : 1. The middle two ratios were the most common. All were high for an American car, but the immense low-speed pulling power of the engine permitted this. Indeed, a few 3 : 1 axle ratios were made to special order. A handful of cars were made with a freewheel device from 1931 onwards.

The chassis frame was available in two standard lengths, giving a short wheelbase of 11 ft. 10½ in. (142½ in.), or a long one of 12 ft. 9½ in. (153½ in.). One J was made with a 14 ft. 10 in. wheelbase (178 in.); the so-called 'Throne Car' or landaulet built for Father Divine, the evangelist. The track was 4 ft. 8 in. (56 in.). The side members, of channel-section alloy steel, dropped and cranked up over the rear axle, were 8½ in. deep. The metal was $\frac{7}{32}$ in. thick. There were six tubular cross members. The second from the front with its diagonal bracing to each side member formed an A-frame. This feature added to the rigidity and stability of the front end of what was already an extremely stiff chassis. The amount of aluminium in the chassis was much advertised: dashboard, differential housing, flywheel housing. sump, camshaft covers, and so forth—and forgings, some of them hollow, were used instead of castings, but a complete limousine would still weigh over 3 tons. The average open four-passenger car turned the scales at over 46 cwt. (5,250 lb.). Half-elliptic springs, aided by Delco-Rémy hydraulic shock absorbers, were fitted at front and rear. With their 1921 Grand Prix cars, Duesenberg had been the pioneers in America of hydraulic brakes, which were also found

on the J. They were of internal expanding type. Vacuum servo assistance was added late in 1929. The degree of assistance available could be adjusted to suit road conditions. The emergency brake, lever-operated, worked on the transmission; a somewhat archaic feature. Nineteen-inch centre-lock knock-off wire wheels were fitted, though 17-in. wheels were optional from 1935.

The standard instrumentation was comprehensive. It included an ammeter, oil pressure gauge, fuel gauge, water temperature gauge, revolution counter, combined clock and stop-clock, 150-m.p.h. speedometer, altimeter, barometer and brake pressure gauge. The most intriguing instrument was the so-called 'timing box' or 'signal box'. A highly complicated reduction gear unit under the bonnet, incorporating 24 sets of planetary gears, was driven from the fuel pump shaft. At the other 'end', on the instrument panel, were four lights. Every 700 miles, one glowed to warn the driver to change his engine oil—an unnecessarily frequent chore, one would have thought. Every 1,400 miles another light came on to tell him to check his battery water level. Every 75 miles the magic 'box' operated a Bijur chassis lubrication pump which delivered lubricant to all chassis points. A red light appeared when it was working and a green one when its reservoir was empty. A reversing light in unit with stop and tail lamps was provided. No mascot was supplied with the car, but from early 1931 the famous 'Duesenbird' became available as an extra.

Control room: interior of the J Victoria by Rollston.
(Photo: William C. Kinsman)

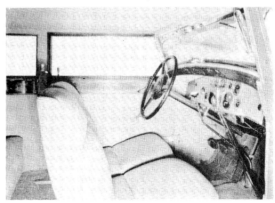

The Duesenberg factory chassis assembly line.
(Photo: William C. Kinsman)

Appropriately enough, each chassis was tested on the Indianapolis Speedway for 500 miles before being passed to the body builder. Straight-line speed and acceleration were the outstanding features of the Duesenberg's performance. Because of its low centre of gravity and great weight, its stability was better than average. The controls—steering, brakes and clutch— were light to operate, in spite of the size of the car, but by 1929 every American buyer of whatever class expected this. The J's strength and long life became legendary, but while its standards of workmanship in construction and finish were far ahead of its American contemporaries, for the ultimate in these qualities the client still had to shop abroad. Like the Hispano-Suiza, one of its nearest rivals, the Duesenberg was not for customers who demanded complete silence in mechanism and exhaust note. Prices were no lower than those obtaining in Europe, before duty was paid. By 1932 the chassis price had climbed to $9,500 (£1,900). It fell to $6,500 two years later, but reverted to $8,500 from 1935 to 1937.

The only major alterations to the J chassis appeared in 1932, when the SJ became available as an alternative. It was fitted with a centrifugal supercharger turning at five times crankshaft speed and giving a 5 p.s.i. boost at 4,000 r.p.m. The engine was given larger crankshaft bearings, tubular steel connecting rods, and stronger

Above: J La Grande Dual Cowl 'Sweep Panel' Phaeton.
Below: J Convertible Roadster by Murphy: cheapest and one of the most popular models.　　　　(Photos: William C. Kinsman)

The longest J built: Father Divine's Throne Car, by Bohman and Schwartz. (Photo: William C. Kinsman)

valve springs to cope with the extra stresses imposed by a power output said to be 320 b.h.p. at 4,750 r.p.m. These mechanical alterations could also be had on the J as options. Following the success of the Duesenberg Special (*q.v.*), a two-carburettor super-charger was supplied. The SJ had stronger front springs than the J, and Watson Stabilators were added at the front. The average open four-passenger phaeton had a claimed speed of 129 m.p.h. in top gear and 104 m.p.h. in second. In spite of a weight of nearly 46 cwt., the roadster could reach 100 m.p.h. in 17 seconds.

Usually, the SJ was sold on the 142½ in. wheelbase, but two SSJ (Short Supercharged) cars were made, for Gary Cooper and Clark Gable, with a 10 ft. 5 in. (125 in.) wheelbase and the 3 : 1 axle ratio. Normal SJs had the 3·78 : 1 axle. The two SSJs were fitted with roadster bodies by the Central Manufacturing Company, an Auburn subsidiary. Outwardly, the SJ could supposedly be identified by its outside exhaust system, rendered necessary by the bulk of the supercharger; but this could be had on the J as an option, to give the impression of an SJ. The 1934 SJ chassis cost $8,000 (£1,600), a figure which had increased to $10,000 by 1935.

The suffixes JN and SJN should be mentioned here because they are confusing, referring not to a chassis variation but to some short-chassis convertible sedans, hardtop sedans and coupés with the distinguishing marks of a lower door line, smaller, bullet-shaped tail lamps and (usually) 17-in. wheels and skirted wings, that were made late in 1934 by Rollston and some other bodybuilders. The skirted wings became a factory option in 1935.

Mention should be made of the new company's only venture into competition work, as it led, as we have seen, to a modification of the SJ. Fred Duesenberg died in July 1932 after an accident in an SJ. His brother August became Chief Engineer in his place, and it was under his auspices that the company reverted briefly to the record-breaking traditions of the Model A. In August 1935 Ab Jenkins, America's

SJ Convertible Sedan by Derham. (Photo: William C. Kinsman)

The Duesenberg Special in road trim.

(Photo: William C. Kinsman)

foremost exponent of this branch of the sport, took a specially-prepared two-passenger SJ to a ten-mile circular course at the Bonneville Salt Flats in Utah. With the racing driver Tony Gulotta as a relief, he captured International Class B records for twenty-four hours at 135·47 m.p.h. and for one hour at 152·145 m.p.h., speeds officially timed by the American Automobile Association. Jenkins was recorded as exceeding 160 m.p.h. His time for the hour beat that set up by Hans Stuck in a Grand Prix Auto Union on the Avus circuit in the previous year by no less than 17·2 m.p.h. John Cobb with his Napier-Railton and Captain G. E. T. Eyston in his 'Speed of the Wind' went on to raise both records still higher at Bonneville during 1935, but with aero-engined vehicles that bore no relation to production road cars.

This Duesenberg Special used a 142½-in. SJ chassis with a twin-carburettor supercharger, and a straight bevel final drive with the 3 : 1 ratio. The revolution counter read up to 8,000 r.p.m. Eighteen-inch wheels were fitted, so that racing tyres could be employed. A streamlined aluminium body was used, that was suitable for either track or road use. The whole machine weighed rather less than 43 cwt. and was designed for speeds of 200 m.p.h.

In 1936 the Duesenberg Special was given a Curtiss Conqueror aero engine and a tail fin for added

stability. Rechristened Mormon Meteor I, it took unlimited class world records from 50 miles to 48 hours, again in Jenkins' hands. With a larger tail fin, it next (in 1937) raised the unlimited-class 24-hour record as Mormon Meteor II. In 1938, the original 1935 SJ engine was reinstalled. Doors, wings and windscreen were fitted, and the Duesenberg Special served Ab Jenkins and his son as a road car for five years and 20,000 miles. It should not be confused with Mormon Meteor III, which was an entirely new machine built by August Duesenberg in 1938 in his shop near the old, closed-down factory, and had no relation to his production cars.

THE BODIES

Being so long, low and stiff, the J chassis was a great favourite with the custom bodybuilders. Every firm, too, that wished to enhance its standing wanted to make bodies for the ultimate in exclusive American makes. However, Duesenberg Inc. were equally concerned to protect their own reputation from the mistakes of clients and bodybuilders alike. Very few bare chassis were sold, and of these almost all went to Europe. As a rule, the client placed his order not direct with the bodybuilder, but with the body design department of Duesenberg Inc. It assumed responsibility for creating designs, to which the

SJ Dual Cowl Torpedo Phaeton by Weymann-La Grande.

(Photo: William C. Kinsman)

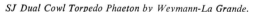

bodybuilder then gave substance, and for exercising close control at all stages. Though they did not have to do so, clients were encouraged to choose from among the wide variety of approved body styles by different builders listed in the Duesenberg catalogue. At the same time, very few of these, when complete, were quite alike in detail. Philip A. Derham, General Manager of the Derham Custom Body Company, was appointed Duesenberg Body Engineer, watching over design and engineering and acting as liaison between the client, Duesenberg Inc. and the bodybuilder. His Chief Designer from 1929 to 1931 was Gordon Buehrig, who was later responsible for the Model 810 Cord.

At least 150, or nearly one-third, of all Js and SJs were bodied by the Walter M. Murphy Company of Pasadena. Bohman & Schwartz bodies were the next most popular. The rest were legion—La Grande (the name used for bodies built by outside firms but trimmed and finished by Duesenberg Inc. themselves), Brunn, Holbrook, Willoughby, Judkins, Locke, Derham, Dietrich, Rollston, Le Baron, Weymann American Body Company. Not all, of course, were included in the Duesenberg catalogue, which embraced only the most popular models, made by builders who were under contract to Duesenberg Inc. These styles, as shown in the first J catalogue, comprised a Phaeton, an All-Weather Cabriolet, a Five Passenger Sedan, Seven-Passenger Sedan, Enclosed Drive Sedan, Convertible Sedan, and Convertible Roadster. The first one and the last two were the most popular; all, significantly, being informal, 'soft-top' bodies. The 1932 catalogue listed no fewer than 18 models, by Derham, La Grande, Le Baron, Rollston, Murphy, Willoughby and Judkins.

No Duesenberg body ever cost less than $2,500 (£500). By 1932 the cheapest, the Murphy Convertible Roadster, was priced at $4,000, while two years later the lowest price was $4,500. In 1932 the prices of complete cars in the catalogue varied between $13,500 and $17,950. The most expensive Duesenberg ever made, a very special order, cost rather less than $25,000 (£5,000). Such figures, not unheard-of in Europe, were fabulous by American standards, and gave rise to much exaggeration later. To the customers of Duesenberg Inc. the price they paid was an indication of status. Most tended to be much-advertised personalities, who either through professional necessity or personal inclination, wanted to keep in the public eye. One way to do this was to buy America's most dashing and flamboyant motor car. Among those who agreed were Mayor Jimmy Walker of New York, the newspaper tycoon William Randolph Hearst, the

Above: SJ 'Twenty Grand' by Rollston. Below: 1933 SJ 'Fishtail' Speedster by Weymann.   (Photos: William C. Kinsman)

SSJ Roadster owned by Clark Gable. This car was one of two built on the ultra-short 125-in. wheelbase.
(Photo: William C. Kinsman)

J Convertible Victoria by Fernandez et Darrin. Its original owner, Greta Garbo, is in the passenger seat beside the present owner. (Photo: William C. Kinsman)

multi-millionaire, much-married Tommy Manville, Elizabeth Arden, Marion Davies, Mae West, Joe E. Brown and, as we have seen, Gary Cooper (who in fact had two), and Clark Gable—to mention only names which are remembered today. Gangsters, too, appreciated the Duesenberg, for its invincible performance and its *panache*.

THE DUESENBERG IN EUROPE

The Model J was unveiled to appreciative European eyes at the Paris Salon in October 1929. Seven chassis had been imported for the occasion, the first of about 50 that crossed the Atlantic. A dozen were made with right-hand drive, so it is reasonable to suppose that not more found their way to Britain, her dependencies and Sweden together. Of these, only about three are known to have been sold in Britain. The chassis price there was £2,380 ($11,900). This compared with £1,900 asked for the chassis of a Rolls-Royce Phantom II, and £1,950 for that of the 45 h.p., 8-litre Hispano-Suiza. The financier Clarence Hatry and the jockey and racing driver George Duller were buyers.

The Duesenberg in Europe immediately attracted an equally famous, if usually rather more sedate clientele, among them the motor-phile King Alphonso XIII of Spain, King Victor Emmanuel of

J Faux Cabriolet by Letourneur et Marchand: the French idiom.
(Photo: Wm. C. Kinsman)

Italy, Queen Marie of Yugoslavia and Prince Nicolas of Roumania. The last-named owned a J with Club Faux Cabriolet bodywork by Letourneur et Marchand, and bought another J chassis to which he added a supercharger and fitted a utilitarian sporting body of his own design that must have horrified Duesenberg Inc. He proceeded to race it all over Europe, with great gusto if not much success. In the Le Mans 24 Hours Race of 1933, Prince Nicolas was disqualified. He entered in 1934, but seized up in practice. When he competed at Le Mans again in 1935 he retired.

Other European bodybuilders who worked on the J chassis were Figoni, Franay, Fernandez et Darrin, Hibbard et Darrin (two Americans, formerly of Le Baron) and Saoutchik in France, Barker and Gurney Nutting in Britain (where Malcolm Campbell Ltd. imported chassis), Vanden Plas and D'Ieteren Frères in Belgium, Castagna in Italy, and Graber of Switzerland.

THE END

The Duesenberg was last shown to the public in 1936, when the 1937 models were displayed. Having survived the Stock Market crash and the worst years of the Depression, it was brought low in the general collapse of the Cord Corporation, which went into voluntary liquidation in August 1937. The purchasers of its holdings decided to discontinue car production. In October the Marmon-Herrington Company of Indianapolis bought the factory. A new company was formed at Auburn, Indiana, in 1938 to supply parts and service for Cord, Auburn and Duesenberg owners. The last Duesenberg, an SJ, was in fact completed during 1938. The order was placed in the previous year by a German client. The factory was closed before the chassis was finished, but work was completed with parts set aside for it. It was assembled in Chicago, and passed by August Duesenberg. The body was made in America by Rollson (formerly Rollston).

Duesenbergs remained in use for many years, often in the hands of their original owners, who saw nothing strange in keeping them on the road. Unlike the average, expendable American car, they were regarded as ageless. Such was the strength of the spell they exerted that as late as 1947, Marshall Merkes of Chicago, backed by Chicago financiers, bought the remaining assets, retained August Duesenberg to help design a new model, and announced his intention of resuming production. The new

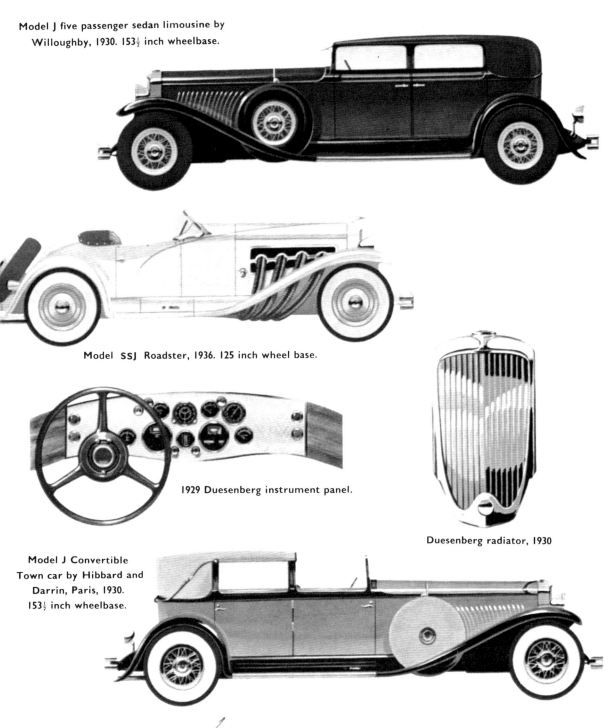

Model J five passenger sedan limousine by Willoughby, 1930. 153½ inch wheelbase.

Model SSJ Roadster, 1936. 125 inch wheel base.

1929 Duesenberg instrument panel.

Duesenberg radiator, 1930

Model J Convertible Town car by Hibbard and Darrin, Paris, 1930. 153½ inch wheelbase.

Model J Boat-tailed Roadster by Walter M. Murphy, Pasadena, California, 1930. 142½ inch wheelbase.

J fabric-bodied 'Saint Cloud' Sedan by Weymann. (Photo: Wm. C. Kinsman)

Duesenberg was to have an eight-cylinder engine with fuel injection. As before, all bodies were to be custom-built. Unfortunately, it was then discovered that the car was going to cost at least $25,000, which effectively killed the project. In 1966, more plans were afoot for reviving the name. The new car was to cost $19,500, and be built at Indianapolis as of old.

No one has yet ascertained the exact numbers of Js and SJs built. Engine numbers ran from J101 to J588, suggesting a total of 488 cars, of which about 36 were SJs. Lycoming dispatch records give a number of 480. Clerical errors help to account for discrepancies, but some engines were used for display outside chassis and others were installed in boats. The engine number of the last complete car built appears to be J586, and of the last chassis sold, J587. Chassis numbers ran from 2125 to 2611, giving a total of 487; but again, some numbers were 'skipped'. It is safe to assume that not less than about 470 complete cars were built, but that is all that can be said at the present time. © *T. R. Nicholson, 1966*

Duesenberg in England: a Barker-bodied J. Formal bodies were in a minority. (Photo: Montagu Motor Museum.)

Belgian J: Convertible Victoria Coupé by D'Ieteren Frères. Last of the line: 1938 Rollson-bodied J. (Photos: Wm C. Kinsman)

SPECIFICATION MODEL J DUESENBERG

ENGINE: Eight cylinders in line. Bore and stroke 95 mm. × 121 mm. (3¾ in. × 4¾ in.), 6,882 c.c. (420 cu. in.). Two chain-driven o.h.c., four valves per cylinder (two inlet, two exhaust). Standard compression ratio 5·2 : 1. Aluminium connecting rods and pistons. Detachable head, integral block and crankcase. Five-bearing crankshaft with vibration damper. Engine rubber-mounted at four points.
Ignition: Delco-Rémy 6-volt. Dual coils.
Carburation: Updraught twin-choke Schebler (1929). From November 1932, downdraught Stromberg. Electric and mechanical fuel pumps, 26-gal. tank at rear.
Claimed output: 265 b.h.p. @ 4,250 r.p.m.
TRANSMISSION
Clutch: Double dry-plate, by Long.
Gearbox: Sliding pinion. Three speeds and reverse.
Final drive: Hypoid spiral bevel. Ratios 3 : 1 (special order only), 3·78 : 1, 4 : 1, 4·3 : 1 or 4·7 : 1.
Freewheel to special order only, from 1931.
CHASSIS
Frame: Channel section steel, dropped, with six tubular crossmembers.
Wheelbase: 11 ft. 10½ in. (142½ in.) or 12 ft. 9½ in. (153½ in.).
Track: 4 ft. 8 in. (56 in.).
Suspension: Half-elliptic front and rear, with Delco-Rémy hydraulic shock absorbers.
Brakes: Duesenberg internal expanding hydraulic. Vacuum servo assistance from late 1929. Handbrake on transmission.
Lubrication: Bijur automatic chassis lubrication.
Wheels: Wire, 19 in. centre-lock knock-off. 17 in. wheels optional from 1935.
Weight: Two tons approx. (4,450 lb.) upwards, depending on wheelbase. Complete car: 44¼ cwt. (5,000 lb.) upwards, according to wheelbase and bodywork.
Price: $6,500 to $9,500, according to year. Complete car: approximately $13,500 to $25,000, according to year and bodywork.
CLAIMED PERFORMANCE (1929 Phaeton)
Acceleration: 10–80 m.p.h. in top gear 22 seconds.
Maximum speeds in gears: 2nd gear 89 m.p.h.
Top gear 116 m.p.h.

SPECIFICATION MODEL SJ

Generally as for Model J, with the following modifications:
ENGINE: Centrifugal supercharger, turning at five times engine speed, 5 p.s.i. @ 4,000 r.p.m. Two carburettors on supercharger from 1935. Outside exhaust system. Larger crankshaft bearings, tubular steel connecting rods, stronger valve springs. All features available as extras for Model J.
Claimed output: 320 b.h.p. @ 4,750 r.p.m.
TRANSMISSION: Final drive ratio 3·78 : 1. 3 : 1 to special order only.
Wheelbase: 11 ft. 10½ in. (142½ in.) normally. Two chassis with 10 ft. 5 in. w/b (125 in.) made.
Suspension: Stronger springs and Watson Stabilators at front.
Price: $8,000 to $10,000 according to year.
CLAIMED PERFORMANCE
Acceleration: 0–100 m.p.h. through gears 17 seconds (Roadster).
Maximum speeds in gears: 2nd gear 104 m.p.h. (Phaeton).
Top gear 129 m.p.h. (Phaeton).

The Bentley 3 & 4¼-Litre

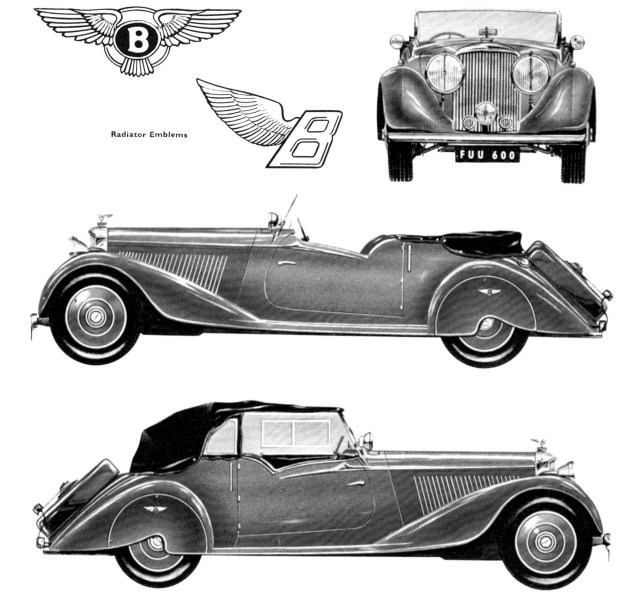

Radiator Emblems

FUU 600

1939, OVERDRIVE SERIES, 4¼-LITRE
BENTLEY TOURER by Vanden Plas,
chassis no. B154MR. Owner: J. R. A.
Green Esquire. (Previous owners:
Hugh Sinclair Esquire, William Riley
Esquire and William Douglas-Home
Esquire).

FUU 600

1   2   3

© GORDON DAVIES

The Bentley 3½ & 4¼-Litre

by George A. Oliver

Sir Malcolm Campbell at the wheel of his 4¼-litre Vanden Plas tourer. (Photo: Rolls-Royce Ltd. and the Bentley Drivers' Club)

After the liquidation of Bentley Motors Limited in 1931 the English firm of D. Napier & Son Ltd. was actively interested in acquiring its assets and re-entering the motor-car market, with a somewhat modified version of the 8-litre model that had been W. O. Bentley's last—and perhaps greatest—achievement up to that time. At an advanced stage of the negotiations Rolls-Royce Ltd. stepped in with a higher offer and secured control, but it was not until the autumn of 1933, almost two years later, that Bentley Motors (1931) Ltd. announced their first car, the engine capacity of which was but half a litre larger than that of the first Bentley of all, the 3-litre model of 1919.

Although the last car made by the old company had been of 4-litres capacity only, it was out of step with a policy that had gradually taken the Bentley farther and farther away from the medium-size sports-car class and into that of the large-engined luxury-car—the very one most seriously affected by the economic slump at the beginning of the 'thirties. This happened despite the fact that engineering advances made since the Armistice had enabled the automobile designer to rely less and less on litres as a means of producing the power necessary for adequate performance.

During the 'twenties the discriminating motorist of means, who sought a combination of high performance with easy running, and comfortable springing with good handling and roadworthiness, was obliged to choose from the automobile élite—from cars of such size and splendour as the 40/50 Rolls-Royce, the 37·2 or 45 h.p. Hispano-Suizas, the straight-eight Isotta-Fraschini, the Lanchester 40, the largest Mercedes-Benz or the 6½-litre Bentley, for example.

But these splendid cars were at once costly to buy, to run and to maintain, and to a greater or lesser degree ownership implied a certain formality of living that was beginning to become irksome to a growing number of people. By the end of the decade road conditions had greatly improved in many parts of Europe and attitudes towards long-distance travel by car were quickly changing; better roads encouraged greater use of them and a demand slowly grew for a medium-size car that would combine high performance, comfort and ease of running.

It is very likely that the 3½-litre Bentley was the first successful example of this type of machine in its class.

In the introduction to their first catalogue its makers outlined their aims in typically well-chosen words:—

"There is at the present time an ever increasing demand for a car of moderate size which can carry in comfort up to four passengers and, at the same time, maintain a high average speed. Such a car must combine the seemingly incompatible qualities of high engine-power and low chassis weight with silence and good riding qualities.

Whereas modern experience gained on the racing track has rendered comparatively simple the production of a car having a high horse-power in relation to its weight, up to the present good road performance in the car of medium size has only been obtainable at the expense of comfort.

The 3½-litre Bentley . . . has been produced to meet the demand referred to above, and its arrival has proved that Performance and Peace can now be reconciled . . . in its docility and absence of fuss under all conditions it is without a rival amongst sporting cars."

For once the claims of a motor manufacturer were not overstated. The new Bentley, a car of medium engine capacity and overall dimensions, united the vivacity of a true sports-car with the delicacy of control and the urbanity of manners of the best type of town-carriage. Unlike so many sporting vehicles of

An unusual 3½-litre which is thought to be a prototype. Note the radiator stoneguard and eared hub nuts.
(Photo: Rolls-Royce Ltd. and the Bentley Drivers' Club)

1934 3½-litre four-door saloon by Park Ward (B189AE). This car was owned by the eminent designer, Sir Roy Fedden, from 1934–1947.
(Photo: Rolls-Royce Ltd.)

earlier years it lacked any kind of mechanical temperament, and while it was enjoyed best on the open road, where it could be given its head, traffic work was no hardship in a car of such flexibility—equipped, what is more, with one of the finest gearboxes ever made.

THE CARS DESCRIBED

For various reasons it was not until late in 1932 that the final design scheme for the new Bentley was approved. After the take-over, according to Mr. W. A. Robotham, then a member of the engineering department at Derby, it was agreed that any new car must be as unlike the current Rolls-Royce models as possible, that silence was of no particular importance, and that supercharging was desirable as a reminder of the sporting activities of earlier Bentleys.

There was no time to design a new engine, but as Rolls-Royce were then experimenting with a scaled-down version of their 20/25 model, called the 'Peregrine', which had a 2·3-litre engine, it was decided to supercharge this unit. The troubles that ensued were many and the delay they caused began to worry a Sales Department with customers but no cars to sell; then someone suggested trying the current 20/25

1934 3½-litre tourer by Vanden Plas. (Photo: Mr. J. R. A. Green)

engine in the 'Peregrine' chassis (fortunately it fitted!) and the result was a lively and likeable car that was quiet and had good handling.

It showed so much promise, in fact, that its further development was sanctioned by Sir Henry Royce, who had been closely involved in the design of the Bentley, according to Robotham, and the whole idea of forced induction was gradually dropped. Sales were persuaded that the idea of a silent sports-car was a good one and during the next 9 months or so what was to become the 3½-litre Bentley went from prototype to production stage.

Comparatively few modifications were made to the

A 3½-litre Barker Sports Saloon supplied to the Marquese de Portago (B27DK).   (Photo: Montagu Motor Museum)

Lord Doune's Abbott-bodied 3½-litre racing two-seater was previously owned by the late Lord Ebury. (Photo: Norval Ltd.)

six cylinder 20/25 engine, the main change being the provision of really efficient lungs—twin S.U. carburetters and a most carefully planned induction system. With a slightly raised compression ratio (6·5 to 1) and little increase in noise the output was raised by about 25 per cent, the b.h.p. of production engines being around 110, unsilenced. At the recommended limit of 4,500 r.p.m. speeds in the gears were approximately 34, 54, 75 and 94 m.p.h. The 4·1 to 1 top gave about 22 m.p.h. per 1,000 r.p.m.

The early cars were rather weak at the front end of the frame and corrective measures included the fitting of an extra cross-member ahead of the radiator and the adoption of the harmonic-stabilising type of front bumper. With this additional stiffening there was a decided improvement in roadholding and ride, and certain body troubles caused by excessive frame flexibility were eliminated.

Towards the end of 1934 ride-control was introduced, the degree of damping provided by the shock-absorbers being varied according to the speed of the car by a gearbox-driven pump. There was an over-riding hand control mounted in the centre of the steering-wheel. The advantages of a system of this sort may better be appreciated when it is realised that a full tank of petrol weighed close on two cwt.—not to speak of the weight of passengers and luggage.

The overdrive cars of 1938–39 had larger-section tyres, to improve riding comfort (a not-very-impressive answer to the adoption of torsion-bar i.f.s. by Lagonda!), and to lighten the driver's burden Marles steering of a lower-geared type than that previously used was fitted.

Engine changes were also few between 1933 and 1941. In the spring of 1936 the larger 4¼-litre engine was offered as an alternative, at £50 extra, and almost immediately was adopted as standard. In detail it differed little from the 3½ but the extra capacity gave better acceleration and pulling-power throughout its range, its top-gear acceleration, for example, being as good as that of the 3½ in third. Both models were quite remarkably economical to run, fuel consumption seldom falling below 17 m.p.g. for either car. Two 3½ models known to the writer still return over 23 m.p.g. on long runs today and a 4¼, which gives an all-year-round average of 18 m.p.g., can give 21 on a journey carried out at high cruising speeds.

The weak point of the 4¼ was its bearings, which

H.R.H. Prince George (father of the present Duke of Kent) ordered this handsome, Barker-bodied 3½, B45AE, in 1933. An unusual feature is the division between front and rear seats. (Photo: Montagu Motor Museum)

gave a good deal of trouble at first. Modifications to the crankshaft oiling system helped until such time as new, longer-lasting bearing materials were developed. When these were fitted bearing life rose from around 40,000 to 60- or 70,000 miles on average, according to post-war company literature, and it is probable that an even higher mileage was possible from the engines of the overdrive chassis. The geared-up top of the latter allowed really safe high-speed cruising on Continental roads.

The basic cause of these bearing troubles was the fact that it was becoming possible to drive long distances at high speeds on the new *autobahnen* and *autostrada* of Germany and Italy, and some owners seemed to think that flat-out driving would do their engines no harm. In a circular to owners of Bentley and Rolls-Royce cars, distributed by their makers in

An Owen-sedanca by J. Gurney Nutting on a 1934 3½-litre chassis—one of the most strikingly handsome cars of the mid-thirties. (Photo: James Young Ltd.)

E. R. Hall's 3½ in its original form (B35AE). (Photo: Rolls-Royce Ltd. and the Bentley Drivers' Club)

1937, it was pointed out that not even the designers of aero-engines expected them to withstand indefinite full-throttle running. Recommendations for *safe maximum continuous cruising speeds* were made—an action as wise as it was courageous. Few, if any, of the critics of the day bothered to notice that in most cases these speeds were as high as the maxima of other cars. . . .

The crankshaft of both 3½ and 4¼ models was absolutely safe up to 4,500 r.p.m. but unwise owners who exceeded this speed could end up with a large bill. Nowadays the high cost of spares is probably the main reason for the comparative lack of interest in restoring these fine cars. To carry out a complete mechanical overhaul could cost upwards of £1,000 and body renovations might conceivably cost even more—but the result would be a car of exceptional character, fascination and long life-expectation.

DRIVING IMPRESSIONS

From the very beginning the 3½ was a success: orders poured in, despite its high price, and deliveries of the AE-series cars began at the end of 1933. At that time the market for expensive open-bodied sports-cars was shrinking and most of the Bentleys made during the next seven years or so were to be fitted with either saloon or convertible coachwork. One of the best-looking sports-tourers of its day, by Vanden Plas, was catalogued at £1,380 but the number sold was not large.

By the standards of 1933–34 (and, indeed, much later) these cars had a spirited performance, a stand-still-to-60 time of less than 20 sec. and a maximum speed of at least 90 m.p.h. putting the 3½ among the really high-performance cars of the mid-'thirties, regardless of engine size. It was not simply on per-

In 1934 and 1935 E. R. Hall finished second on handicap in the Ulster Tourist Trophy race with his works-supported 3½. In the 1936 race he was again second driving the same car (seen here)— now with a new body and a 4¼-litre engine. (Photo: *The Motor*)

formance that the Derby Bentley sold so well, however: it had much more to offer the seasoned driver than that alone, and because a fair number of these cars survives in tip-top condition it is possible still to find out by actual trial just what their attractions were —and are.

The present writer began road experience of Derby Bentleys in 1941, since when he has sampled many different models as passenger, driver and owner, and while he freely admits to a partiality for the make he has taken the trouble to try as many other cars of quality as possible in order to establish standards of comparison. So far he has driven no other car of the 'twenties or 'thirties that has given him more all-round driving satisfaction than the Derby Bentley, especially in its earliest form.

An early 1934 car tried some time ago was in such good mechanical order that when driving it one felt very much as one supposes the commentators of 1933 must have felt when they first tried the new Rolls-Royce-made Bentleys in the autumn of that year. After

During 1938 and 1939 close on 500 standard steel saloon bodies were built on 4¼ chassis by Park Ward & Co. Ltd. The complete car cost about £1,510. (B31MX).
(Photo: James Young Ltd.)

1938 4¼-litre drophead coupé by Windover. (Photo: Mr. J. R. A. Green)

only a few miles one realised that the blend of qualities was so beautifully balanced that no one feature stood out as being superior, or inferior, to any other. As a result everything the car was asked to do it did in such an unobtrusive manner that one felt it to be an extension of oneself and one's will—yet it was in no way lacking in personality.

In dense traffic it could be 'town-carriaged' like a Rolls-Royce, using third and top gears almost all the time, and the extreme quietness of both engine and gearbox—inherent and not the result of skilful sound-damping, incidentally—was notable *even by present-day standards.* Out of town the speedometer and rev.-counter needles could be made to sweep swiftly round their respective dials to chosen speeds, but even at full throttle there was no fuss and at 70 m.p.h. or more the engine was really quiet.

It was not at all obtrusive at 60 in the silent third, and at 30 or so in second (another silent ratio) one sometimes made to change into top in the mistaken belief that one was already in third. The synchromesh on third and top was as light as it was effective, so that the short lever on the driver's right seemed to fall into either gear without conscious effort. To engage second or first on the move demanded some small skill in double-declutching, but in spite of the fact that the gear-wheels were cut to Rolls-Royce standards of accuracy the margin of permissible error in matching the respective speeds of the revolving and engaging ones was more generous than one might have expected.

In a car of half the weight and size the steering would have been considered especially light yet it was high-geared, requiring little more than two turns

The 1939 4¼ Vanden Plas "All-weather" tourer.
(Photo: Mr. J. R. A. Green)

from one lock to the other, absolutely accurate and without lost motion. Its immediacy of response was matched by that of the servo-operated brakes, which responded with astonishing smoothness and effectiveness to remarkably low pedal pressures. Fully to realise how effective they were, indeed, one had to watch the swift drop of the speedometer needle on application. . . .

Although Rolls-Royce were themselves working on an independent front-wheel suspension system for their forthcoming Phantom III model quite early in the 'thirties, conventional semi-elliptics were used for the Bentley—flat under normal conditions of loading at the front and reverse-cambered at the rear. They were most effectively controlled by shock-dampers of the Rolls-Royce hydraulic type, those at the front being connected to the axle beam by typically neat triangulated links that served also to absorb brake reaction. In combination with a frame that had a certain degree of flexibility this straightforward system gave an above-average standard of riding comfort, along with really first-rate roadholding.

"Razor-edge" coachwork was fashionable in 1938 and 1939, and this fine H. J. Mulliner body, on the overdrive 4¼-litre chassis (B184MR) is typical of the best work of that time.
(Photo: James Young Ltd.)

Facia of the 1939 4¼-litre. (Photo: Mr. J. R. A. Green)

Although one was aware of car movement over rough surfaces little of this was actually transmitted to the occupants, the phasing of seat-cushion springs and padding having been carefully considered as an important part of the suspension system. The high level of actual comfort had much to do with the ability of these cars to cover long distances in short periods of time without in any way tiring their occupants. In this respect, as in so many others, the claim for Performance with Peace was fully justifiable still.

THE OPPOSITION

In 1933 the 3½ had no rivals in its class. The trend that it started for quiet, fast, medium-sized sporting cars took some time to get under way, and its importance, historically speaking, is perhaps not yet fully appreciated. Towards the end of 1933 Lagonda introduced their Meadows-engined 4½-litre model, which was a little faster and a little cheaper than the 3½ but a good deal less refined. The current Alvis Speed 20 had i.f.s. and was very well made but its power-to-weight ratio restricted performance. The new Hudson-engined 4·1-litre Railton had a most advantageous combination of lightness and power, and its performance was spectacular. Like other Anglo/American hybrids of similar type, however, it lacked the sheer quality and staying power of the best English makes.

After W. O. Bentley joined Lagonda, in 1935, to take over as technical director, almost the first thing he did was to improve the manners of the current 4½-litre model. It is worth emphasising here that this was not something picked up during his years with Rolls-Royce; it dated back to the mid-'twenties, in fact, when his 6½-litre car proved that it was possible to unite quiet, smooth running with sporting performance, and during its brief production life the 8-litre had impressed the world with the same features, albeit on an even higher level.

To compete on more equal terms Alvis enlarged the engine of their Speed Twenty in 1936 and in 1938 introduced the 4·3-litre, which, like the contemporary 4½ Lagonda, was both faster and cheaper than the 4¼ Bentley. In terms of absolute quality and in sheer refinement the latter was probably still their superior but in one respect it lagged behind. Independent front-wheel suspension was a feature of both the Alvis and the Lagonda and while the Bentley still outsold them its margin of superiority was narrower than it had been previously.

Other rivals were the Talbot 110—from all accounts a good car—the Hudson-engined Brough-Superior and the Lammas-Graham. Although they were in a

very much lower price-range the S.S. 'Jaguars' made from 1936 onwards may have had some slight effect on Bentley sales. In 2½- and 3½-litre form these cars offered fine performance, considerable refinement of running and very well-equipped coachwork, at prices that were almost unbelievably low. Their resemblance to the Bentley, outwardly at least, was close—especially in profile—and it was easy enough to mistake the Coventry car for its more distinguished contemporary. All the same those 'Jaguars' were a remarkable commercial achievement.

If performance alone was the sole criterion certain foreign cars offered as much, or more, than the Bentley. The Type 57 Bugatti that appeared in 1934 was both quiet and quick, and from all accounts much less fickle than some of its forebears. A total production (according to Mr. Hugh Conway) of less than 800 cars compares unfavourably with the figures for Bentleys over approximately the same period—1,191 3½-litres, 1,241 4¼-litres and about a dozen Mark V cars were made between late 1933 and 1941.

Other French cars that could give the 4¼ a run for its money were the 3½-litre Delahaye, the Paris-Nice Hotchkiss and the 4-litre Talbot. The larger Type 500 Mercedes-Benz, and the later Type 540K, gave a slightly better performance at the cost of dreadful fuel consumption, an accelerated rate of wear if the supercharger was engaged for longer than the permitted time, and a vast increase in noise. Their only real advantage lay in the fact that they had independent suspension of all four wheels.

Good as the springing of the 3½- and 4¼-litre Bentleys was, it did impose a limit on speed over bad surfaces, and as many of these cars were used for foreign travel technically-minded owners probably wondered at the apparent reluctance of their makers to adopt i.f.s. It had been a feature of the Phantom III Rolls-

Inlet and exhaust sides of the 1939 4¼-litre engine.
(Photos: Mr. J. R. A. Green)

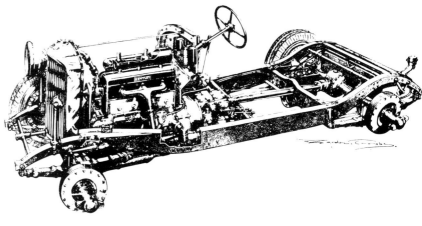

This F. Gordon Crosby drawing shows the chassis of the 1933–34 3½-litre. Of the double-dropped type, it was sturdy yet light in weight.

(*Autocar* drawing)

Royce since 1935, and of the smaller 'Wraith' from the autumn of 1938. Perhaps Bentley Motors (1931) Ltd. were too busy coping with the continued high demand —in 1938 and most of 1939, for example, Park Ward alone were building 10 'standard' saloon bodies a week for the 4¼ chassis —to do much about a change really somewhat overdue; but whatever the reason it was not until well on in 1939 that an independently sprung Bentley appeared.

THE MARK V

This, the Mark V model, was built in small numbers and few have survived. Its main difference from the previous MR- and MX-series overdrive chassis lay in the adoption of coil-spring and wishbone i.f.s., along the same lines as the Rolls-Royce system already mentioned. With some modifications it was continued after the war, in the highly successful Mark VI and 'R' type cars.

In other respects the Mark V was an interesting link between the traditional sports-car, as exemplified by the 3½ and 4¼ models, and the latter-day type, softly-sprung yet impressively roadworthy, quiet yet very fast, and luxuriously equipped. Its body shape clearly anticipated that of the post-war standard steel saloon without, however, losing a family resemblance to earlier Park Ward bodies created specifically for the Bentley car. Indeed this coachbuilder (owned since the early 'thirties by Rolls-Royce) had pioneered a form of all-steel construction for 'bespoke' or 'custom' bodies that was remarkably successful and paved the way, as it were, for the standard bodies fitted to Rolls-Royce and Bentley cars until the recent advent of the 'Silver Shadow' and 'T'-series models.

In appearance and in its up-to-date suspension the Mark V was forward-looking, but its engine and transmission were a continuation of well-tried principles, which is nearly always wise, technically and commercially speaking. The result—either in the normal form or in the higher-performance 'Corniche' model—won high praise from the small number of experts actually able to try these cars.

IN COMPETITION

Stamina was always an outstanding feature. Along with the superb steering, brakes and roadholding it attracted the attention of experienced racing drivers, prominent among whom were George Eyston, Raymond Mays and E. R. Hall. Both Mays and Hall used their Bentleys for pre-race practice on many occasions and the latter was able, by means best known to himself, no doubt, to secure official backing for entry of his 3½ in the 1934 Ulster Tourist Trophy Race. As the last time Derby had taken an official part in competition was as far back as the Alpine Trial of 1913, the magnitude of Hall's achievement may be the more clearly judged.

Hall's car was a 1933 chassis, B35AE, and for the race he had it fitted with a specially designed open body that closely resembled its original one. A certain amount of attention was paid to reducing drag but the main alterations were to the engine, gearbox and suspension. With raised compression (7·35 to 1) and a straight-through exhaust conforming to T.T. regulations 131 b.h.p. was developed and the car could reach about 110 m.p.h. With a rear-axle ratio of 3·75 to 1 its overall gear ratios were raised to such an extent that 50 m.p.h. was possible in first.

Hartford friction shock-dampers supplemented the hydraulics already fitted and the other changes were an increase in tank capacity to 26 gal. and the fitting of an extra oil tank. In spite of the fact that the T.T. course did not favour the larger cars Hall took second place to Dodson's M.G. 'Magnette', averaging 78·40 m.p.h. for 478 miles and losing on handicap by only 17 sec.

In the same year he took first place in his class at the famous Shelsley Walsh hill-climb and made fastest time for any sports-car over 1,500 c.c. capacity.

In the 1935 Tourist Trophy Hall was again backed by the works and with only one or two modifications

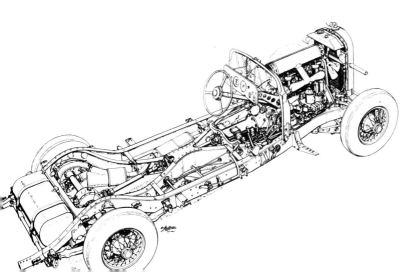

The frame of the Mark V was very much stiffer than that of its predecessors and featured independent front-wheel suspension. (*Autocar* drawing)

The Park Ward body of this 1940 Mark V (B16AW) resembles in many respects the post-war Mark VI standard steel saloon.
(Photo: Rolls-Royce Ltd. and Mr. Dennis Becker)

B35AE took the field in an even more powerful form. The compression was raised to 8·35 to 1, the inlet valves were of increased size and larger carburetters and induction manifolds were fitted, as a result of which power went up to 152 b.h.p. Because larger diameter tyres were fitted the rear-axle ratio was lowered, and the wheel-nuts (which had given trouble the year before) were suitably modified.

Once again Hall came in second on handicap, this time 13 sec. behind the Riley of Freddie Dixon. In 1934 his main duel had been with the 4½ Lagondas, which he defeated decisively, and in 1935 he was up against two Lagondas and three Bugattis of the 8 cylinder, 3·3-litre type. Earl Howe was driving one of these French cars and another experienced driver, the Hon. Brian Lewis, was in charge of a second. It says much for Hall and his car that they disposed of this strong opposition so effectively that they finished almost 3 minutes ahead of Earl Howe.

For the 1936 race B35AE was fitted with a tuned 4¼ engine of 163 b.h.p. Hall had been given permission to enter it for the Le Mans race of that year and in preparation for such a gruelling event it had been endurance-tested for 24 hours at full-throttle. It was a great pity that because of political troubles in France the race did not take place after all—but the car distinguished itself in the T.T. by averaging 80·81 m.p.h. for 410 miles and although it was second on handicap

once more (this time to the Riley driven with such brilliance by Freddie Dixon and C. J. P. Dodson) it finished almost 9 minutes ahead of the 4½ Lagonda that was second in Class C and fourth overall in the race. Of the 6 3½-litre Delahayes entered only one finished.

And if proof were still needed of the stamina of this splendid machine consider the fact that it took eighth place in the 1950 Le Mans 24 hour race driven by E. R. Hall and T. G. Clarke, at an average of 82·9 m.p.h. A year or two earlier it had been racing in South Africa.

In 1938 a specially bodied 4¼ was built to the order of the late Walter Sleator and with George Eyston in charge it covered almost 115 miles in the hour at Brooklands. In 1949 this car was driven by its owner H. S. F. Hay, and Tommy Wisdom, into sixth place at Le Mans (averaging 73·5 m.p.h.) and in 1950, with H. Hunter sharing the driving, it finished fourteenth, at an average of 78·6 m.p.h.

Both the 'Corniche' Mark V of 1940 and the 'Continental' R-type of 1951 owed much to the lessons

In 1949, the car in which Captain G.E.T. Eyston put 114.6 miles into an hour at Brooklands in 1939, was driven in the Le Mans 24-hour race by H. S. F. Hay and T. H. Wisdom. It was placed sixth and averaged 73.5 m.p.h. In 1950 it was 14th at an average of 78.6 m.p.h. driven by Hay and Hunter
(Photo: Mr. Louis Klemantaski)

The "Corniche" of 1939–40 was the high-performance version of the Mark V, with a top speed of well over 100 m.p.h. It was, perhaps, the ugliest Bentley ever made.
(Photo: Rolls-Royce Ltd.)

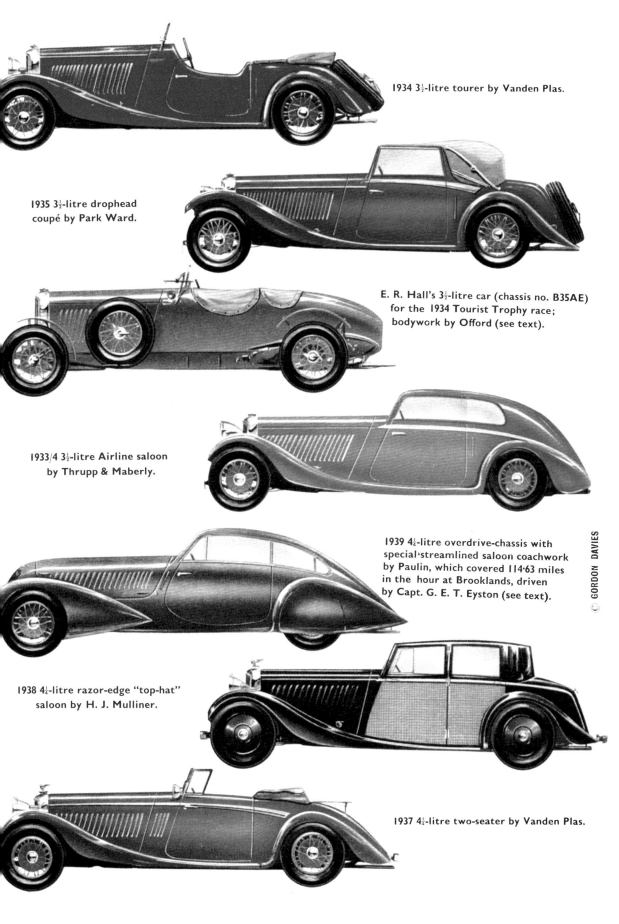

1934 3½-litre tourer by Vanden Plas.

1935 3½-litre drophead coupé by Park Ward.

E. R. Hall's 3½-litre car (chassis no. **B35AE**) for the 1934 Tourist Trophy race; bodywork by Offord (see text).

1933/4 3½-litre Airline saloon by Thrupp & Maberly.

1939 4¼-litre overdrive-chassis with special streamlined saloon coachwork by Paulin, which covered 114·63 miles in the hour at Brooklands, driven by Capt. G. E. T. Eyston (see text).

1938 4¼-litre razor-edge "top-hat" saloon by H. J. Mulliner.

1937 4¼-litre two-seater by Vanden Plas.

© GORDON DAVIES

Le Mans, 1950: Eddie Hall's 4¼, veteran of the pre-war Tourist Trophy races, in the early stages of the event with the head lamp covers still in position. Note the coupé top and cowled-in radiator. Driven by E. R. Hall and T. G. Clarke, the car came eighth at an average speed of 82.9 m.p.h. (Photo: *Autocar*).

learned from the Sleator car of 1938, and to experimental work carried out even earlier on the 3½ chassis by H. I. F. Evernden. In 1933 the latter carried out trials of a 3½ fitted with a body of streamlined shape that differed only in comparatively unimportant ways from the later 'wind-cheating' bodies.

*   *   *

During the seven years of their production the

Derby Bentleys established a lasting reputation for sheer quality of construction, extreme durability, high yet refined performance and great economy of running. More than 30 years after the first cars reached their owners it is still possible to prove that this reputation was in no way a false one. The Bentley was not only 'The silent sports-car'—it was the durable sports-car, *par excellence*.

© George A. Oliver, 1966

SPECIFICATIONS OF 3½-LITRE, 4¼-LITRE AND MARK V MODELS, 1933–1941

3½-LITRE BENTLEY

ENGINE: 6 cyl. monobloc. 3¼ in. bore, 4½ in. stroke, 3,669 c.c. R.A.C. rating 25·3 h.p.; approx. 110 b.h.p. (see text). 7 bearing crankshaft with patent vibration damper at front. 6·5 to 1 compression ratio.
Overhead valves, push-rod operated. Pressure-feed lubrication.
Twin S.U. carburetters, fed from 18 gal. rear tank by dual electric pumps; 2 gal. reserve.
Coil and distributor ignition with automatic advance and retard and over-riding hand control. 12-volt, 50 amp. hour battery.
Constant voltage control.
Cooling by pump and fan, with thermostatically-controlled radiator shutters.

TRANSMISSION: single dry-plate clutch.
4 speeds and reverse gearbox in unit with engine; right-hand, gate-change. Overall ratios: 4·1, 5·1, 7·08 and 11·3 to 1.
Open propeller shaft: hypoid bevel final drive with fully-floating half shafts. Standard ratio 4·1 to 1 (3·9 to 1 optional).

BRAKES: mechanical servo-operated four-wheel brakes; hand-brake operates on separate set of shoes in rear drums.

STEERING: worm and nut.

SUSPENSION: semi-elliptic springs, front and rear: hydraulic shock absorbers (automatic regulation of dampers by gearbox-driven pump, with over-riding hand control from chassis BICW, 1934).

CHASSIS DETAILS: wheelbase: 10 ft. 6 in.; track: 4 ft. 8 in.; overall length: 14 ft. 6 in.; overall width: 5 ft. 9 in.; ground clearance: 6 in. Tyres: 5·50 in. × 18 in., on centre-lock wire wheels. Chassis weight approx. 2,250 lb.
Chassis price £1,100.

4¼-LITRE BENTLEY

As for 3½-litre Model, with the following differences:

ENGINE: 6 cyl. monobloc. 3½ in. × 4½ in. 4,257 c.c. R.A.C. rating 29·4 h.p.; approx. 125 b.h.p.; 6·8 to 1 compression ratio.
60 amp. hour battery: ventilated dynamo; cooling, from chassis B2MR, 1939, pump and fan: thermostat and dummy radiator shutters.

TRANSMISSION: Borg and Beck single dry plate clutch: gearbox from chassis B2MR—overall ratios: overdrive top 3·6 to 1; direct drive 4·3 to 1; second 6·4 to 1; first 10·3 to 1; final drive ratio from chassis B2MR—4·3 to 1.

STEERING: Marles steering from chassis B2MR.

CHASSIS DETAILS: overall length: 16 ft.
Tyres: from chassis B2MR—6·50 in. × 17 in.
Chassis weight approx. 2,558 lb.
Chassis price £1,150.

MARK V BENTLEY AND 'CORNICHE' CAR
ENGINE: compression ratio 6·4 to 1.
Twin S.U. carburetters with automatic choke; 16 gal. tank ('Corniche' 19 gal.).
55 amp. hour battery.

TRANSMISSION: overall gear ratios: overdrive top 3·6 to 1; direct drive 4·3 to 1; second 6·15 to 1; first 10·5 to 1. 'Corniche'—overdrive top 3·1 to 1; direct drive 3·73 to 1; second 5·33 to 1; first 9·10 to 1. 'Corniche' semi-floating half shafts. Standard final drive ratio 4·3 to 1; 'Corniche' 3·73 to 1.
STEERING: cam and roller.
Independent front wheel suspension by coil springs and wishbones.

CHASSIS DETAILS: wheelbase: 10 ft. 4 in.; track, front 4 ft. 8¼ in., rear 4 ft. 10 in.; overall length 15 ft. 11 in. Tyres: 6·50 in. × 16 in., on centre-lock wire wheels. 'Corniche' 5-nut steel disc wheels. Chassis weight approx. 2,719 lb.

The Vanwall Grand Prix Car

8

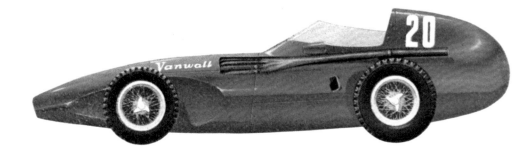

The 2½-litre Grand Prix Vanwall, winner of the 1957 British Grand Prix (Grand Prix d Europe) driven by Tony Brooks and Stirling Moss. 90 laps = 270 miles. Average speed: 86.80 m.p.h. The first victory in a *Grande Epreuve* by a British driver in a British car since 1923 (H. O. D. Segrave, Sunbeam, French Grand Prix).

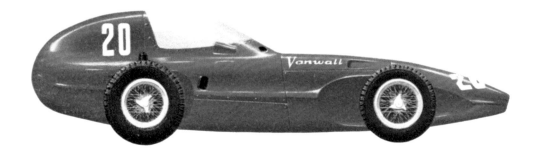

The Vanwall Grand Prix Car

by Denis Jenkinson

In 1957 the Vanwall team began to dominate Grand Prix racing, and in September they achieved their first truly undisputed victory when they won the Italian Grand Prix at Monza. The team in the first three positions on the starting grid, about to set out on one of their finest races: (left to right) Stuart Lewis-Evans, Stirling Moss and Tony Brooks.

The Vanwall Grand Prix car started as the hobby of Mr. Guy Anthony Vandervell and developed into an obsession and a passion that nearly ruined his health, but in that time it won the Manufacturers' Championship in Grand Prix racing and set a standard in motor racing that is still hard to match. Tony Vandervell was interested in motor racing many years ago and when the B.R.M. was planned in 1945 he gave it his full support, but as that idealistic scheme for a Grand Prix car got into worse and worse muddles in its early days, Vandervell left the syndicate and started his own racing department in his factory at Park Royal in West London where he had the headquarters of his great Vandervell Bearing concern.

For a number of years his team raced Ferrari cars, bought from Italy and extensively modified by themselves, and called Thinwall Specials, after the trade name of his shell-bearings. Vandervell had close connections with the Norton motorcycle racing team, and it was from this association with the racing 500 c.c. single-cylinder motorcycle engine that the idea of a 2,000 c.c. 4-cylinder engine developed, this being the size of engine for the 1952/53 seasons of Grand Prix racing. Vandervell had a personal desire to see a British car beat the Italian cars at motor racing, for they were in complete command, with Alfa Romeo, Ferrari and Maserati cars.

It was for this reason that he first of all supported the British Racing Motor project, but having started his own team the idea of a Vandervell-built car beating the Italians began to be more than just a dream. Norton Motors started to build a 4-cylinder 2-litre engine, based on their extensive knowledge, while Vandervell began the design and construction of a chassis. Not unnaturally the basic layout of the car followed Ferrari principles, as the team had had a lot of experience with the Italian cars, but progress was slow and the 1952/53 seasons were finished before the car was even nearing completion.

It was 15th May 1954 before the Vanwall Special first appeared in a race, which was the International Trophy at Silverstone, where the car was driven by Alan Brown. By this time the formula for Grand Prix racing had been changed to a capacity limit of $2\frac{1}{2}$ litres, so that the Vanwall was handicapped by its smaller 2-litre engine, but already work was underway designing a new $2\frac{1}{2}$-litre version. The new car went well, finishing sixth in its heat, but in the final it was

put out by a broken oil pipe. As an interim measure a second engine of 2·3 litres was built and installed in the car in place of the original 2-litre engine, and in this form the car took part in the British Grand Prix, again on the Silverstone circuit, but this time driven by Peter Collins. Trouble developed in the cylinder head of this new engine, and a water leak caused the car to be withdrawn after only 17 laps of the race, but these sort of things were put down as 'teething troubles' and it was hoped that the future would see better things.

The great desire to beat the red Italian cars saw Vandervell sending his team off to Italy next, for the Italian Grand Prix at Monza, with Collins as driver once again. Unfortunately the new $2\frac{1}{2}$-litre engine gave trouble while on test, shortly before the team left home, so the earlier 2·3-litre version was installed and in spite of being under-powered compared with its rivals, it ran well and finished seventh, after a pit stop to repair an oil leak.

Back in England the car was driven in four short-distance events, two at Goodwood and two at Aintree, and it gave a good account of itself, finishing 2nd at the former circuit, driven by Collins, and 2nd at the latter circuit driven by Mike Hawthorn. Both these events were for Grand Prix cars, and though the opposition was not strong, it was quite representative so that the car's performance could be judged. For these events it was using the new $2\frac{1}{2}$-litre engine, and at both meetings it also ran in Formula Libre events, finishing 4th at Goodwood, but retiring at Aintree after spinning off on to the grass. These outings in small races were most encouraging and though Vandervell did not need anything in the way of support from the racing world, everyone became eager to help, as in the Vanwall Special they could see a car that was worthy of wearing the British Racing Green in Grand Prix racing.

Very late in the 1954 season the Spanish Grand Prix took place on the outskirts of Barcelona, and the Vanwall Special was entered, driven by Collins, but during practice he made a driving error and turned the car over, doing so much damage that it could not be repaired in time for the race and the entry was withdrawn. This was a sad ending to a first season of this new car, but Vandervell was not unduly disturbed, as he was determined to develop the car and strive for better things, already planning a new chassis and the formation of a two-car team for 1955.

The first time the Vanwall Special appeared in a race was for the 1954 Daily Express Trophy Race at Silverstone, where it was driven by Alan Brown, in very wet conditions. Unusual feature was the externally mounted surface radiator, which was later cowled in, but eventually abandoned in favour of an orthodox radiator block.

A CHANGE OF NAME

Mike Hawthorn was signed up to drive in 1955 and as a second car was being built Ken Wharton was taken into the team. The name of the car was changed to Vanwall, the Special part being dropped, and the two cars being ready for the first important race at Silverstone, which was the International Trophy. The engines had been greatly improved by the addition of Bosch fuel injection, the injectors being in the inlet tracts, with the bodies of Amal carburetters being used to provide throttle slides. It looked as though this season was going to be a good one for Vandervell, with a first-rate driver in the team, and two cars to challenge the opposition. However, things did not turn out as expected, and in the first race both cars retired, Hawthorn with a gearbox oil leak, while Wharton had the misfortune to crash, the car catching fire and being badly damaged. This bad start was to put the team into a muddled state, and trouble plagued them at Monaco and Belgium, after which Hawthorn terminated his contract and joined another team. As a replacement Vandervell signed on Harry Schell, a Franco-American driver of no great skill, but enormous enthusiasm and courage and he proved to be just what the team wanted. Small troubles continued to plague the cars but when things were right Schell drove with great spirit and convinced many people that the Vanwall had the makings of a winning Grand Prix car, if only it could get over its 'teething troubles', which were going on too long.

It was Vandervell's plan to race his cars only in the major Grand Prix events, where the opposition would be strongest, and in particular where the 'red cars' would be. He was not interested in 'pot hunting', by racing his cars in small events against little opposition, but during 1955 he was forced to do this as a number of the big Continental events were cancelled during the summer. Consequently Schell and Wharton finished 1st and 2nd in a race at Snetterton, and Schell was 2nd at the Crystal Palace, but these successes did not impress Vandervell as the opposition had been negligible. A more serious proposition faced the Vanwall team when they went to Monza at the end of the season and though both cars retired, Schell put up a good fight, showing once more that the Vanwall was fast, though still fragile. All that was left of the 1955 season were two small British events, so that Vandervell was more or less forced to run his cars in these, in order to get more experience for the cars, drivers, mechanics and his own organisation. Against quite good opposition at Oulton Park the Irishman Desmond Titterington finished 3rd, while Schell won two short races at Castle Coombe airfield circuit.

By the end of the season Vandervell was ready to field a team of three cars, this being his ultimate aim so that he could combat the big foreign teams with the same amount of equipment as they themselves had. Throughout 1955 the Vanwalls had been fast enough, but handling and road holding was not the equal of some of the rival makes, even though a coil spring suspension had been used in place of the original transverse leaf spring suspension. Before the 1956 season began Vandervell called upon Colin Chapman of Lotus, to assist in the design of a new chassis, while a new gearbox was designed, giving 5 speeds instead of the previous 4 speeds. Chapman had been making a name for himself with his Lotus chassis designs, as well as streamlined sports cars with bodywork designed by Frank Costin, so Vandervell wisely contracted for these two to design a new Vanwall to take the powerful 4-cylinder engine built at Acton. The resultant work produced an entirely new Vanwall that was received by the motor racing public with mixed feelings. It was aerodynamically correct, even if not aesthetic by current racing car standards, and was devoid of slots, openings, louvres, bulges and so on, and had a remarkably small radiator opening in the nose, while the

The 2½ litre Vanwall Special on the left, driven by Mike Hawthorn in a Formula Libre race at Goodwood in 1954, is alongside its parent car, the 4½ litre Ferrari "Thinwall" Special, driven by Peter Collins. Much of the experience gained with the big car, especially as regards chassis and brakes, was passed on to the smaller car in its first design stages.

A partly assembled Vanwall 2½ litre Grand Prix engine, showing the separate inlet ports, the gear drive train to the camshafts and the magneto and fuel injection unit mounted on the front of this drive train.

In 1955 two cars were built and the word "Special" was dropped from the name. Early in the season, at Silverstone Ken Wharton had an unfortunate accident, from which he escaped, but in which the car was burnt out. This sort of disaster and financial loss did not deter Tony Vandervell from carrying on with his plans for a full team of cars to ultimately defeat the Italian teams.

A driver who instilled a great deal of team spirit and enthusiasm in the face of setbacks, into the Vanwall team was the Franco-American Harry Schell. Here he is seen driving a Vanwall at the Crystal Palace circuit in 1955.

cockpit and windscreen blended into a high and bulbous tail, the driver being completely enclosed by the bodywork, apart from an opening on the top of the cockpit. Even the multiple pipe exhaust was let into a recess in the bodywork, to avoid unnecessary breaks in the airflow across the body.

The whole aspect of this new Vanwall was one of functional efficiency rather than any sops to traditional racing car shape, and underneath this shape the Chapman influence had been applied in the same way to the chassis frame of small-diameter tubing, and to the suspension. While some of Vandervell's rivals were still using drum brakes, and others were experimenting with disc brakes, he had been using Goodyear disc brakes on his cars from the beginning with complete success. These brakes incorporated radial drilling of the disc to assist cooling, and even in 1965 this problem of perforated discs was still causing one of his rivals trouble. The Vanwall/Goodyear disc brakes had been developed on the old Thinwall Special Ferrari, and the knowledge and experience carried on to the smaller Vanwall.

There was now every intention of fielding a full three-car team, the only problem being to find suitable drivers, for Vandervell was a difficult man to satisfy and had very fixed ideas on what he wanted from a driver, tending towards drivers with wide experience of all types of circuit rather than a very fast 'aerodrome racer'. This was because his real interest was the series of World Championship Grand Prix races, on the circuits of Europe, no two of which bear any resemblance to each other. Harry Schell remained with the team and was joined by Maurice Trintignant, a driver who was not outstandingly fast, but was absolutely reliable and very experienced in the ways of Continental Grand Prix racing. The Vanwall 4-cylinder engine was now giving a very good power output, in excess of 270 b.h.p. and certainly equal to

most of the rivals' makes. With Daimler-Benz having retired from racing, some of their engineers and consultants from Bosch assisted Vandervell with his fuel-injection system, so that he was able to perfect its working, though the installation was still giving him problems.

A MAJOR VICTORY

The intention for 1956 was to concentrate on the World Championship events, and all entreaties from organisers of small races were ignored, even at the risk of upsetting people, for Vandervell knew what he intended to do with his cars and nobody was going to sway his decision. He relented as regards the International Trophy at Silverstone, as it was on the same circuit that the British Grand Prix was due to be run later in the season, and it provided a useful 'practice' session. For this race he was fortunate in having Stirling Moss drive one of the new cars, Schell naturally having the other one, and the two new sleek Vanwalls were on the front row of the starting grid. Schell was forced out by a broken fuel injection pipe, but Moss drove magnificently to win the race against quite strong opposition, but not over a full Grand Prix distance. This was a wonderful debut for the new cars, and it caused a lot of people to take a very different view of the Vanwall team.

All along Tony Vandervell had ignored popular publicity and the Press, believing that results were the things that would impress people, not a lot of talk before anything happened. Being a very wealthy man, quite capable of financing the cars from his own resources, he had little need of outside publicity and in consequence the sporting world did not know a great deal about the team other than what could be seen, and this suited Vandervell. He was out to conquer the Grand Prix world and in particular 'beat the bloody red cars' as he used to say, and when he had done that there would be time enough for talking, and he hoped that by that time everyone would know about the Vanwall team anyway, by reason of their success.

With the success of the new car on its first outing

The new aerodynamic Vanwall had its first victory at Silverstone, in the International Trophy, 1956.

By the middle of the 1956 season the Vanwall proved itself to be the fastest car in Grand Prix racing, but not the most reliable. During the 1956 French Grand Prix at Rheims Schell has just passed the Lancia/Ferrari V8 cars of Collins and Castellotti.

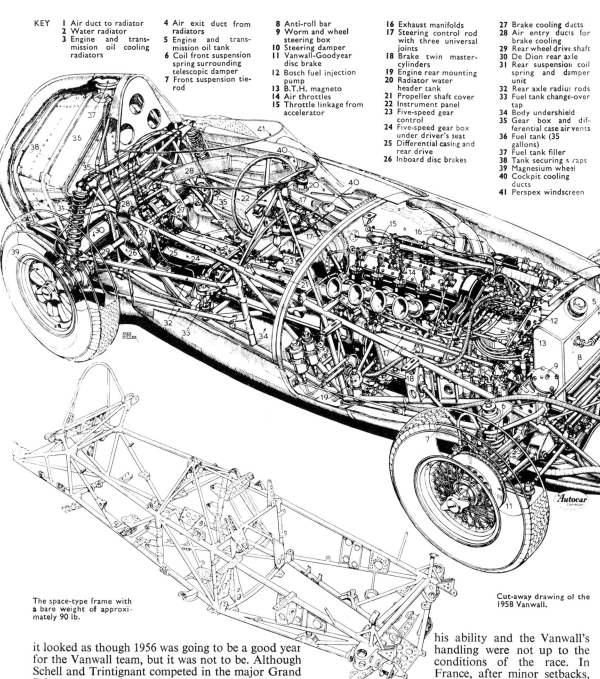

1	Air duct to radiator	4	Air exit duct from radiators	8	Anti-roll bar	16 Exhaust manifolds

1 Air duct to radiator
2 Water radiator
3 Engine and transmission oil cooling radiators
4 Air exit duct from radiators
5 Engine and transmission oil tank
6 Coil front suspension spring surrounding telescopic damper
7 Front suspension tie-rod
8 Anti-roll bar
9 Worm and wheel steering box
10 Steering damper
11 Vanwall-Goodyear disc brake
12 Bosch fuel injection pump
13 B.T.H. magneto
14 Air throttles
15 Throttle linkage from accelerator
16 Exhaust manifolds
17 Steering control rod with three universal joints
18 Brake twin master-cylinders
19 Engine rear mounting
20 Radiator water header tank
21 Propeller shaft cover
22 Instrument panel
23 Five-speed gear control
24 Five-speed gear box under driver's seat
25 Differential casing and rear drive
26 Inboard disc brakes
27 Brake cooling ducts
28 Air entry ducts for brake cooling
29 Rear wheel drive shaft
30 De Dion rear axle
31 Rear suspension coil spring and damper unit
32 Rear axle radius rods
33 Fuel tank change-over tap
34 Body undershield
35 Gear box and differential case air vents
36 Fuel tank (35 gallons)
37 Fuel tank filler
38 Tank securing straps
39 Magnesium wheel
40 Cockpit cooling ducts
41 Perspex windscreen

The space-type frame with a bare weight of approximately 90 lb.

Cut-away drawing of the 1958 Vanwall.

it looked as though 1956 was going to be a good year for the Vanwall team, but it was not to be. Although Schell and Trintignant competed in the major Grand Prix races the only result they could show was a 4th place by Schell in the Belgium Grand Prix on the very fast Francorchamps circuit. For the rest it was retirement after retirement, from engine breakages, suspension breakages, drive shafts, fuel systems, accidents, overheating, gearbox troubles, in fact just about everything that could go wrong did so during the season, and a lesser man than Vandervell would have withdrawn against such bitter odds. However, during this holocaust there were moments of brightness that drove everyone on to overcome adversity, for it was clear that the Vanwall was a good and fast car and well capable of winning a Grand Prix, if only the odds could be in its favour for a short time. In Belgium Schell showed that it was faster than its rivals, though

his ability and the Vanwall's handling were not up to the conditions of the race. In France, after minor setbacks, he again showed the speed of the Vanwall, giving rise to great concern in the Ferrari team, while the same thing happened at Monza, but always retirement after these efforts was the result.

This constant attacking by Schell and the Vanwall was first-class stuff, and by the end of the season everyone was agreed that if reliability could be found success was inevitable, and even the Italian opposition agreed with this. Many top drivers with ability far greater than that of Harry Schell were made conscious of the Vanwall's performance and were thinking what would happen if they drove the car. During the season the Vanwall racing department continued to build chassis, engines and gearboxes, and twice they attempted to run a team of three cars but the 1956 'gremlins' got at them

A third car was entered for the French Grand Prix for Colin Chapman to drive, he having good possibilities as a driver as well as a designer, but an unfortunate accident in practice damaged the car beyond repair for the race. In the British Grand Prix three Vanwalls actually got on the starting grid, the third one driven by the Argentinian Froilan Gonzalez, who had driven the old Thinwall Special for Vandervell in the past. A drive shaft broke as he let in the clutch at the start, and the team were back to their usual two-car team again. Eventually the full team got under way at Monza, when Piero Taruffi joined them for the Italian Grand Prix, but all three cars retired. The Italian teams were watching all this with great interest, having seen the first Vanwall Special appear at their track in 1954; two years later there being a team of three very advanced cars that only lacked reliability. Coming from Great Britain this was something new, for in the past most attempts at Grand Prix racing that stemmed from Great Britain, not only suffered from poor reliability, but were seldom fast enough, the engines giving insufficient power. Now there was a green car with a British engine that was the equal in power output to anything from Italy, or anywhere else for that matter.

TEAM OF THREE

At the end of the season a single car was meticulously prepared for Stirling Moss to try, and after numerous long-distance tests he agreed to sign up with Vandervell to lead the Vanwall team in 1957 in the World Championship battle. To do this meant leaving the Maserati team, and they in turn signed on Juan Manuel Fangio, the only driver who was superior to Moss. This now made the Vanwall future very bright, and it pleased Vandervell to think that the forthcoming season was not only going to be a battle between his green cars and the red ones, but that the two best drivers in the world were shared, one on each side. As second driver to Moss Vandervell signed on Tony Brooks, a relative newcomer to Grand Prix racing, but a driver with uncanny skill and judgment, a

smooth and fast driving style and a very serious and scientific approach to motor racing. The excitable Harry Schell left the team, having done them a power of good and raised them from the depths of despair by his spirited fighting and gay disposition.

There was a third car ready to race but until a driver could be found who was capable of staying with Moss and Brooks, Vandervell preferred not to race it. In actual fact there were many more than three cars available, for the Park Royal factory spent the winter months hard at work on the production of engines, gearboxes, frames and so on, in order that no car needed to be raced twice in succession. Vandervell was only interested in the Championship races, and the policy was to send the cars back for a complete overhaul after each event, so that the drivers always started a race with fresh cars. This meant an outlay in men, materials and money that was so great that nobody was prepared to hazard a guess at the total cost, apart from saying it was astronomical.

Vandervell could see his goal in sight when Moss agreed to drive for him, and in spite of the setbacks of the 1956 season, the good signs had been so encouraging that he threw everything he had into the battle, and worked and worried himself as much as anyone in the team. What had started out as a single car and nothing much greater than a hobby, 'instead of playing golf' he used to say, had turned into an obsession and he was now driving himself and the whole works at full pressure for he could see that the Italian teams were beginning to stumble in their efforts to stay ahead of his cars.

The first part of the season saw a repetition of 1956, the cars had not been changed radically, except for replacing the leaf spring rear suspension by coil springs, and improving numerous details, but reliability still eluded them. All the time the cars were proving very fast, Moss and Brooks being the equal of any opposition, but little troubles still beset the cars. The Vanwall cars set fastest laps but seldom finished, apart from a very good second place by Brooks at Monaco, but it was second to Fangio and the Maserati, the deadly enemy. In mid-season the two regular drivers were unwell and unfit to race, so for two races Roy Salvadori and Stuart Lewis-Evans filled the gaps. The latter driver was fresh to Grand Prix racing, but had had a lot of experience with

The first World Championship victory for the Vanwall was in the 1957 British Grand Prix at Aintree, when Stirling Moss took over the car being driven by Tony Brooks, and went right through the field to victory. He is being greeted by two Vanwall mechanics, to whom such a moment more than compensates for years of work, worry and disappointment.

smaller cars, and he took to the Vanwall in a most impressive manner, and but for an oil leak from the engine he would have won the Grand Prix on the fast Rheims circuit. His performance so impressed Vandervell, and everyone else for that matter, that he was signed on as the third member of the team when Moss and Brooks were fit once more.

At last the fortunes of the Vanwall team began to improve and in the British Grand Prix at Aintree one of the cars came home in first place, having been driven by Brooks to start with and then being taken over by Moss, who gave a fantastic display of driving, the car standing up to every minute of it. The Ferrari and Maserati opposition had misfortune right at the end of the race, which allowed the Vanwall to romp home to its first real victory, and Britain's first Grande Epreuve victory since the mid-twenties (see page 2). This success spurred the team on and apart from a slight set-back at the German Grand Prix, they went on to better and better things, the 'gremlins' seemingly being ousted at last. At Pescara, in Southern Italy, Moss trounced Fangio and the Maserati well and truly, scoring Vanwall's second win of the season, and after that the team went to Monza, Vandervell's greatest challenge.

Monza is the home of Italian racing and apart from the World Championship it was Vandervell's ambition to trounce the Italians on their home ground. After the success at Aintree and Pescara the whole team was in fine spirit and the three drivers dominated practice and gained the first three positions on the starting grid, and a fine sight it was to see the three sleek Vanwalls on the front row of the Italian Grand Prix, with red cars in row upon row behind them. The opening laps were classic in Grand Prix racing, with two Maseratis trying to beat the three Vanwalls, but the British team drove superbly and dominated the Italian cars, while the rest of the entry were left way behind. A price had to be paid for this domination, and Brooks and Lewis-Evans had mechanical troubles, but so did the Maseratis and Moss swept on to the first undisputed victory of the Vanwall, and Tony Vandervell's finest hour of glory, all the disappointments and frustrations of the past three years being swept away as Moss received the winner's flag. The Ferrari team were never in the picture and the Maserati team were vanquished in open battle; Vandervell was indeed a happy man that night.

This magnificent victory was spoilt when the team returned to England, for Moss insisted on doing a 10-lap high speed demonstration with the car at Goodwood, just as it had finished the race. This was too much

In 1956 the Vanwall appeared in an entirely new guise, with a very advanced aerodynamic bodywork designed by Frank Costin. Here Tony Vandervell is driving the prototype car while it was on test at Goodwood. Unlike many prototype cars the Vanwall was unchanged in its racing form, the only additions to the sleek body being regulation rear view mirrors, which also acted as inlets for cockpit cooling air.

for the engine and it broke in an ignominious cloud of steam before the short demonstration was completed.

This vastly improved 1957 season ended with a race in Morocco, near Casablanca, and though the team put up a good fight it could only manage a second place, Maserati getting their revenge.

THE CREST OF THE WAVE

The Vanwall team was now in as strong a position as any Grand Prix team has ever been, the cars were the match of any opposition, the three team drivers were unequalled as a well-knit trio, the resources of materials and equipment behind the racing cars was second to none, and the whole organisation was geared to victory. In 1958 they competed only in World Championship events, putting all their efforts into these important Grand Prix races, and they went into battle fully prepared. Fangio had virtually retired, leaving Moss as the uncrowned champion of Grand Prix driving, while Maserati had succumbed to the Vanwall onslaught and withdrawn their official team, though Ferrari was still as strong as ever.

The Vanwall cars did not need to be altered in any major respect, except that new racing rules limited fuel to ordinary petrol, whereas Vandervell had been using special alcohol fuels in 1957. A lot of development work had to be done on the engines, still 4 cylinders and virtually the same design as the original 1954 2-litre engine, in order to make them give sufficient reliable power on the poorer fuel. Race distances were reduced in length so that the cars could be made lighter, having less fuel load to carry; with the need for tyre changes gone, it was possible to use fixed wheels, and experiments were done with alloy non-detachable wheels, but the basic design of the Vanwall remain unchanged, as did the body shape, although experiments were tried with completely enclosed cockpits and fully streamlined bodywork.

The 1958 season was not one of 100 per cent reliability, but it was one of success, and the trio of Moss, Brooks and Lewis-Evans were virtually unbeatable. Of the nine Grand Prix races entered the Vanwalls won six, being 2nd in one and 4th in another, the first race of the season seeing all three cars retiring with engine troubles. Victories were gained at the expense of failures, but Vandervell did not mind this as long as one of his cars was first, and by winning the Grand Prix races of Holland, Belgium, Germany, Portugal, Italy and Morocco he was acclaimed World Champion Manufacturer for 1958, and received numerous coveted awards of merit, as befitted this magnificient achievement. By the end of 1958 the Vanwall team was all-conquering, winning the last four events in a row, but once again this supreme effort had to be paid for, and it was Tony Vandervell

A justifiably proud Tony Vandervell holds aloft the victor's trophy after one of his cars had won the 1957 British Grand Prix at Aintree. On his right is Tony Brooks who drove the car in the opening stages of the race, and on his left is Stirling Moss who took over, when his own car gave trouble, and drove to the fine victory.

The Vanwalls were adapted for the peculiarities of various circuits, and Tony Brooks is seen in the 1957 Monaco Grand Prix, in which he finished 2nd, in a car with specially shortened nose cowling, to avoid damage in the crowded opening laps, and a cutdown perspex wind shield to permit more cooling air into the cockpit on this slow and twisty circuit.

who paid the price, not in money, but in health.

Throughout the four years existence of the Vanwall team he had been in sole command, an absolute dictator in his own empire, but a worthy one, at times ruthless, at times a bit muddled, but it was his team and they were his cars, and he drove everyone on to greater and greater efforts all the time, and no-one more than himself. He was not a young man, reaching his 57th birthday on the day of his first victory at Monza in 1957, and he took all the responsibility of the team upon his own shoulders. What had started out as a game and a hobby had become an obsession and he suffered mental anguish during a race, not only for the outcome but also for the safety of his drivers, and the lives of all the people he employed. A race completed was a great relief for him, and he used to pace up and down in front of the pits, a tired and worried man as a race drew to a close.

All this strain told on his health, for in addition to running the Vanwall team he was still head of the vast Vandervell Bearings empire, a multi-million business into which he had put all his efforts and capital. In the last race of the season Lewis-Evans crashed and sub-sequently died from his injuries, and this affected Tony Vandervell deeply, as he felt he was directly responsible. He would say, 'if it wasn't for my bloody silly passion for racing cars, and my obsession to beat the red cars, this wouldn't have happened'. All these things were mounting up against him as the victorious 1958 season wore on, and by the end of it he was completely spent, and his doctor ordered a complete rest before a serious nervous breakdown took place.

THE END OF AN ERA

Tony Vandervell had achieved his ambitions, so reluctantly he disbanded the Vanwall team at the height of its glory, and the race at Casablanca on 19th October 1958 was the last appearance of this fine team of Grand Prix cars from Britain, proudly wearing the colour of British Racing Green. They went out on the crest of the wave, and drivers, mechanics, team personnel dispersed into other parts of the motor racing world, leaving Vandervell and his cars in the quiet of his Park Royal factory.

After a year of rest there were small stirrings again in the Vandervell factory and a single new car was built and made a very brief appearance, but it never developed, for by this time Grand Prix racing was almost completely dominated by British cars, the Continental teams never really recovering from their crushing defeat by the Vanwall team. Tony Vandervell found no pleasure at all in racing his car against his fellow countrymen, 'If there is not an International battle it's not interesting' he would say, and the Van-

wall withdrew from the scene of its former triumphs. In 1961 it looked as though Inter-Continental Formula racing might produce some 'foreign' opposition, and Vandervell built another new car, this time in the modern idiom with the engine behind the driver, and John Surtees drove it, but the old spark of battle was not there and it was not a Vanwall of the great days of 1957/58, it was more a Vanwall Special of the early days, but without any objective behind it.

The Vanwall cars were true factory racing cars, only driven by factory employed drivers, and none of them ever left the works team to go into private hands, as happens with a lot of factory cars. Every time a Vanwall competed in a race it was under the watchful eye of its originator, Guy Anthony Vandervell, maker of Thinwall Shell Bearings, builder of the Thinwall Specials and the victorious Vanwalls.

Denis Jenkinson, 1966

The 1958 Vanwall Grand Prix Car—Specification

ENGINE: Four cylinders in line, with twin overhead camshafts gear-driven from front of crankshaft. Liquid-cooled cylinders and dry-sump lubrication. Engine front mounted.

Bore 96 mm, stroke 86 mm, capacity 2,490 cc. Two valves per cylinder at included angle of 60 degrees, operated by overhead camshafts through cylindrical tappets and exposed hairpin valve springs. Two sparking plugs per cylinder fired by double-bodied Bosch magneto mounted in front of engine. Cylinder head of R.R.50 aluminium alloy with inserted valve seats. Cylinder block, separate cast iron liners spigotted into cylinder and crankcase, surrounded by light alloy water jacket. Crankcase of aluminium alloy.

GEARBOX: Five speeds forward and one reverse. Porsche syncromesh on upper four ratios. Gearbox in unit with differential/crownwheel and pinion housing. Aggregate mounted at rear of chassis, under driving seat. Left-hand operated gear change lever in open gate. ZF limited-slip differential. Gearbox ratios: top 1·0, 4th 1·12, 3rd 1·40, 2nd 1·96, 1st 2·80. Final drive ratios: optional between 3·27 and 6·06.

CLUTCH: Vandervell designed multi-plate.

BRAKES: Vandervell-Goodyear disc brakes, with hinged calipers and radially perforated discs and Lockheed master cylinders and pipework. Front discs 12 in. diameter—brakes hub mounted. Rear discs 11·75 in. diameter—brakes mounted inboard, on each side of gearbox/axle unit.

SUSPENSION: Front: unequal length wishbones with coil spring/shock-absorber units and anti-roll bar. Rear: de Dion axle, with cross tube located by double radius arms on each side and Watts linkage at centre of tube. Coil spring/shock absorber units each side to top of frame.

BODYWORK: Aerodynamic aluminium body, panelling held by Dzuz fasteners. Aluminium petrol and oil tanks.

WHEELS: Borrani alloy rim wire-spoke wheels with Rudge Whitworth centre lock hubs. Pirelli tyres until end of 1957, then Dunlop tyres. Front 5·50 × 16 in. Rear 7·00 × 16 in.

COLOUR: Dark green.

For the 1958 the Vanwalls experimented with cast light-alloy wheels, which were subsequently only used on the rear, their increased stiffness on the front affecting handling, while the solid alloy disc form restricted brake cooling. Slight changes were made to the tail shape, and a shorter exhaust system was used, with a "muff" around the tail pipe, through which cooling air flowed. Stuart Lewis-Evans is seen at the wheel of one of the ultimate versions of the Vanwall.

The Vanwall disc brakes were built to Goodyear patents, and incorporated a perforated disc to provide radial cooling air flow, and used a pivotted caliper. This view shows a front wheel unit.

Unless a driver specified differently the Vanwalls used a three spoke steering wheel. The instrument panel was finished matt black and instrumentation was strictly functional, the two large dials being r.p.m. on the left, and water temperature on the right. The gear-lever was on the left of the seat.

DIMENSIONS: Wheelbase: 7 ft. 6¼ in.
Track, front: 4 ft 5¾ in.
rear: 4 ft. 3¾ in.
Overall length: 14 ft 0 in.
Overall height: 3 ft. 9¼ in.
Weight dry: 12½ cwt.
PERFORMANCE: 280 b.h.p. at 7,400 r.p.m. on alcohol fuel.
265 b.h.p. at 7,400 r.p.m. on petrol.
Maximum speed: approx. 175–180 m.p.h.

LIST OF DRIVERS WHO DROVE IN VANWALL TEAM, 1954/58
Alan Brown (1954) now retired.
Peter Collins (1954) killed in Ferrari, 1958, at Nurburgring.
Mike Hawthorn (1954–55) killed in road accident, 1959.

Ken Wharton (1955) killed in Australia in Ferrari in 1957.
Harry Schell (1955–56) killed Silverstone in Cooper, 1960.
Stuart Lewis-Evans (1957–58) died after crash at Casablanca in Vanwall, 1958.
Desmond Titterington (1955) now retired.
Stirling Moss (1956–58) now retired.
Froilan Gonzalez (1957) now retired.
Piero Taruffi (1956) now retired.
Tony Brooks (1957–58) now retired.
Roy Salvadori (1957) now retired.

ANALYSIS OF ENTRIES BY VANWALL TEAM 1954–58
Number of cars started in races: 88.
Number of cars finished in races: 40.
Number of retirements: 48.
Number of victories: 13.

RACING RESULTS

1954

Date	Event	Circuit	Driver	Result
May 15	International Trophy	Silverstone	Alan Brown (Heat 1)	6th
			(Final)	Ret.
July 17	British Grand Prix	Silverstone	Peter Collins	Ret.
Sept. 5	Italian Grand Prix	Monza	Peter Collins	7th
Sept. 25	Goodwood Trophy	Goodwood	Peter Collins	2nd
Sept. 25	Woodcote Cup	Goodwood	Mike Hawthorn	4th
Oct. 2	Daily Telegraph Trophy	Aintree	Mike Hawthorn	2nd
Oct. 2	Formula Libre Race	Aintree	Mike Hawthorn	Ret.
Oct. 24	Spanish Grand Prix	Barcelona	Peter Collins	crashed practice

1955

Date	Event	Circuit	Driver	Result
May 7	International Trophy	Silverstone	Mike Hawthorn	Ret.
			Ken Wharton	Ret.
May 22	Monaco Grand Prix	Monte Carlo	Mike Hawthorn	Ret.
June 5	Belgian Grand Prix	Spa	Mike Hawthorn	Ret.
July 16	British Grand Prix	Aintree	Ken Wharton/Schell	9th
			Harry Schell	Ret.
July 30	International Trophy	Crystal Palace	Harry Schell	2nd
Aug. 13	Redex Trophy—F1	Snetterton	Harry Schell	1st
			Ken Wharton	2nd
Aug. 13	Formula Libre Race	Snetterton	Harry Schell	Ret.
Sept. 11	Italian Grand Prix	Monza	Harry Schell	Ret.
			Ken Wharton	Ret.
Sept. 24	Gold Cup Meeting	Oulton Park	Harry Schell	Ret.
			Desmond Titterington	3rd
Oct. 1	Avon Trophy—F1	Castle Coombe	Harry Schell	1st
Oct. 1	Empire News Trophy— F. Libre	Castle Coombe	Harry Schell	1st

1956

Date	Event	Circuit	Driver	Result
May 5	International Trophy	Silverstone	Stirling Moss	1st
			Harry Schell	Ret.
May 13	Monaco Grand Prix	Monte Carlo	Harry Schell	Ret.
			Maurice Trintignant	Ret.
June 3	Belgian Grand Prix	Francorchamps	Harry Schell	4th
			Maurice Trintignant	Ret.
July 1	French Grand Prix	Reims	Harry Schell	Ret.
			Mike Hawthorn/ Harry Schell	10th

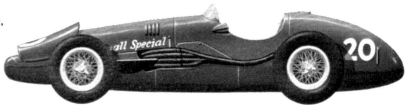

...4 Vanwall Special for British Grand Prix,
...verstone, with ducting over surface
...iator; 2.3-litre engine. Driver: Peter
...lins.

1954 end-of-season Vanwall Special for
Goodwood, with orthodox radiator;
2½-litre engine. Driver: Peter Collins.

...5 Vanwall for International Trophy race,
...verstone. Driver: Mike Hawthorn.

...6 Vanwall for French Grand Prix, Reims, showing Chapman/
...stin influence in design. Driver: Harry Schell.

1957 Vanwall for Monaco Grand Prix, with shortened radiator
cowl and cut-away windscreen. Driver: Tony Brooks.

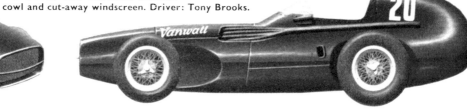

1957 Vanwall for Reims Grand Prix, with
all-enveloping body-work. Used for practice
only. Drivers: Roy Salvadori and Stuart
Lewis-Evans.

...Vanwall for Belgian Grand Prix,
...with cast-alloy wheels
...modified exhaust system.
...er: Tony Brooks.

This rear view of the 1958 Vanwall minus its bodywork, shows the enormous rear mounted fuel tank, of riveted aluminium. For long races it was supplemented by an auxiliary tank alongside the cockpit. For 1958 the racing rules allowed only normal petrol to be used, while the withdrawal from racing of the Italian Pirelli tyre firm caused Vandervell to change to Dunlop tyres.

July 14	British Grand Prix	Silverstone	Harry Schell	Ret.
			Maurice Trintignant	Ret.
			Froilan Gonzalez	Ret.
Sept. 2	Italian Grand Prix	Monza	Harry Schell	Ret.
			Maurince Trintignant	Ret.
			Piero Taruffi	Ret.

1957
April 7	Siracuse Grand Prix	Sicily	Stirling Moss	3rd
			Tony Brooks	Ret.
April 22	Glover Trophy	Goodwood	Stirling Moss	Ret.
			Tony Brooks	Last
May 19	Monaco Grand Prix	Monte Carlo	Stirling Moss	Ret.
			Tony Brooks	2nd
July 7	French Grand Prix	Rouen	Roy Salvadori	Ret.
			Stuart Lewis-Evans	Ret.
July 14	Reims Grand Prix	Reims	Roy Salvadori	5th
			Stuart Lewis-Evans	3rd
July 20	British Grand Prix	Aintree	Stirling Moss	Ret.
			Tony Brooks/	
			Stirling Moss	1st
			Stuart Lewis-Evans	7th
Aug. 4	German Grand Prix	Nurburgring	Stirling Moss	5th
			Tony Brooks	9th
			Stuart Lewis-Evans	Ret.
Aug. 18	Pescara Grand Prix	Pescara, Italy	Stirling Moss	1st
			Tony Brooks	Ret.
			Stuart Lewis-Evans	5th
Sept. 8	Italian Grand Prix	Monza	Stirling Moss	1st
			Tony Brooks	7th
			Stuart Lewis-Evans	Ret.
Sept. 28	Demonstration 10 laps	Goodwood	Stirling Moss	Ret.
Oct. 27	Moroccan Grand Prix	Casablanca	Stirling Moss	Non-starter
			Tony Brooks	Ret.
			Stuart Lewis-Evans	2nd

1958
May 18	Monaco Grand Prix	Monte Carlo	Stirling Moss	Ret.
			Tony Brooks	Ret.
			Stuart Lewis-Evans	Ret.
May 26	Dutch Grand Prix	Zandvoort	Stirling Moss	1st
			Tony Brooks	Ret.
			Stuart Lewis-Evans	Ret.
June 15	Belgian Grand Prix	Francorchamps	Stirling Moss	Ret.
			Tony Brooks	1st
			Stuart Lewis-Evans	3rd
July 6	French Grand Prix	Reims	Stirling Moss	2nd
			Tony Brooks	Ret.
			Stuart Lewis-Evans/	
			Tony Brooks	Ret.
July 19	British Grand Prix	Silverstone	Stirling Moss	Ret.
			Tony Brooks	7th
			Stuart Lewis-Evans	4th
Aug. 3	German Grand Prix	Nurburgring	Stirling Moss	Ret.
			Tony Brooks	1st
Aug. 24	Portuguese Grand Prix	Oporto	Stirling Moss	1st
			Tony Brooks	Ret.
			Stuart Lewis-Evans	3rd
Sept. 7	Italian Grand Prix	Monza	Stirling Moss	Ret.
			Tony Brooks	1st
			Stuart Lewis-Evans	Ret.
Oct. 19	Moroccan Grand Prix	Casablanca	Stirling Moss	1st
			Tony Brooks	Ret.
			Stuart Lewis-Evans	Ret.

Winner of Manufacturers' Championship for 1958

The Auburn Straight-eight

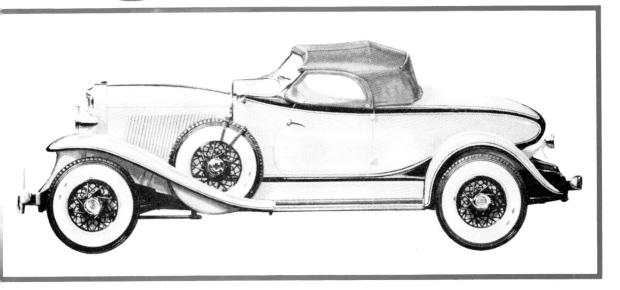

9

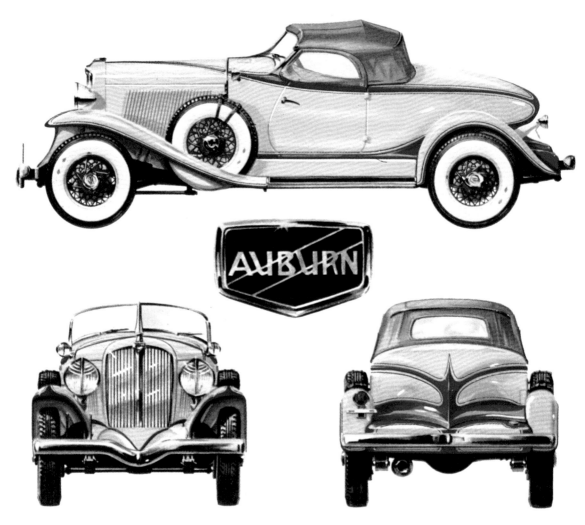

1932 MODEL 8-100A AUBURN SPEED-STER, with 8-cylinder-in-line Lycoming engine (3″ × 4¾″: 268·6 cu. ins.) producing 98 b.h.p. at 3,400 r.p.m.

0′   5′

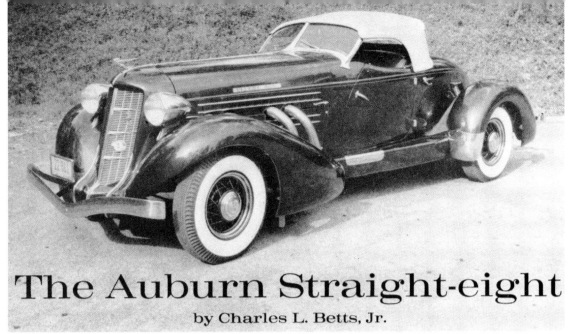

The Auburn Straight-eight

by Charles L. Betts, Jr.

The 1935 Model 851 Supercharged Speedster, designed by Gordon Buehrig. All supercharged models had four chrome plated flexible exhaust pipes emerging from the right side of the bonnet (hood). (Photo: William C. Kinsman)

The Auburn automobile derived its name from the town in the north-eastern corner of Indiana where it started life at the turn of the twentieth century. It was the product of one of forty-odd American firms who started in the automobile business in 1900, a year in which less than 4,200 motor vehicles were manufactured in the United States.

The Auburn Automobile Company was the outgrowth of the Eckhart Carriage Company, founded in 1874. The first Auburns were of the single-cylinder variety, and the firm remained small and relatively unknown until after World War I, when a desire for national prominence and distribution was aroused in the hearts of the founders, Charles and Morris Eckhart.

Feeling that re-organisation was desirable, the control of the company was sold to a group of capitalists in June 1919. At the same time the advertising and sales programme was greatly enlarged, and, as a matter of fact, considerable progress was enjoyed under this new management who did a great job in promoting the Auburn Beauty Six during the early 1920s.

In June 1924, E. L. Cord, a man of unusual talent and foresight in the automotive industry, was hired as general manager. He was quickly elevated to vice-president, and in 1926, at the age of 31, he was elected president of Auburn. One of his first moves after taking this office was to develop the Auburn straight-eight. Introduced the year previous as the 'Eight-in-Line', the 1926 Model 8–88 embodied little change in general design of the chassis, but the engine bore was increased from 3⅛ to 3¼ inches, adding greatly to its power and performance. This model greatly enhanced Auburn's reputation in the automotive industry and was responsible for creating a phenomenal growth in sales for the firm.

Under Cord's influence, Auburn emerged from a somewhat commonplace automobile to one of distinctiveness and dash. Leading the 1926 model

parade was a smart roadster with a snug-fitting top and a rumble seat that could be entered through a special door on the right side. The closed models featured Brewster-type windshields with fixed sun visors. The 2–3 passenger coupé was furnished with a body finished in Meritas fabric. This material was stretched over padding mounted on a special steel base supported by the usual wood body frame. The body itself was not painted since the fabric was dyed with the desired colours before applying it to the frame, thus eliminating surface checking and peeling. The Auburn's appearance was made particularly distinctive by having a belt line which swept up gracefully over the top of the bonnet (hood).

The Auburn 8–88 had performance and durability to match its atmosphere and beauty. J. M. Crawford, Auburn's chief engineer, saw to it that the chassis was designed to give maximum performance and comfort over a long period of time. The frame was pressed from heavy gauge high carbon steel having 6-inch deep section side rails with wide flanges, rigidly held together with seven cross members, front and rear being tubular. Suspension was by semi-elliptic springs front and rear, constructed of many thin leaves with special shackle design to ensure smooth riding qualities. "Gabriel Snubber"-type shock absorbers were fitted as standard equipment.

The engine, of conventional L-head design, having eight cylinders in line with a bore and stroke of $3\frac{1}{4} \times 4\frac{1}{2}$ inches, displaced 298·6 cubic inches and developed 68 horsepower at 3,000 r.p.m. Built to Auburn specifications by the Lycoming Manufacturing Company, Williamsport, Pennsylvania, these engines incorporated such features as a semi-automatic spark advance, a full forced-feed pressure lubrication system controlled by the opening and closing of the throttle instead of the speed of the engine, and a link-belt silent chain with automatic tightener. The intake manifold was of a special Swan type which distributed the gas evenly to all cylinders

Model 8–88 Touring Car of 1928. Note the fixed glass shields on each side of the windshield—an Auburn feature of that year. (Photo: William C. Kinsman)

The 1928 Model 8–88 Roadster with rumble seat, showing special door for entering rumble seat on right side, thus eliminating the ordinary awkward situation of having to climb up over the rear wing (fender). (Photo: William C. Kinsman)

to make cold weather starting easy as well as to provide smooth and rapid acceleration. The Schebler carburettor engineers worked closely with the Auburn design staff, and it was only after exhaustive tests on the Indianapolis Motor Speedway that the Schebler carburettor was perfected for use with the Auburn 8–88 engine.

The overall gear ratio was 5·11 to 1, with the three-speed and reverse transmission providing direct drive in third, 1·69 to 1 in second, 3·11 to 1 in first and 3·78 to 1 in reverse. It is interesting to note that an oversize transmission, larger than any used in comparable automobiles, was selected for the eight-cylinder Auburn.

The test room at the factory in Auburn, Indiana, was large enough so that as many as forty engines, complete with electrical equipment, carburettors, transmissions and clutches, could be run at one time. Each engine was hooked up to a heavy propeller, which rotated outside the building, to produce a load equivalent to pulling up a hill at 25 m.p.h. with a wide open throttle. Under the watchful eyes of expert inspectors, every engine that went into an Auburn chassis was run for a period of eleven to fourteen hours, or a distance of approximately 300 miles at a 25 m.p.h. speed. Since these inspectors were responsible to the Sales Department rather than to the Production Department, they would readily reject any unit not measuring up to standard requirements, regardless of any production demands.

After having tested both hydraulic and mechanical four-wheel braking systems, the Auburn engineers came to the conclusion that the mechanical system would be the most satisfactory from the owner's point of view. It is true that this type was then being used by Packard, Pierce-Arrow and Cadillac, and this fact may have had some bearing on their choice.

Steering was accomplished through a Ross variable ratio gear of the cam-and-lever type. This arrangement made the steering practically irreversible in mid-position or on the straight-away, thus eliminating road shocks and holding the car to a straight line through mud and sand. In turning a corner or in cramping the car into a tight space at the curb, the variable ratio feature necessitated only a minimum turning effort at the steering wheel.

All instruments were located together in one panel under glass on the instrument board and were illuminated at night by a concealed light. Included in this group was a petrol (gas) level gauge operated by air pressure, an engine heat indicator, an oil pressure gauge, an ammeter and a speedometer with a mileage indicator (odometer). For ease of operation and convenience, the ignition switch as well as the light switches were located on the steering wheel column. The only lever in the front compartment was the gear shift device; the emergency brake handle was located below the dash line, thus removing this projection from the front compartment. It was within easy reach yet

1929 Model 115 Pheaton (convertible sedan). (Photo: William C. Kinsman)

unobtrusive, controlling an easily operated brake drum on the transmission shaft.

Each closed model was equipped with a heater, while door openings were especially wide for easy entry and exit. These Auburn cars were unusually low, giving them a certain individuality and 'foreign' look, yet the bodies provided ample head room, even for persons of more than ordinary height. The width of the seats was such as to make it possible for three persons to ride comfortably abreast, even in the winter season when heavy clothing was worn.

The Auburn 8–88 was built on a chassis having a wheelbase of 129 in. and was equipped with 30 × 5·77 in. balloon tyres. The roadster (with body by McFarlan) carried a price tag of $1695, while the coupé, brougham and sedan (all with bodies by Limousine) sold for $1,745, $1,795 and $1,995 respectively.

The Auburn 8–88 was continued for 1927 with little change in either design or appearance—they were simply 'improved' versions of the 1926 models. The dimensions of the Lycoming engine remained the same, but Nelson Bohnalite pistons were fitted and the five-bearing crankshaft was equipped with a Lanchester vibration dampener. This and other refinements increased the output to 72 horsepower at 3,000 r.p.m.

Auburn always endorsed a rigid frame, and in 1927 the $\frac{7}{32}$ × 6-in. deep channels were firmly braced with seven cross members, three of them tubular. The wheelbase was increased to 130 in. and Lovejoy hydraulic shock absorbers became standard equipment.

The low design pioneered by Auburn was further promoted by the adoption of small wheels, only 19 in. in diameter. These provided increased road stability at high speeds, elimination of all side sway and top-heaviness, greater riding comfort and increased braking efficiency.

The Auburn 8–88 played an important rôle when stock car racing was revived by the Contest Board of the American Automobile Association. In March 1927 Wade Morton reeled off 1,000 miles at nearly

70 m.p.h. on the Culver City Speedway in California, and in the 75-mile stock car race at the Atlantic City Speedway in May he finished second, less than one second behind the winner. On 4th July, Morton won a 100-mile stock car race on the boards at Salem, New Hampshire, this time the Auburn averaging just a shade under 90 m.p.h. Later in the summer, two

A 1928 Model 115 Speedster, advertising Auburn's 108·460 m.p.h. record made at Daytona Beach by Wade Morton. (Photo: William C. Kinsman)

The 1929 Model 120 Speedster: a big powerful car, still in great demand by collectors. (Photo: William C. Kinsman)

Two views of the 1928 Model 115 Speedster. Even though the hood (top) *provided good protection during rainy weather, the appearance and dash of the car was spoiled.* (Photos: William C. Kinsman)

roadsters and a sedan set off on long-distance stock car speed records at the Atlantic City Speedway—the roadsters averaged better than 60 m.p.h. for 15,000 miles.

A fully-equipped Auburn 8–88 roadster entered the annual Pike's Peak Hill Climb classic in 1927, the first time the Penrose Trophy had been offered to the stock car making the fastest time of the day. Wade Morton, in his first race up the Peak, finished third in the stock car class with a time of 24 min. 26 sec. for the 12-mile ascent. This was the year that Auburn coined the slogan, 'The Car Itself is the Answer'.

The 1928 Auburn Model 115 featured a completely new chassis on a 130-in. wheelbase. Lockheed internal four-wheel brakes, having an automatic supply tank integral with the master cylinder, replaced the former mechanical system. Improved riding with more perfect stability at high speed was obtained through the adoption of a very stiff frame, weighing 410 lb. and having a depth of 7 in. and a flange width of 3 in. These cars were equipped with a Bijur central chassis

lubricating system—one kick of a lever on the dash before starting on the day's journey forced an adequate supply of fresh lubricant to all chassis points, as well as to the clutch, water pump and fan bearings.

The dimensions of the eight-cylinder L-head Lycoming engine remained the same, the increase in power resulting largely from improved manifolding—a $1\frac{1}{4}$ in. dual carburettor now fed a dual intake manifold. A mixture heat control valve, operated from the instrument panel, permitted adjustment of the amount

1929 Model 115 Sedan chassis. (Photo: William C. Kinsman)

The Model 115 Cabin Speedster was a unique design—the frame actually went underneath the rear axle. (Photo: William C. Kinsman)

of exhaust heat supplied to the intake manifold. A muffler by-pass (cut-out) was furnished which could be opened by a valve within reach of the driver.

The Model 115 featured new body lines set off by a higher, narrower radiator made distinctive by a vertical nickeled band down the centre. Count Alexis de Sakhnoffsky was engaged to design a distinctly new speedster which set a trend for the next six years. This body was boat-tailed, with doors set at a rakish angle

and a top that disappeared completely when not in use. Spare wheels were carried in side mounts in the front wings (fenders) and a Vee-type windshield was placed well back on the unusually long cowl. Wade Morton took one of these speedsters to Daytona Beach in March and established a speed of 104·37 m.p.h. over the measured mile straightaway. Later in the year and with the help of Eddie Miller, he covered 2,033 miles in 24 hr. (84·7 m.p.h. average) in a 115 speedster on the

Two views of the 1934 Model 850 Convertible Coupé. Auburns of this particular vintage are extremely rare today. (Photos: William C. Kinsman)

Model 851 Supercharged Speedster details: radiator (above), exhausts and . . .

Atlantic City Speedway, in addition to setting a new record of 21 min. 45·4 sec. for stock cars at Pike's Peak to win the Penrose Trophy for Auburn.

Another new model introduced by Auburn in 1928 was the phaeton-sedan, essentially a sport touring car easily convertible into a regular sedan. Heretofore this type of body had been obtainable only on special order from custom coachbuilders. The Auburn 115 phaeton-sedan was unusually attractive and distinctive in design, having four doors and a straight-type windshield, and was equipped with a large touring trunk in the rear. All the top bows (hood frames) were nickel finished on the inside, and all the windows turned down completely flush with the door edges. According to Robert E. Turnquist, author of *The Packard Story*, the phaeton-sedan and the convertible coupé were designed by the Walter M. Murphy Company of Pasadena, California, designs that Auburn used for the next five years. Due to the distance involved and quantities required, Murphy sub-contracted the work of actually building these bodies to the Limousine Body Company of Kalamazoo, Michigan, a firm that was purchased by Auburn in the late 'twenties.

There was very little change in the Auburn eight for 1929 and 1930. The Model 120 for 1929 retained the

unusually stiff frame and was reinforced from a point at the rear engine support to the radiator by a second frame which was pressed into the regular frame channel and securely riveted. The purpose of this extra rigidity at the front end was to eliminate all radiator shimmy and bonnet (hood) vibration. The engine remained the same, but, in addition to a standard compression ratio of 5·25 to 1, an optional head was available with a ratio of 6·56 to 1. Styling was pretty much the same as the Model 115, but Auburn introduced a special wood artillery-type wheel with ten spokes, extra strongly constructed, while Dayton wire wheels of the centre-lock racing type could be had on all models at a small additional cost.

Auburn unveiled the Cabin Speedster, a subtle compound of racing car and airplane, sky-styled and designed by the famous racing driver and aviator, Wade Morton. The Cabin Speedster was radical—a special, distinct and far advanced creation. The height, from the ground to the highest part of the body, was only 58 in. Unusual features included cycle-type individual fenders (wings) that literally rode with the wheels, no running boards, frame side rails that dipped under the rear axle, two wicker basket airplane-type seats, a body made entirely of aluminium. The wheelbase was only 120 in., and it was equipped with the high-compression 125 h.p. Lycoming straight-eight engine. An extra wheel and tyre was carried on the inside of the V-shaped taper of the body's rear deck, while the battery was located under the bonnet (hood). The entire car, complete with gas, oil and water, weighed only 3,000 lb. and was certified to have attained a speed of 100 m.p.h. or more. Its styling closely resembled that of Barney Oldfield's famous 'Golden Submarine', and Auburn advertised the Cabin Speedster as 'a racing car with the comfort of a closed car'. It is unfortunate that the Cabin Speedster and the Great Depression made their appearance at the same time—today there are few indeed who ever saw this great automobile.

In 1930 the Contest Board of the American Automobile Association and the Indianapolis Motor Speedway Corporation opened the door to racing cars equipped with modified stock car engines up to 366 cu. in. capacity. For the annual 500-mile race that year, Marion Trexler built and drove a modified Auburn straight-eight which was called the Trexler Special. It had a $3\frac{1}{4} \times 4\frac{1}{2}$-inch Lycoming 8-cylinder

. . . windshield treatment. (Photos: Guy Griffiths)

Buehrig back: Model 851 Supercharged Speedster at Silverstone. (Photo: Guy Griffiths)

engine of 298 cu. in. displacement, fitted with a Packard carburettor, Defiance spark plugs, Long clutch, Warner gearbox, Columbia axles, 3½ to 1 gear ratio and six Hartford shock absorbers. Trexler qualified this machine at 93 m.p.h. for 32nd position in a field of 38 starters.

During the actual race, Red Roberts (Duesenberg), who was driving relief for Peter de Paolo, skidded in the path of Babe Stapp (Duesenberg) on entering the north turn after leaving the backstretch on the 20th lap. Trexler (Trexler), who was immediately behind, tried to slow down too suddenly and also went into a skid, right in the path of Deacon Litz (Duesenberg). Stapp collided with Roberts, and Litz hit Trexler's left front wheel which was so badly damaged that Trexler was forced to withdraw from the race.

The Model 120 became the Model 125 in 1930, with practically no changes in either mechanical design or outward appearance. But the Model 8–98 was an entirely new automobile for 1931. The 8–98 appeared more massive in spite of the fact that it was actually smaller—the wheelbase had been reduced to 126 in. What made it appear more massive was the fact that smaller, 17-in. wheels were now used which lowered the roof line. It was more graceful too, featuring long,

sweeping front wings (fenders)—in fact this year's Auburn looked almost like a small version of the famous Duesenberg.

In keeping with Auburn tradition, the frame was stronger than ever—8-in. deep channel with 3-in. wide flanges of $\frac{5}{32}$-in. stock. These side members were rigidly braced with conventional cross members front and rear and with a 6-inch deep channel of $\frac{5}{32}$-in. stock forming an 'X' cross-member with a spread of 75 in. bracing the centre of the frame. This marked the first time that bracing of this form had ever been offered in a rear-drive automobile.

The L-head, straight-eight cylinder Lycoming engine, known as Type GU, was a bored-out version of their 1927 Type GT, with a bore and stroke of $3 \times 4\frac{3}{4}$ in., displacing 268·6 cu. in. and developing 98 h.p. at 3,400 r.p.m. Such items as Bohnalite pistons with invar strut construction, five-bearing crankshaft with balancer (formerly called a vibration dampener), large water passages to ensure adequate cooling and rear engine supports mounted in rubber were carry-overs from the 1930 models.

The Model 8–98 was equipped with an L.G.S. Free Wheeling unit mounted on the rear of the transmission case, controlled by a short lever located behind the floor-mounted gear shift lever and directly in front of the driver's seat. Lovejoy double action hydraulic shock absorbers were standard equipment, and the underslung front spring construction allowed a much straighter front axle with a much heavier frame over it to eliminate front end shimmy. The Model 8–98 was also equipped with the automatic Bijur chassis lubrication system.

The Auburn 8–100 was introduced as the 1932 model with very little change in powerplant or styling. The wheelbase had been extended one inch, to 127 in. and the standard gear ratio changed from 4·45:1 to 4·70:1. This change afforded snappier acceleration with only a small sacrifice in top speed.

The big, new feature for 1932 was a two-speed Columbia rear axle; Auburn labelled it 'Dual Ratio'. With this device, it was possible to select the ratio that would give the most desirable performance in accordance with load, speed and road conditions. The two ratios available were 5·1 to 1 and 3·4 to 1. The

The 1929 Model 120 Pheaton-Sedan: one of the lowest-priced convertibles on the market and a great hit with movie stars. (Photo: William C. Kinsman)

The Model 125 Deluxe Cabriolet of 1930 was a favourite of the women. In fair weather, with the hood (top) down and the rumble seat open, it provided a thrilling open car for four. (Photo: William C. Kinsman)

shift from one ratio to the other was made by taking advantage of the vacuum off the intake manifold through a valve actuated by a hand lever located on the instrument panel. The lever, indicating high and low positions, could be moved from one position to the other at speeds below 40 m.p.h. This shift was accomplished by lifting the foot off the accelerator pedal momentarily, depressing the clutch and then turning the Dual Ratio control lever to either the 'High' or 'Low' position.

Auburn continued to build the same eight-cylinder automobile during 1933, the designation for this year being Model 8–105. It had the same Lycoming engine, the same 'X' braced frame, the same free-wheeling unit, the same dual-ratio rear axle and the same bodies. But the 8–50 model introduced in 1934 was new. And, much to the regret of the younger set, the famous speedster model was discontinued for the first time since its introduction in 1928. These were the first Auburns to carry skirted wings (fenders) and a completely re-designed front grille and bonnet (hood) treatment. Mechanically they were quite similar to their predecessors, including such items as an exceptionally stiff frame, dual ratio axle (now controlled by a lever on top of

the steering column), and L.G.S. free-wheeling unit. The Lycoming engine, known as Type GG, had a bore and stroke of $3\frac{1}{16} \times 4\frac{3}{4}$ in., displacing 279·9 cu. in. Fitted with an aluminium head giving a 6·2 to 1 compression ratio, it developed 115 h.p. at 3,600 r.p.m. Old features retained for 1934 included Nelson-Bohnalite pistons with two compression rings and two rings for oil control, and a five-bearing crankshaft with Lanchester vibration dampener, while new devices included such items as a Bendix vacuum-operated clutch and a Bendix BK vacuum booster for braking.

The 1935 Model 851 was announced in September 1934; this was a continuation of the 1934 line with minor changes in body and radiator grille design. Greatest noticeable change was the elimination of the

1931 8–98 Speedster, showing instrument panel, lid for concealing the hood (top), and the side door for access to the compartment under the rear deck. (Photo: Charles L. Betts, Jr.)

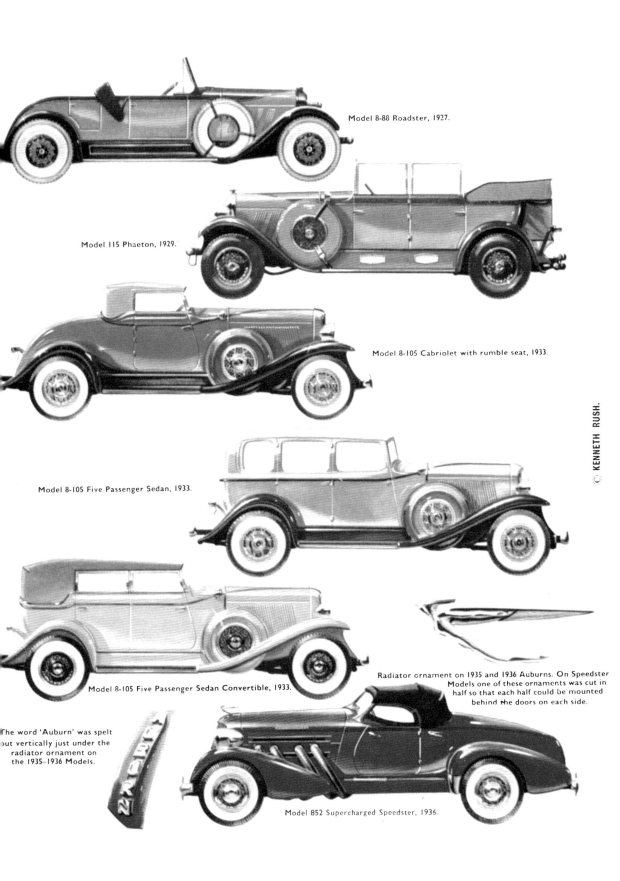

Model 8-88 Roadster, 1927.

Model 115 Phaeton, 1929.

Model 8-105 Cabriolet with rumble seat, 1933.

Model 8-105 Five Passenger Sedan, 1933.

© KENNETH RUSH.

Model 8-105 Five Passenger Sedan Convertible, 1933.

Radiator ornament on 1935 and 1936 Auburns. On Speedster Models one of these ornaments was cut in half so that each half could be mounted behind the doors on each side.

The word 'Auburn' was spelt out vertically just under the radiator ornament on the 1935–1936 Models.

Model 852 Supercharged Speedster, 1936.

Auburn 'hallmark'—the side belt that ran up over the top of the bonnet (hood). And in January 1935 Auburn introduced a line of six body styles with a super-charged engine developing 150 h.p. at 4,000 r.p.m. The chassis was identical with the unsupercharged version which produced 115 h.p. at 3,600 r.p.m. The supercharger (Schwitzer-Cummins) was of the centrifugal type running at six times crankshaft speed. Planetary gearing of the frictional type was used to step up the speed of the impeller.

Gordon Buehrig, best known for his design of the Model 810 Cord, was responsible for the design of a new Auburn speedster, featuring a tapering tail, deeply skirted wings (fenders) and no running boards. Four 3-in. exhaust pipes of flexible stainless steel tubing protruded through the left side of the bonnet (hood).

This new speedster proved to be a star performer in the hands of Ab Jenkins who piloted it to new stock car speed records at the Bonneville Salt Flats in Utah during July 1935. The standing mile was covered in 51·9 sec. (equivalent to an average speed of 69·4 m.p.h.), and the flying mile was covered in 34·56 sec. (104·17 m.p.h.). When Jenkins completed a twelve-hour run averaging 102·9 m.p.h., the Auburn Super-charged Eight Speedster became the first fully-equipped American stock car to exceed 100 m.p.h. for a twelve-hour period of sustained speed.

The Auburn Model 852, which was introduced in 1936, was practically the same as the former Model 851, and it marked the end of the line for Auburn. Altogether, only about 500 Auburns were manufactured during 1935 and 1936.

© *Charles L. Betts, Jr. 1966*

AUBURN STRAIGHT-EIGHT SPECIFICATIONS

	1925	1926	1927	1928	1929	1930	1931	1932	1933	1934	1935	1936
Year	1925	1926	1927	1928	1929	1930	1931	1932	1933	1934	1935	1936
Model designation	8-in-line	8–88	8–88	115	120	125	8–98	8–100	8–105	850	851	852 s/c
Engine make and type	Lycoming Straight-8 cast en bloc 5-bearing L-head											
Bore and stroke (inches)	3⅛ × 4½	3¼ × 4½					3 × 4¾			3 1/16 × 4¾		
Displacement (cubic inches)	276	298·6					268·6			279·9		
N.A.C.C. rating *	31·0	33·8					28·8			30·0		
Developed (Brake) horsepower	65	68	72	115		125	98	100		115		150
R.p.m. at peak horsepower	2700	3000		3300		3600	3400			3600		4000
Carburettor	Schebler							Stromberg				
Crankcase capacity (qts.)	8											
Coolant capacity (qts.)	20		22		20		21	19		20		
Gas tank capacity (gals.)	18						20		25	20		
Compression ratio	4·61		5·25 (6·55 optional)				5·26			6·20		6·50
Rear axle gear ratio	5·11		4·45				5·00 low and 3·47 high (dual ratio)					
First gear ratio (low)	3·11						2·87					
Second gear ratio (intermediate)	1·69						1·68					
Third gear ratio (high)	1·00 (direct)						1·00 (direct)					
Reverse gear ratio	3·78						3·76					
Suspension, front and rear	Semi-elliptic											
Wheelbase (inches)	129		130		129		126	127		126	127	
Track/tread (inches)	56 (F and R)								60 (F) 62 (R)	59 (F)	62 (R)	
Tire size (inches)	30 × 5·77	30 × 6·00	30 × 6·20	6·20 × 18			6·00 × 17			6·50 × 16		
Foot (service) brake	4-wheel mechanical			4-wheel hydraulic			4-wheel mechanical	4-wheel hydraulic				
Hand (emergency) brake	Propeller shaft behind gearbox						All 4 wheels			Rear wheels only		
Shock absorbers	Gabriel	Lincoln	Lovejoy						Delco	Spicer		Delco
Chassis lubricator	(None)			Bijur						(None)		
Free wheeling unit	(None)						Type L.G.S.			(None)		
Factory price (5-passenger sedan)	$1895	$1995	$2095	$2195	$1895		$995	$1195	$1245	$1125	$1045	$1545

* *N.A.C.C. Rating: The National Automobile Chamber of Commerce used the empirical formula* $\frac{D^2 \times N}{2\cdot5}$ *in which D equals cylinder bore in inches; N equals number of cylinders; 2·5 is a constant (based on the average view of eminent engineers as to a fair, conservative rating for a 4-cycle engine at 1000 ft. per minute piston speed).*

The Type 35 Grand Prix Bugatti

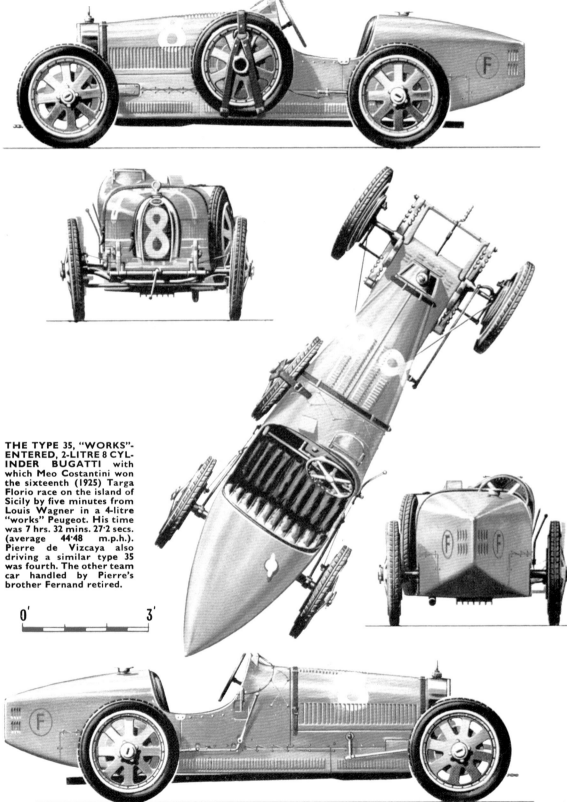

THE TYPE 35, "WORKS"-ENTERED, 2-LITRE 8 CYL-INDER BUGATTI with which Meo Costantini won the sixteenth (1925) Targa Florio race on the island of Sicily by five minutes from Louis Wagner in a 4-litre "works" Peugeot. His time was 7 hrs. 32 mins. 27·2 secs. (average 44·48 m.p.h.). Pierre de Vizcaya also driving a similar type 35 was fourth. The other team car handled by Pierre's brother Fernand retired.

0'   3'

The Type 35 Grand Prix Bugatti
by Godfrey Eaton

First race appearance of the 2-litre type 35. The cars lined up for the French Grand Prix (also first European Grand Prix) at Lyons on August 3 1924. No. 13 (not an unlucky number on the Continent) was driven by E. Friderich. Meo Costantini drove car No. 22. Due to rear-tyre troubles Bugattis could finish no nearer than 7th and 8th. (Photo: *Autocar*)

The type 35 Bugatti has been described by many writers as 'a classic' in racing car design. Aesthetically it was what most people would call a *real* racing car being both beautifully fashioned and having a superb finish. It did, however, have a somewhat complex engine, which nevertheless proved itself most successfully in its various forms over a period of some six to seven years.

Incidentally the type 35 was not solely a 'works' car, as it could be, and indeed was, purchased by anyone. This fact of course contributed to the claimed 2,000 or so racing successes of the type during its period of manufacture, from 1924 to 1931.

The engine was basically that of the unsuccessful 1923 tank-bodied, type 30, 8-cylinder cars which had two major weaknesses—a three-bearing crankshaft and a lubrication system for the big ends of the connecting rods which left a great deal to be desired. These and other minor defects were remedied by the 1924 season and with a modified and considerably improved chassis and better brakes the 2-litre type 35 emerged.

Before embarking on details of engine and chassis design, one should understand the overall development of the type 35, which was due in some respects to the bewildering changes of the formulae for Grand Prix races and in others to the special requirements of important events during the period 1924 to 1931.

Type 35. An unblown 8 cylinder-in-line car, first catalogued in 1924, with a bore of 66 mm. and a stroke of 88 mm. giving 2,000 c.c. It had, as did all but one of the types 35, cast aluminium wheels with eight flat spokes and detachable rims (these were done away with on subsequent models).

Type 35A. Similar in many respects to the 2-litre type 35 it had an identical body and chassis but used the type 38 engine with a three ballbearing crankshaft and plain big ends. Ignition was by battery and

distributor, not magneto, and it had wire wheels. Known as the 'Tecla', it is a rare model today. It is not a racing model in the strict sense but is capable of more than 90 m.p.h. at 4,500 r.p.m. in top gear.

Type 35. The factory produced a limited number of 1½-litre cars for Grand Prix events in 1925. They were unblown with bore and stroke 52 mm. × 88 mm.

Type 35. For the 1926 Alsatian Grand Prix three special 1,100 c.c. supercharged cars were made. Bore and stroke were 51·3 mm. × 66 mm. This was basically a type 39 engine with smaller bores.

Type 35T. This model made its appearance in the 1926 Targa Florio, the affix 'T' denoting Targa. Unblown, it had a capacity of 2·3 litres as the stroke had been lengthened to 100 mm.

Type 35B. A logical sequence to the successful type 35T and, by 1926, Ettore Bugatti had decided to add a supercharger. The radiator was enlarged and moved further forward. Other improvements to the basic design were also gradually evolved—such as a larger brake drum and bigger tyres. The engine capacity, however, remained at 2·3 litres.

Type 35C. A variant of the type 35B with a 2-litre engine. Otherwise it was similar in all respects and produced at the same time, i.e. from 1926.

Type 39. Whilst having the number 39 it was, however, a variant of the type 35. Produced in 1926 it had an almost square engine with bore and stroke 60 mm. × 66 mm. Not many of these 1½-litre cars were made.

Type 39A. This was the supercharged version of the type 39 and had a number of successes in Grands Prix and also in less exalted events. Essentially a 'works' car, not many were produced, and it is not really certain whether the blown or unblown car came first.

THE CHASSIS

The type 35 had a wheel-base of 7 ft. 10½ in. with a

Ernest Friderich coming out of the Virage de la Mort on the winding descent to Les Sept Chemins during the European Grand Prix at Lyons in 1924. During practice Friderich demolished a lamp standard and quite a yardage of so-called protective chestnut fencing, but kept going without any apparent concern. (Photo kindly loaned by Capt. T. A. S. O. Mathieson)

In the paddock at Montlhéry prior to the French Grand Prix of July 26 1925. Meo Costantini takes in the scene behind him, obviously no pre-race nerves even if the car is number 13. Note rims on the early type 35 wheels. 1925 was the first year in which mechanics were no longer carried.
(Photo kindly loaned by Capt. T. A. S. O. Mathieson)

track of 3 ft. 9 in. The track on some models varied from 4 ft. 1 in. at the front to 3 ft. 11 in. at the rear (types B and C). The chassis was of channel section with side members varying in depth from $\frac{3}{4}$ in. at the front dumb irons, which were tied by a tube, to $6\frac{3}{4}$ in. at the central point. It also varied gracefully in width—narrow at the front end, widening at the bulk head and amidships and then curving inwards towards the tail. For extra rigidity at the front, the engine was anchored to the frame members at four points while the gearbox (a separate unit from the engine) held the central section firm. The rear of the frame was held rigid by transverse tubular members.

The Bugatti patent wheels were of cast aluminium alloy with eight flat broad spokes, integral with rims and brake drums. The early 2-litre type 35 had a detachable rim secured by 24 set screws, but this outer flange was discarded on later models. With this layout the brake-shoes were revealed on removing the wheels making for easy access, and also rapid wheel changing when racing. This method of construction also saved up to 30 lb. of unsprung weight. A spare wheel was always carried on the near-side of the cars.

The semi-elliptic front springs passed through forged slots embodied in the polished front axle, which was tubular and hollow, dipping at the centre but tapering and upswept at the outer sections. The rear portion of the spring was held in a trunnion and not the usual shackle. The reversed quarter-elliptic springs at the rear were unique. They were held by shackle-bolts to the rear axle and, to deal with driving thrust, two external radius rods ran forward with ball joints to connect them to the frame. The rear springs faced inwards towards the tail which concealed them, thereby giving the back end of the car a very clean line.

All the moving parts in the steering box were of massive proportions and steering was by worm and helical wheel. A leather universal joint was placed on the steering column to compensate for any misalignment of the steering if untoward loads were placed on the steering or the steering box. The steering arms were exceptionally strong and tapered, and were able to withstand almost any load placed upon them.

Brakes were cable-operated with chain and bevel gear compensation. The hand-brake was placed on the right, outside the body, and operated the rear-brakes only. There was a certain degree of servo action, since the brake camshafts were forward of the front wheel axis. Drums were integral with the wheels (see above) and initially the shoes were lined with cast-iron segments with inset rollers for the brake cams.

The gearbox was neat in construction due to the layshaft being placed alongside the main shaft and thereby saving on depth. The gear was gate-operated with the lever again on the right side and protruding through a slot in the bodywork (see page 11). There were four forward speeds and reverse, with direct drive on top.

The rear axle casing was fabricated in two pieces in cast aluminium alloy and enclosed the bevelled gears which had straight-cut teeth. The axle ratios were 15/54, 14/54 and 13/54. The half-shafts were $\frac{3}{4}$-floating and encased in steel tubes flanged and bolted to the bevel box casing.

A 20-gallon petrol tank was housed in the tail and situated to the rear of the axle.

THE ENGINE

This was a beautiful and neat piece of engineering which shows the touch of the artist in Ettore Bugatti. The 8 cylinders were cast in two blocks of four but had a common light alloy camshaft housing. The camshaft ran in drip lubricated plain bearings with three cams to each cylinder. The valves were adjusted for clearance by inserting steel shims in the caps located on top of the valve stems. The single camshaft operated through rocking fingers which opened the vertical valves in the head, there being three per cylinder (two inlet and one exhaust) with a larger exhaust

The 1½-litre type 35 of Meo Costantini leads a team-mate during the French Grand Prix of 1925 held on the Linas-Montlhéry circuit. Costantini finished fourth and the other four works-entered Bugattis filled fifth to eighth places after a race distance of 621 miles on the 7·7 mile 'road' and track course.
(Photo kindly loaned by Capt. T. A. S. O. Mathieson)

Fernand de Vizcaya raises the dust with the works 2-litre type 35 during the 16th Targa Florio on May 3 1925. Meo Costantini won the race — Fernand retired. This photo was inscribed by Fernand to his friend 'Julot' (Bugatti racing driver Jules Goux).

(Photo kindly loaned from the H. G. Conway Collection)

than inlet area. Due to the layout of the head, the valves were long, but they had short guides.

The crankcase was split horizontally in half, the lower portion locating the engine/chassis attachments at four points. The centre of the built-up crankshaft had two webs which were held together by taper and key and the various sections of the shaft were anchored by the use of pins and tapers. In comparison to the three bearing crankshaft of the type 30 engine, the type 35 had five main roller or ball bearings, the three inner bearings (roller) being held from the top half of the crankcase. The diameter of the main journals was 3 in. with roller bearings of $5\frac{1}{2}$ in. in diameter, in which they ran, held in split steel races and supported by three caps to the top part of the crankcase. The outer bearings were ball whilst the big ends had roller bearings, which incorporated 17 rollers for each connecting rod. The connecting rods were in one piece and, at the small end, held the short pistons near the base of the skirt with gudgeon pins 16 mm. in diameter. The pistons therefore had a large top land with three compression rings and, on some engines, an oil ring was placed low down on the skirt.

Lubrication was by means of a normal gear-type pump which fed oil at around 15 p.s.i. through jets. To keep the oil cool the sump had deep fins and it also housed 13 copper tubes running from the front to the back. This method of oil cooling proved highly efficient. The water-cooling system, while proving satisfactory—and it must therefore have been efficient since it did its work—appeared to leave something to

Pierre de Vizcaya cornering at Le Far during the French Grand Prix on July 26 1925. There was a pre-race dispute between Ettore Bugatti and the Delage team manager concerning the streamline cover over the mechanic's vacant seat on the Bugattis. Ettore withdrew his cars but was finally persuaded to run them, which he did but without removing the covers!
(Photo kindly loaned by Capt. T. A. S. O. Mathieson)

be desired. The short valve guides had almost minimum contact with the water and the eight plugs, which were placed on the inlet side of the engine and located in solid metal, had to be content with narrow water passages at the top and bottom. The water pump operated from a transverse drive off the vertical drive shaft for the valve gear. Although it was mounted on

On the Lasarte circuit near San Sebastian the front row line-up for the start of the 1926 European Grand Prix (Spanish G.P.) held on July 18. Left to right: Meo Costantini (Bugatti), Louis Wagner (Delage), Jules Goux (Bugatti). It was during this fantastic race that the Delage drivers had their feet roasted! (Photo kindly loaned from the H. G. Conway Collection)

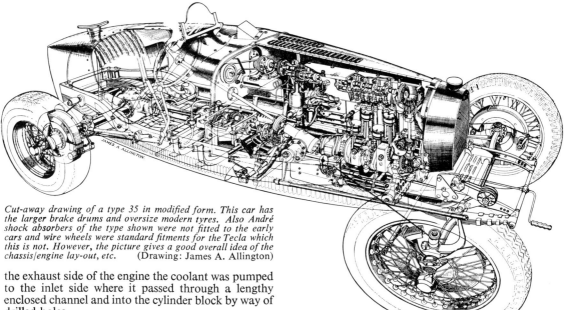

Cut-away drawing of a type 35 in modified form. This car has the larger brake drums and oversize modern tyres. Also André shock absorbers of the type shown were not fitted to the early cars and wire wheels were standard fitments for the Tecla which this is not. However, the picture gives a good overall idea of the chassis/engine lay-out, etc. (Drawing: James A. Allington)

the exhaust side of the engine the coolant was pumped to the inlet side where it passed through a lengthy enclosed channel and into the cylinder block by way of drilled holes.

The three-lobed rotor Roots supercharger fitted to some of the types 35, was placed centrally and driven at engine speed by a chain of gears at the front of the engine. The fuel mixture was drawn from a vertical carburettor (usually a Zenith) and, from the super-charger, went to a pipe with a T branch, thence to two separate manifolds which were water-heated. Each manifold fed a cylinder block. Two cylinders in each block shared a 1 in. × 2 in. inlet port. In all, the mixture had a tortuous journey through six right-angles on its way to the valve head, but for all this the system seemed to work with efficiency! The unblown cars had two Solex carburettors.

A great deal of attention had been paid to the flow of the exhaust gases since each block of cylinders had a four-branch Y exhaust manifold. There were no sharp bends and the whole led to a central steel chamber, thence to a single tail pipe which was carried under the car and therefore out of sight, thereby adding to the general neat appearance of the car.

The firing order was certainly unique for an 8-in-line engine for, taking each section separately, it was 1, 2, 3, 4 for the front and 5, 6, 7, 8 for the rear block, which comes out at 1, 5, 2, 6, 3, 7, 4, 8.

Jules Goux, winner of the 1926 European Grand Prix, does his own water-carrying during a pit stop—very primitive! This was the 1½-litre supercharged type 39A, of which only a very few were built. Meo Costantini driving a similar car backed up Jules by taking second place after covering 484 miles! (Photo kindly loaned from the H. G. Conway collection)

The small diameter clutch was of the wet multiplate type and designed by Ettore Bugatti. It had virtually no fly-wheel effect, the mass of the crankshaft making this unnecessary. The plates could never be disengaged in a positive manner, but pressure from the pedal operated a swinging yoke and toggle levers which released two thrust buttons which held the plates together. Engagement of the clutch was provided initially by a light spring followed by the centrifugal effect of the levers.

Except for the type 35A, ignition was by a single Bosch or Scintilla (in the early models) magneto driven from the rear end of the camshaft and placed in the fascia. (See page 11.) Advance and retard was operated by the unique method of a lever placed to the left of the magneto and through a slot on the fascia.

Many design features of the engine were against normally accepted engineering practice, being precision-built with no tolerances. 'Fit' was the keyword and machining allowed for no errors, skill being required both in workmanship and assembly. Gaskets were unheard of as metal rested on metal. It was an extremely successful design!

IN THE TARGA FLORIO

The author feels that Bugattis achieved their greatest triumphs on the Medium Madonie Circuit for the Targa Florio, and the shorter course for the Coppa Florio races, on the Isle of Sicily. All these successes between the years 1925 and 1929 were with the type 35 in its various guises against stiff opposition such as was not to be found on the Grands Prix Circuits at that time. Other *marques* opposing the type 35 during these years numbered no less than twenty-two at one time or another, including such famous names as Peugeot, O.M., Mercedes, Maserati, Itala, Alfa Romeo and Fiat.

Descriptions of this tortuous course are to be found in a number of books and it is only necessary to say here that the Circuit was undoubtedly the toughest in the world. Usually five laps of the circuit, totalling 335½ miles, had to be covered for the **Targa**

Mme F. Junek from Prague, with Cav. Florio, sitting on her type 35 prior to the start of the 19th Targa Florio on 6th May 1928. The lady, lying second, pressed Albert Divo (Bugatti) very hard for some 270 miles but finally fell back to finish fifth.
(Photo kindly loaned from the H. G. Conway Collection)

In 1928 the Linas-Montlhéry circuit was used for a great variety of races, one of these being La Coupe des Dames won on this occasion by Mme. F. Junek. Madame is seen with her early type 35 and the victor's laurels.
(Photo kindly loaned from the H. G. Conway Collection)

Florio, and 268½ miles (one lap shorter) for the Coppa Florio.

For the race on 3rd May 1925 (the 16th Targa Florio), 13 cars lined up with the 'works' team of 2-litre type 35 Bugattis, handled by Meo Costantini and the brothers Pierre and Fernand de Vizcaya, opposed by the 'works' 4-litre sleeve valve Peugeots of Boillot, Wagner, Rigal and Dauvergne; the remainder of the field was in the hands of private owners.

After the first circuit Peugeots were in the first three positions, with Boillot leading and Meo

The up-and-coming young French driver, Louis Chiron, won the Rome, Marne, Spanish and Italian Grands Prix in the 1928 season. He is seen here in his early type 35B after one of his victories. This photograph is inscribed 'to my very dear friend Jules Goux'.
(Photo kindly loaned from the H. G. Conway Collection)

Costantini fourth. Then trouble overtook the Peugeots. Boillot suffered tyre-troubles, then Dauvergne overturned his car, which caught fire; Wagner gave what help he could and was delayed. This allowed Costantini to take the lead and he won by five minutes in 7 hr. 32 min. 27·2 sec. (44·48 m.p.h. average) from Wagner. Pierre de Vizcaya took fourth position, but his brother Fernand retired.

In 1926 the 'works' team of Bugattis was again led by Costantini, this time with a type 35T (2·3 litres) and supported by two other well-known racing drivers, Jules Goux and Minoia—a truly formidable team. While Bugatti had made a name for himself and his cars as early as 1911 he was now really beginning to make his mark, the three 'works' cars were supported by a number of well-known amateur drivers, including André Dubonnet. In all, eight other Bugattis were in a field of 33 starters and these included both the 2- and 1½-litre types 35.

Opposition was strong. Ernesto Maserati had entered a new 1½-litre 8-cylinder car. Peugeot 'works' cars were to be driven by Wagner and Boillot, and the Delage team of René Thomas, Robert Benoist and Albert Divo had the fantastic 2-litre 12-cylinder supercharged cars with which to do battle.

Costantini and Minoia led the field and kept their places throughout the race to finish in that order, the winner's time being 7 hr. 20 min. 45 sec., a race average of 44·77 m.p.h. Jules Goux was third, followed by Materassi driving the Hispano-Suiza-engined Itala and André Dubonnet in a privately-owned 2-litre Bugatti fifth. Three other Bugattis completed the course. During the race a fine amateur driver, Count Masetti, was killed when his non-'works' entered 12-cylinder Delage overturned. Brake trouble had bothered the Delage team and the tragedy might have been due to this. In any case, the Delage 'works' team called it a day. Of the twelve cars which finished the race in the time limit, seven were Bugattis.

Meo Costantini retired in 1927 but supported Bugatti by acting as team-manager and also supervising the privately-entered Bugattis. Once more the *marque* dominated the race, but Minoia retired with both a broken torque arm and universal. 'Sabipa' ran out of road, taking one of the many bends at an excessive speed, and disappeared into an orchard

50 feet below road level, but was luckily quite unhurt.

For the first time a lady driver competed, Mme Junek, in a 2·3-litre supercharged Bugatti. Although completing the first circuit in fourth place only 70 sec. behind the leader, she had the misfortune to run off the road and lose a wheel due to the steering box cracking.

The race was won by Materassi in the 2-litre supercharged Bugatti with Count Conelli taking second place in a supercharged 1½-litre model. The race time was 7 hr. 35 min. 55·4 sec., an average of 44·15 m.p.h. Of the eight official finishers, five competed in Bugattis.

The 19th Targa Florio of 1928 could be called a vintage year—not only in respect of cars, but also as regards drivers. Various type 35 Bugattis were piloted by Divo, Minoia, Louis Chiron, Count Conelli, Materassi, Count Brilli-Peri, René Dreyfus, Foresti, Mme Junek, the up-and-coming Tazio Nuvolari and others. Maseratis were in the hands of Ernesto Maserati, Fagioli and Borzacchini, and the works 1½-litre 6-cylinder supercharged Alfa Romeos were led by the incomparable Campari, with Marinoni and Sillitti in support.

The race held very little in the way of incident, apart from some exhuberant driving by the Countess d'Einsiedel (Bugatti) who eventually clouted a low wall without damage to anyone or anything, but thereafter proceeded more cautiously to finish twelfth. The main excitement was provided by Divo who was hard-pressed for some 270 miles to keep ahead of Mme Junek in her black and yellow Bugatti. She was never more than a mile astern and was lying second at the time, eventually to finish fifth.

Albert Divo in a 2·3-litre Bugatti averaging 45·6 m.p.h. won in 7 hr. 20 min. 56·6 sec. from Campari (Alfa Romeo). Bugattis held the next four places and, out of twelve finishers, nine were cars of the *marque*.

The Polizzi Course was used for the 1929 race, four laps for the Coppa Florio and an additional circuit of 67 miles for the Targa. The Alfa Romeo team, again led by Campari, with Varzi and Count Brilli-Peri, opposed a strong onslaught from the 'works' Bugattis of Divo, Minoia, Wagner, Conelli, Foresti and three others. The field of 19 was completed by a trio of Maseratis, two Fiats, a Salmson and another Alfa Romeo. The race was hard-fought between the Bugattis of Divo and Minoia and the

A type 35 driven by Delmo on La Course de Cote du Mont Ventoux, a hill climb event — the course being 13 miles 750 yards.

Ettore Bugatti, in a sun helmet, looks on as Meo Costantini brings his 1½-litre type 35 Bugatti to a standstill. On this occasion Meo won the 1925 Grand Prix de Tourisme at Montlhéry.
(Photo kindly loaned by Capt. T. A. S. O. Mathieson)

Alfa Romeos driven by Brilli-Peri and Campari who finished in that order. The lap record was broken repeatedly, pushing the race time down to 7 hr. 15 min. 41 sec., an average of 46·2 m.p.h. A heavy toll was extracted from the machinery, and only four cars finished in the time limit.

This race ended Bugatti's dominance in Sicily, but his cars, driven by Louis Chiron and Conelli, were placed second and third behind Varzi in a 'works' Alfa Romeo in 1930.

Opposed by cars of equal merit, there is no doubt that the superior road-holding of the Bugattis contributed largely to their successes, plus the fact that their pit management was superb when one considers the primitive facilities available. To change four wheels, take on oil, fuel and water in 60 sec., or less, was certainly fantastic.

IN GRAND PRIX RACING

Bugattis had been successful on the race circuits of Europe before 1925, but it was in that year, after the introduction in 1924 of the type 35, that considerable success came to the works at Molsheim and for six seasons, with one exception, the *marque* dominated the motor racing scene.

It is a pity, however, that from 1924 and for almost a decade there was a decline and deterioration in Grand Prix racing. The writer feels that, apart from the intervention of the brilliantly designed 1½-litre supercharged Delage of 1927, the type 35 Bugattis of the period never had a proper chance of showing their true worth. It can, however, be guessed at if one takes as a guide the results of the Targa Florio races from 1925 to 1929 inclusive.

The type 35 made its début at Lyons on 3rd August 1924, for the French Grand Prix (this was also the first European Grand Prix). Six of the 2-litre cars (including a reserve), one of which was piloted by Ettore Bugatti, were driven under their own power from the works to the race.

Commercially the race was not a success for *Le Patron* (as he was called) as none of his cars finished 'in the money'. Two of his cars finished 7th and 8th but defeat was due neither to mechanical defects nor to lack of power for, though the cars were unblown, they proved faster on certain sections of the circuit than either their blown or unblown rivals which included 'works' teams from Alfa Romeo, Sunbeam, and Fiat and a privately-entered Miller. Lack of success was attributed to failure of the rear-wheel tyres which kept throwing their treads due to faulty vulcanisation.

Their other appearance in 1924 was in the Spanish Grand Prix at San Sebastian on 25th September. The eleven-mile circuit was in an appalling condition, made worse at the corners where clay had been deposited, instead of sand, by the officials. The crash rate was high. After 386 desperate miles Segrave in a Sunbeam won by a mere 90 sec. from Costantini in his 2-litre Bugatti, the latter taking the lap record at 69·7 m.p.h. This race saw the first appearance of an official Mercedes team in a Grand Prix after the war and included 'works' entries from Delage and Diatto, apart from Sunbeam and Bugatti and a lone Schmid car.

1925 saw the final year of the 2-litre formula and manufacturers turned their attention mainly to the 1½-litre formula for the following season which called

A completely restored, to Pur Sang specification, type 35 B owned by B. Lindblad of Sweden. During the rebuild the car was featured in the studio of Swedish television.

Three-quarter front view of B. Lindblad's type 35 B during rebuild. Note depth of chassis frame at bulkhead.

Peter Stubberfield, a former well-known speed hill climb exponent, clips the curb at Pardon Hairpin on the Bugatti Owner's Club course at Prescott, near Cheltenham. The car is a type 35B with a monoposto body and, to obtain better adhesion for speed events, twin rear-wheels were fitted. The driver and car held the Bugatti record at Prescott from 1951 to 1957.
(Photo: Guy Griffiths)

for a minimum weight of 600 kg. The only change for 1925 was the dropping of the participation of riding mechanics.

The French Grand Prix was held on the newly-opened Montlhéry circuit on 26th July with a race distance of 621 miles—80 laps of the 7·7-mile 'road' and track course. Fourteen cars lined up, including 1½-litre Bugattis driven by Costantini, Goux, Foresti, Pierre and Fernand de Vizcaya. Placed fourth to eighth, they were not disgraced as Costantini was only 60 sec. behind Masetti (Sunbeam) who was third. The cars were, however, down on power by as much as 40/50 b.h.p. as far as the Sunbeams were concerned and 60/90 b.h.p. in comparison with the Delage and Alfa Romeo 'works' entries. This lack of power was undoubtedly due to the fact that Bugatti was still unconvinced that supercharging would improve the performance of his cars. By 1926, however, he had altered his mind.

The Italian Grand Prix over 800 km. run on the Monza Circuit took place on 6th September. Although a race for 2-litre cars, Costantini on one of the new 1½-litre unsupercharged Bugattis held third place at the finish but won the race for Voiturettes. To wind up the season Meo Costantini driving a 2-litre type 35 took the lap record at 82·75 m.p.h. in the Spanish Grand Prix. Other successes for Bugatti during the season were the Rome G.P., La Baule G.P. and Alessandria and Bordino Circuit G.P.

Grand Prix racing was reaching its lower depths in 1926. Manufacturers were finding it increasingly expensive, and one supposes that Ettore Bugatti could only keep going because he offered his production racing cars for sale. To illustrate the point the French Grand Prix, run on 27th June, was a complete fiasco. Only the type 39A Bugattis of Jules Goux, P. de Vizcaya and Meo Costantini lined up for the fall of the flag—Goux finished first at an average of 68·2 m.p.h. There were 21 entries for the European Grand Prix (also the Spanish Grand Prix) but the only teams to appear were the 1½-litre blown type 39A Bugattis of Costantini, Goux and Minoia and the new 1½-litre supercharged 8-cylinder-in-line Delages handled by Benoist, Morel and Louis Wagner. The Delages, classical in design and purposeful to look at, were the inspiration of M. Lory, but had one very bad

Rear wheels just beginning to really grip as John P. G. Horton moves off the start line at Prescott in his beautifully restored type 35. The original narrow section tyres are a feature of this car.
(Photo: Pim Faber)

design fault which, on the very hot day on which the race was run, cost them dearly. The twin superchargers were placed on the near-side of the engine which meant that the exhaust pipes passed within inches of the accelerator pedal causing the driver's feet to be roasted with dire result. The race run on the Lasarte circuit near San Sebastian on 18th July was full of drama, and although only two teams were competing it was thrilling to watch. Jules Goux won, covering the 484 miles in 6 hr. 51 min. 52 sec. (average 65·5 m.p.h.), with Costantini second. Despite the grim conditions, every car was running at the finish— from which it would seem that these small cars were extremely reliable and very fast.

Malcolm Campbell was the sole Bugatti entry for the first British Grand Prix held at Brooklands on 28th August. A somewhat dull and uninteresting race over 287 miles was won by the Delage of Louis

Exhaust arrangement of type 35B engine. Top half of the water pump can be seen at bottom left, filter at centre and blower oil reservoir mounted on bulkhead at right.

Wagner and his co-driver Robert Sénéchal at an average speed of 71·6 m.p.h., while Campbell, who finished second, trailed four laps in arrears in the 1500 c.c car.

Bugattis were also successful in a number of other minor Grands Prix during the 1926 season: Italian ('Sabipa', type 39A), Milan (Costantini, 35C), Rome (Maggi, type 35), Alsace (Dubonnet, 1100 c.c. type 35), Boulogne (Eyston, type 35), Provence (Williams, type 35), Cote d'Azur (Williams, type 35), Marne (Lescot, type 35), Tripoli (Eysermann, type 35), Pescara and Coppa Acerbo (Spinozzi, type 35), Garda Circuit (Maggi, type 35), Alessandria and Bordino (Alloati, type 35).

From 1927 onwards Grands Prix races had arrived at a farcical state for, while formulae were laid down, they were not always strictly adhered to as fuel consumption, weight restrictions and other innovations were introduced in the hope of making the races of greater interest.

The outstanding feature of the year was the re-designed 1½-litre supercharged car from the Delage équipe. It had 'looks', speed and power, and completely dominated the circuits. So much so that 'works' Bugattis were non-starters in the French and European Grands Prix (the former run at Montlhéry on 3rd July and the latter at Monza in September) but turned up for the British race on 1st October where they were trounced by these cars.

The type 35 Bugattis in various forms were successful, however, in a number of less important Grands Prix at Boulogne (Campbell), Marne (Etancelin), Baule (Eyston), Tripoli (Materassi), Rome (Nuvolari), Garda (Nuvolari), San Sebastian (Materassi), Burgundian 4-hour (Philippe), Montenero Circuit and Coppa Ciano (Materassi), Alessandria and Bordino (Bona).

Type 35B (1926) front-end showing larger radiator which was also more forward. Type 35B was first supercharged Bugatti.

© JAMES LEECH

Showing outboard position of gear-lever (through slot in bodywork) and brake-lever (the hand-brake only operated on rear wheels).

The cockpit. Facia had the usual clock (left), small tachometer (extreme right), Scintilla magneto (placed centrally), advance/retard lever (left of magneto), petrol gauge (left bottom), oil gauge (next petrol gauge), ammeter (right of magneto).

Type 35A (1925) known as the "Tecla" usually had wire wheels, type 38 8-cylinder engine and battery/distributor instead of magneto.

For sprint hill climbs and short sprint races owners often use twin rear-wheel for better adhesion.

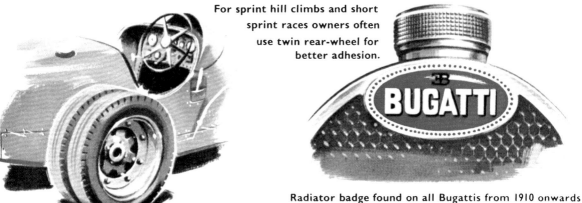

Radiator badge found on all Bugattis from 1910 onwards Note knurled radiator cap, also typical.

Rear view of John Horton's type 35. The driver is negotiating Ettore's Bend on the new loop section at Prescott.
(Photo: Photographic Craftsmen)

Malcolm Campbell won the important J.C.C. 200-mile race at Brooklands in the same year in his Bugatti, and the Gaillon and Klausen hill-climbs fell to Bugattis driven by Mme. Jennky and Louis Chiron respectively.

Delage, Talbot and Fiat withdrew from racing in 1928 leaving the field clear for the Bugattis—not a very wholesome prospect for important international motor races. There was no official formula laid down other than *formule libre*.

During the three years 1928 to 1930 there were exclusive Bugatti Grands Prix races at Le Mans, presumably run for 'les boys et girls'. First three in 1928 were A. Dubonnet, G. Philippe and Delzaert with J. Zanelli, Gauthier and 'Sabipa' placed in that order for the 1929 race. The final event was also won by Zanelli, with M. Fourny and Mlle. Helle-Nice in the minor positions.

For all that, many of the races during this period were exciting, and it brought to the fore one of the 'greats' of motor racing, namely Louis Chiron, who took most of the honours that were going during the 1928 season, including the Marne, Rome, Italian (also European) and Spanish Grands Prix.

The type 35 had virtually run its course by 1929, but notched up four Grand Prix wins, including the first Monaco race which was won by W. Williams driving a type 35B. It did, however, win a number of less important events during the next few years. The type 35 was succeeded by the type 51—a car similar in many respects, but having a twin overhead camshaft engine.

There are no official figures giving the maximum speeds of the various types 35, but it is safe to assume that all the models could exceed 100 m.p.h. Some idea of their potential may be guessed at, however, as a type 35B can still reach 115 m.p.h. at 5,500 r.p.m. in top gear on the straight at Silverstone—forty years after it was first designed!! In 1930 the same type reached 124·4 m.p.h. and at a post-war speed trial at Brighton the well-known monoposto type 35B of Peter Stubberfield crossed the kilometre finishing line at 120 m.p.h., achieving this speed with unsuitable speed hill-climb gearing.

THE TYPE 35 TODAY

The types 35, 35B, C and T are still found racing today, particularly in the United Kingdom, in short distance races and speed events, including speed hill-climbs. These cars are in the hands of enthusiastic amateurs steeped in Bugatti lore.

It will not be out of place to suggest that, apart from Bugattis *being* Bugattis and thereby keeping a special niche for themselves as racing, sporting and touring cars in the world of motoring, the fame of the *marque* will be carried on for many years, if not for all

time, by the clubs formed specially to keep the name alive.

The premier Club, founded in 1929, is the Bugatti Owners Club Ltd. with an international membership and registered offices at Newbury, Berkshire, England. Other clubs fostering the name of the *marque* are The Nederlands Bugatti Club, Bugatti-Club Deutschland, American Bugatti Club and Bugatti Club de France. In addition, both Australia and Czechoslovakia keep special registers.

© *Godfrey Eaton, 1966*

SPECIFICATION

TYPE: 35, 35B, 35C and 35T.
MODEL: Grand Prix.
MADE: 1924 to 1930/1.
ENGINE: Cylinders 8-in-line; two blocks of four. Bore and stroke mm.: 35 and 35C—60 × 88, 35B and 35T—60 × 100. Capacity c.c.: 35 and 35C—1,991, 35B and 35T—2,262. B.H.P.: 35 approximately 90, 35B, 35C and 35T—120/135. R.P.M.: 35 and 35C—5,500, 35B and 35T—5,000. Camshaft: 1 overhead, front drive by bevel gears. Valves: Vertical 3 per cylinder (2 inlet and 1 exhaust). Valve timing: I.O. 15 mm., E.C. 40 mm., E.O. 90 mm., I.C. 60 mm., on flywheel 214 mm. dia. Valve clearance (cold): Inlet 0·5 mm. Exhaust 0·5 mm. Crankshaft bearings No. and type: 3 journal roller and 1 thrust ball, 2 roller and roller rods. Supercharger: 3-lobed rotor Roots driven at engine speed (35B and 35C) (manifold pressure 10 lb. boost). Carburettor: 35 and 35T—two Solex, 35B and 35C—one Zenith. Ignition and timing: magneto mounted on fascia; timing on flywheel 85 mm. Plugs: 1 per cylinder on inlet side. Firing order: 1, 5, 2, 6, 3, 7, 4, 8. Clutch: wet multi-plate.
GEARBOX: Separate from engine. 4 forward speeds and reverse. Direct, 0·41, 0·54, 0·77.
REAR AXLE: Ratios 15/54, 14/54, 13/54.
BRAKES: 4 wheel cable operated. Hand brake to rear wheels.
WHEELS: Bugatti patent, aluminium alloy casting with eight broad spokes. Integral with brake drum. Early type 35 had detachable rims.
WHEELBASE: 7 ft. 10½ in.
TRACK: 3 ft. 9 in. (type 35). 4 ft. 1 in. front, 3 ft. 11 in. rear (types 35B, T and C).
TYRE SIZE: Original: 710 × 90 mm., later 5·00 × 19.
OIL: Sump: 6 litres.
FUEL: Tank: 100 litres.
WEIGHT: 750 kg. approximately.
OVERALL DIMENSIONS: 12 ft. 1 in.
HEIGHT TO SCUTTLE: 3 ft. 6 in.

The Alvis Speed Twenty & Twenty-Five, 3½ & 4.3-litre Models

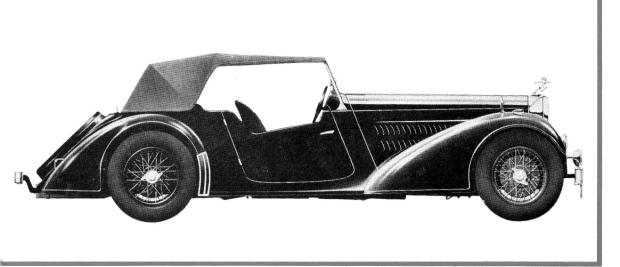

11

1939 ALVIS 4·3-LITRE TOURER by Vanden Plas. Owner: R. A. Parker, Esquire. Road tested by *The Autocar*, this car gave a mean average maximum speed of 100·84 m.p.h.

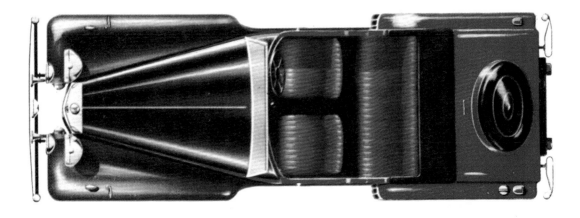

The Alvis Speed Twenty & Twenty-Five, 3½- & 4.3-Litre Models

4·3-Litre Charlesworth Saloon on the short chassis, entered in the 1938 RAC Blackpool Rally. (Photo: Photographic Advertising)

by T. R. Nicholson

Since it first appeared before the British motoring public in 1920, the name of Alvis had been associated primarily with a combination of high-speed reliability and good roadholding at reasonable cost. Alvises were solidly built from fine materials, which made for long life. Their most popular models, while being exceptionally fast, handling well, and exuding character, were of conventional, proved design. Therefore they were thoroughly practical all-round road cars, not world-beaters in competitions. There were sound economic reasons for this. When the Alvis Car & Engineering Company Ltd. had devoted most of their efforts to vehicles of the latter type, they had found themselves in dire financial trouble through catering for an over-specialised market. By 1931 they had learned their lesson.

In that year the prototype of a new high-performance, medium-sized six emerged from the Holyhead Road works in Coventry. It was shown late in the same year as a 1932 model. This Speed Twenty supplemented a range which included earlier, staider versions of it that were basically similar—permutations of the smooth, fairly quite Silver Eagle—and also smaller, four-cylinder cars on the theme of the 12/50 h.p. model; a car which had saved the company and provided the backbone of its sales. Up to the war, the character of the Alvis range remained the same: the Speed Twenty and its developments were the glamorous models, backed up by a variety of less

exciting, if in some cases more popular, 'bread-and-butter' four- and six-cylinder machines.

The new car was an immediate success, because it combined the qualities of the other Alvises with exceptionally low, handsome lines. It was described as a 'speed model' or a 'fast tourer' ideal for long-distance high-speed motoring, and was greeted lyrically by the motoring press as 'the best Alvis so far produced'. There was almost nothing like it on the British market at the time. As a rule, the few fast tourers were comparatively rough and noisy, while the new popular breed of small sports car was usually cheap and nasty.

The men behind the Speed Twenty had made the firm, between them. Thomas George John had run the financial and administrative sides of the firm since the beginning. He was described in the 1929 catalogue as 'an idealist who believed that ideals could be achieved within the realms of commercialism'. He was a strong man, too, and was always the biggest shareholder, as he did not hesitate to remind anyone who made difficulties at company meetings. Captain George Thomas Smith-Clarke had been Assistant Works Manager with the Daimler Company Ltd. before becoming Chief Engineer, Chief Designer and Works Manager of Alvis in 1922. He had been responsible for the money-spinning 12/50, and had been appointed a Director in 1931.

Smith-Clarke had designed and built his new car in

Left: 1934 Speed Twenty, showing near side of engine and independent front suspension. (Photo: Radio Times Hulton Picture Library). *Right: Offside of engine, 1936 Speed Twenty.* (Photo: A. R. Buck)

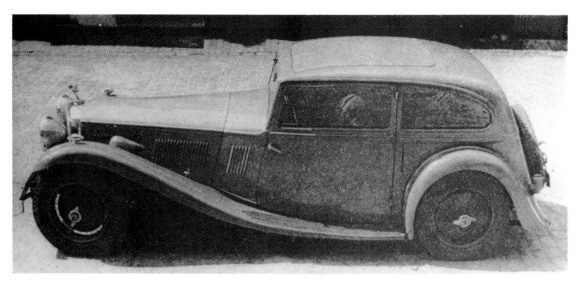

1934 Speed Twenty Vandem Plas Sports Saloon. (Photo: Guy Griffiths)

about three months; a *tour de force* which, unlike so many of its kind, produced an exceptionally good machine. The engine had six cylinders of 73 × 100 mm., totalling 2,511 c.c. Rated at 19·82 h.p., it was a development of a power unit already in service in the 20 h.p. version of the Silver Eagle, but modified to give a greater output with larger ports and a higher compression ratio, and strengthened to cope with this with a heavier crankshaft. The latter had four bearings, was heat-treated, and was statically and dynamically balanced. The camshaft, chain-driven from the rear of the engine (an unusual feature), operated two overhead valves per cylinder through pushrods and rockers.

Three SU carburettors looked after the induction. The mixture was controlled by a knob on the instrument panel, through a system of complex linkages. Fuel feed was by a mechanical pump from a 14½-gallon tank at the rear. The exhaust manifold was on the same side as the inlet manifold, giving a hotspot. Cooling was by pump, though there was no fan. A thermostat and water temperature gauge were, however, provided. The block was furnished with aluminium frost plugs. The cylinder head gasket was not expected to act as a water joint, separate porting being provided at the rear of the head and block.

The electrical system was 12-volt. There was dual ignition on the offside of the engine, by a combined BTH coil and magneto unit. A change-over switch enabled the driver to use the coil for starting, and as a standby, while the magneto was brought into operation for normal running. The magneto and the dynamo were both driven from the water pump shaft, in that order from the rear of the engine. All the auxiliaries were very accessible. This engine was rubber-mounted to the chassis. Notably smooth and flexible, it gave 87 b.h.p. at 4,200 r.p.m.

The single dry-plate clutch was of Alvis manufacture. The gearbox was made in unit with the engine; the first instance of this kind of construction in an Alvis. It was of normal, sliding-pinion 'crash' type, with four forward speeds. Two alternative sets of ratios were offered—in the case of the lightest of the models, the open four-seater sports tourer, 4·55, 6·42, 9·3 and 14·3:1. Standard ratios with the heavier cars

were 4·77, 6·6, 10, 16·9:1. Though not exceptionally so for the day, these ratios needed to be fairly low, because of the quite small engine for the size and weight of car; a disadvantage imposed by the penal British horsepower tax, which was based on engine bore. As the clutch and flywheel assembly was heavy, upward changes were slow, except in expert hands, and though the short, stiff gearlever was pleasant to operate, the gearbox needed knowing. The massive open propellor shaft, designed for well over 6,000 r.p.m., was in keeping with the rest of the car: there was no skimping. It drove to a fully-floating spiral bevel rear axle.

The normal chassis, which was similar to that of

1932 Speed Twenty saloon by Carlton. (Photo: Guy Griffiths)

One of the first Speed Twenties: 1932 Vanden Plas Sports Tourer.
(Photo: C. W. P. Hampton)

128

1935 Speed Twenty Charlesworth Saloon. (Photo: Guy Griffiths)

the Silver Eagle, had a wheelbase of 10 ft. 4 in., though an 11 ft. wheelbase was listed. The track was 4 ft. 8 in. The frame, dropped and cranked up over the rear axle, had rigid, deep side members. There was a normal beam front axle. Half-elliptic springs were fitted, those at the rear being underslung. All were damped by Hartford friction shock-absorbers. Luvax-Bijur one-shot chassis lubrication was adopted. The Marles-Weller steering was excellent. The 14 in. brakes were first-class, stopping the Speed Twenty in 25 feet from 30 m.p.h., but they needed heavy pressure. This chassis gave handling that was taut and of 'perfectly uncanny steadiness', to quote a test report.

A bare chassis could be bought for £600, but customers usually plumped for one of the standard body styles. They were designed by Charles Follett Ltd., the London and Home Counties distributors, in conjunction with Vanden Plas (England) 1923 Ltd., and other firms. (Follett had put money into the company in 1931, and had agreed to take part of the output.) Styles comprised the four seater, four-door Sports Tourer, and two four-door Sports Saloons by Vanden Plas and Charlesworth, priced at £695, £750 and £825 respectively. A little later, a four-door tourer by Cross & Ellis was also listed.

The range for 1933 included a Vanden Plas Sports Tourer, now £725, the Vanden Plas saloon at £865, a Vanden Plas four-seater Drophead Coupé at the same figure, a Thrupp & Maberly saloon at £895, and a third saloon by the Mayfair Carriage Company Ltd. Other coachbuilders built to special order on bare chassis, Carlton, Duple, Mulliner, Ranalah and Bertelli, among them. It was already becoming apparent that most customers were demanding comfortable closed bodies. Correspondingly, the sporting note of early Speed Twenty advertising was damped down. In fact, all the bodies fitted to Speed Twenty were notably comfortable and roomy of their kind. Heavy bodies and heavy chassis meant that the Sports Tourer weighed 26 cwt., and the Drophead Coupé 3 cwt more.

In spite of this, the performance of the new car was

entirely out of the ordinary for its type. A 1933 Vanden Plas Sports Tourer would exceed 85 m.p.h. in top gear, though most would not quite touch the 90 m.p.h. claimed by their makers. It would also throttle down to 15–20 m.p.h. in the same gear. Top speed in third gear was between 60 and 70 m.p.h. The latter figure was regarded as the maximum sustained cruising speed. Forty m.p.h. was attainable in second gear. From rest, the Sports Tourer took about 14 seconds to reach 50 m.p.h., around 18 seconds to reach 60, and 25 seconds to reach 70. It would also return a fuel consumption of up to 18 m.p.g. overall, driven hard; the Drophead Coupé a little less.

With the Speed Twenty, Alvis had no competition among other 1932 models. The only opposition in its class for performance, refinement, quality and comfort came from the Talbot 105, the saloon model of which cost £895 and the tourer £835.

DEVELOPMENT OF THE SPEED TWENTY

The Speed Twenty was still a fast car, but from 1934 its makers' emphasis on comfort and convenience in fact grew, even though in that year their literature went so far as to call it a sports car. The models for 1934 incorporated two major and several minor changes. First, in the interests of passenger riding comfort, independent front suspension of the type that had been fitted to the Crested Eagle since its inception early in 1933 was introduced on its faster sister. Independent suspension was no novelty at Holyhead Road, for the production front-wheel-drive cars of 1928 had used a system of four quarter-elliptic springs with parallel link action at the front and swing axles with quarter-elliptics at the rear. However, the new type consisted of a single transverse leaf—the first example to appear on any British car—with wishbone linkages below. Alvis-designed front shock absorbers supplemented it. André Telecontrol shock absorbers, adjustable from the driver's seat were fitted at the rear. In fact this suspension did not fulfil its purpose of affording a softer ride, but it did improve roadholding and steering a little, at the cost of added weight. The

1935 Speed Twenty Charlesworth Drophead Coupé. (Photo: Guy Griffiths)

trackrod was moved back behind the sump.

Secondly, an all-synchromesh gearbox was fitted; the first to appear on a British car. It incorporated General Motors patents. Unit construction was abandoned—this gearbox was a separate entity. An inertia lock made premature meshing impossible, allowing a virtually 'unbeatable' change. The box was split on the horizontal centre line, permitting a centre bearing for the mainshaft and layshaft. This box was very expensive to make, but was a beautiful piece of mechanism, quiet and hard-wearing.

The valve springs were now of Alvis's own, peculiar design, intended to prevent valve bounce at high revolutions. They consisted of a cluster of tiny, multiple planetary springs to each valve. The frame was stiffened up by means of a cruciform central cross-member. DWS permanent hydraulic jacks were added. Finally, the mixture control by long linkages was done away with in favour of an easy-starting unit, which consisted of a small additional carburettor that was fitted to one of the existing instruments, usually that at the front. It was controlled from the dashboard by wire cable.

The chassis price remained at £600, with these refinements, and the cost of complete cars for 1934

Sporting breed: two Speed Twenty Tourers—1932/33 Vanden Plas (foreground) and another, possibly a modified 1932 car by Cross & Ellis—on the starting line in a 1949 Vintage Sports Car Club Silverstone speed trial. (Photo: Guy Griffiths)

actually went down. The standard bodies this year were the Cross & Ellis Tourer at £695, the Charlesworth Saloon at £825, and a Drophead Coupé by the same builders at the same price. For what was offered, in the way of quality, performance and amenities, there was nothing but the Talbot 105 (the saloon version of which now cost £795) to touch the Alvis Speed Twenty at its price. Bentley and Lagonda offered comparable machines for more or less the same market, but their saloons cost £1,460 and £895 respectively.

The added weight of their improvements persuaded Alvis to increase the power output of the Speed Twenty engine for 1935. This was done by lengthening the stroke to 110 mm., giving a capacity of 2,762 c.c. A fan was added. This engine, which was capable of higher r.p.m., was mounted at two points at the front instead of one as hitherto, a braced crossmember being added for the purpose. This allowed the trackrod to be brought forward to a more normal position in front of the sump, eliminating the two long draglinks on either side. André Telecontrol shock absorbers were now fitted at the front as well, replacing the Alvis instruments, which had tended to wear quickly. A further improvement was the substitution of a lighter, Borg & Beck clutch for the previous Alvis affair. Silencing was improved—the exhaust note of earlier Speed Twenties was a little too healthy for the more sedate owners who predominated. The accelerator pedal was moved from a central position between the clutch and brake to their right, as was normal, and the capacity of the fuel tank was increased to 16 gallons.

The Sports Tourer now weighed 27 cwt., and the Vanden Plas Sports Saloon no less than 31½ cwt. However, the latter's maximum speed was still in excess of 80 m.p.h. The chassis price was unaltered, but complete cars were a little more expensive, the Sports Tourer costing £700, and the Sports Saloon and Drophead Coupé £850.

Nineteen thirty-six was the last year of the Speed Twenty. The models for the new season were little changed, except for the provision of wider bodies, and

A 1932/33 Cross & Ellis two-seater, one of the most attractive models. (Photo: Guy Griffiths)

1936 3½-Litre sedanca by the Mayfair Carriage Co. (Photo: K. J. Jenner)

Bertelli-bodied 3½-Litre, powered by a 4·3-Litre engine, owned by H. Widengren, the racing driver. (Photo: William Boddy Collection)

1937 Speed Twenty-five Drophead Coupé by Charlesworth. (Photo: Guy Griffiths)

dual electric fuel pumps instead of the single mechanical instrument. Prices were unaltered.

Alvis themselves had ceased to race officially in 1930. The Speed Twenty in normal trim was hardly suitable for this type of exercise, but Charles Follett, and also C. G. H. Dunham, the Alvis dealer of Luton, competed energetically on Brooklands Motor Course. It is said that a special car was built for Follett for the 1932 Tourist Trophy, but was too late to enter. In early 1933 Sir Henry Birkin had another built for him to suit A.I.A.C.R. regulations, but he did not live to race it. After the war B. Chevell used a lowered, rebodied and mildly-tuned 2,511 c.c. Speed Twenty in club racing, later fitting it with a 4·3-Litre engine. It is now raced by A. Charnock in Vintage Sports Car Club events.

THE 3½-LITRE

Late in 1935, Alvis introduced a new car alongside the Speed Twenty, as an alternative that combined the performance of the earlier, lighter Speed Twenties with new standards of smoothness, quietness and comfort. The 3½-Litre was in fact a luxury car with sports-car speed and acceleration. It was greeted, in its turn, as the best Alvis yet made. The engine was basically the same as that of the Speed Twenty. Its bore was enlarged to 83 mm., giving a cubic capacity of 3,571 c.c. and a rating of 25·63 h.p. Light alloy pistons were used. A new, seven-bearing crankshaft with a vibration damper fitted at its front end gave smoother and more flexible running. The exhaust was quieter, and the carburettors were fitted with an air silencer. This engine produced 110 b.h.p. at 3,800 r.p.m. Maximum revolutions were 4,500 r.p.m. The gear ratios were slightly closer-spaced. There were two alternative sets of ratios: 4·11, 5·9, 8·34, and 12·95:1, or 4·33, 6·22, 8·79, and 13·65:1. The ride was softer, but there was no pitch or roll. The fuel tank was increased in capacity to 17 gallons. Specifications were otherwise similar to the 1936 Speed Twenty.

The wheelbase was lengthened to 10 ft. 7 in,. to accommodate the finely-appointed Saloon and Drophead Coupé bodies which were normal wear. The roof line of the saloon was 1 in. higher than of the Speed Twenty. The company sold only the bare chassis, at £775, but many bodybuilders designed coachwork specially for it. The Mulliner and Charlesworth Saloons cost £1,170, that by the Mayfair Carriage Company £1,175, and the Vanden Plas and Freestone & Webb Saloons £1,270. Vanden Plas and

1938 3½-Litre Saloon by Vanden Plas. (Photo: Anthony Pritchard)

1938 Speed Twenty-five Cross & Ellis tourer. (Photo: A. R. Buck)

132

1937 Speed Twenty-five Vanden Plas tourer with special 'Continental' body. (Photo: A. R. Beck)

Mystery car: possibly a 4·3-Litre, with special body. (Photo: R. Kirby)

1938 4·3-Litre short chassis drophead coupé by Whittingham & Mitchell. (Photo: K. Malcolm Hardy)

Mann Egerton Drophead Coupés were also available.

The Freestone & Webb Saloon weighed 35 cwt., but even so, the new car was a little faster than the Speed Twenty. Maximum speed in top was in excess of 90 m.p.h., and it could be throttled down to 5 m.p.h. in the same gear. Well over 60 m.p.h. was available in third, and nearly 50 m.p.h. in second. Acceleration figures for the saloon almost equalled those for the Speed Twenty Sports Tourer. From rest, the 3½-Litre took 14 seconds to reach 50 m.p.h., less than 21 seconds to 60 m.p.h., and about 28 seconds to 70 m.p.h. At 3,000 r.p.m. the cruising speed was between 70 and 75 m.p.h. At the same time, fuel consumption was no heavier.

THE SPEED TWENTY-FIVE

The 3½-Litre was so clear an improvement on the Speed Twenty that a replacement for the latter, developed from the former, was introduced in autumn 1936 for the 1937 season. While retaining the 3½-Litre's comfort and refinement of running, the new Speed Twenty-five offered still more performance, and kept the Speed Twenty's lowbuilt, dashing appearance, that had been lacking in the 3½-Litre, even though its roof line was no lower than on the last-named. Not surprisingly, the new Alvis was regarded as a still better car than any of its predecessors, and even today many people think that it was the finest to come from Holyhead Road before the war.

The engine of the 1937 model was generally the same

as that of the 3½-Litre, and the choice of gearbox and axle ratios was unchanged. Important chassis differences comprised the Speed Twenty's 10 ft. 4 in. wheelbase for all models, the addition of Dewandre vacuum servo assistance for the brakes—a much-needed innovation—and the substitution of Luvax finger-tip control shock absorbers for the André Telecontrol system. They had three positions: hard, normal and soft. The Speed Twenty-five handled perceptibly lighter than the Speed Twenty.

The bare chassis was the same price as that of the Speed Twenty: £600. The open Four Seater Sports model cost £700, and the four-door Saloon and Drophead Coupé £850 each. Offord and Lancefield were among bodybuilders who created coachwork to special order for the Speed Twenty-five at various times. For 1938, prices went up to £625, £735 and £885 respectively. The engine was given better exhaust extraction, and at the same time made quieter, by the provision of dual exhaust manifolds and pipes, each furnished with three silencers. The front of the chassis was boxed in and so stiffened up. The 1938 Saloon weighed a little over 36 cwt., but fuel consumption remained at 16–19 m.p.g. The Charlesworth Saloon was a very fast car indeed. It could exceed 95 m.p.h. in top gear. Speeds in the other gears were about the same as for the 3½-Litre, but acceleration was much better. It took a shade over 11 seconds to reach 50 m.p.h. from rest. To 60 m.p.h. the figure was 15 seconds, and to 70 m.p.h., just under 22 seconds.

The 1939 models included a new standard Saloon and Drophead Coupé without running boards. Prices were unchanged for that and the following season, but for 1940 engine location was made more positive by the addition of two tie rods to the frame at the rear of the power unit.

THE 4·3-LITRE

At the same time as the Speed Twenty-five made its bow, the 4·3-Litre was introduced. It was initially regarded as a replacement for the 3½-Litre. It was one of the fastest catalogued cars of its period, but lacked a little of the refinement and quietness of running of the Speed Twenty-five, and was thirstier. Neither was it quite so good-looking, for although the bonnet was 1 in. lower than that of the 3½-Litre, it was still higher than that of its companion model.

The cylinder bore was enlarged once again, to 92 mm., giving a cubic capacity of 4,397 c.c. and a Treasury rating of 31·48 h.p. This unit provided 123 b.h.p. at 3,600 r.p.m. Maximum revolutions were unchanged. The engine's other mechanical features were the same as for the Speed Twenty-five, except for the provision of dual coil ignition in place of the coil and magneto. The same choice of gearbox and axle ratios was available. There was only one chassis

C. G. H. Dunham's Speed Twenty leaves the line at Brooklands, 1935. (Photo: Sport and General Press Agency Ltd.)

Charles Follett's Speed Twenty at Brooklands. (Photo: Barratts Photo Press)

length to be had at first; the 10 ft. 7 in. of the $3\frac{1}{2}$-Litre. The steering was slightly higher geared, but otherwise the 4·3-Litre shared the improvements of the Speed Twenty-five, as to Dewandre vacuum servo assistance for the brakes and Luvax shock absorbers.

The chassis cost £750. For the first model year of 1937, the four-door Saloon by Charlesworth, cost £995 complete. The Mulliner Sports Saloon was priced at £1,145, and the Vanden Plas pillarless Saloon at £40 more. The Drophead Coupé cost £1,065. The very odd-looking 'O.F.' Enclosed Continental Tourer by Offord carried a price tag of £1,225. The $34\frac{1}{2}$-cwt. Charlesworth Saloon could just reach 100 m.p.h. Its acceleration figures were also truly outstanding—9 seconds from rest to 50 m.p.h., 13 seconds to 60 m.p.h., and 18 seconds to 70 m.p.h. Fuel consumption however, had now increased to between 15 and 16 m.p.g. Its nearest competitors might compare with the 4·3-Litre in speed, but not in price. The V12 Lagonda saloon cost £1,450, and the $4\frac{1}{4}$-Litre Bentley Saloon £1,510.

For 1938 the range was unaltered except for the deletion of the ill-advised 'O.F.' Tourer, and the addition of a new, even more shattering machine in the shape of the Vanden Plas Special Short Chassis Sports Tourer, at £995. It was made on a 10 ft. 4 in. wheelbase, which was also available with other bodies, and had higher, better-spaced gear ratios than the heavier cars: 3·82, 5·46, 7·75, and 12·02:1. (These ratios, too could be had with other coachwork.) In spite of a weight of $32\frac{1}{2}$ cwt., it was capable of a clear 103 m.p.h. in top gear, with 80 m.p.h. on third and 56 m.p.h. on second. Its acceleration figures were the best ever noted in the press for a catalogued car: 0–50 m.p.h. in 8·3 seconds, 0–60 in under 12 seconds, and 0–70 in a little over 16 seconds. A 1939 model improved further on these figures, returning 0–50 in 7·6 seconds, 0–60 in 11·3 seconds, 0–70 in a shade over 15 seconds, and 0–80 in 21 seconds, By this time, a 19-gallon fuel tank was fitted.

For 1940, the compression ratio of the 4·3-Litre was raised, and a further new model was offered: the Vanden Plas 'razor-edge' Saloon at £1,195. The other styles remained the same. Then war came, this line of splendid cars came to an end, and the Holyhead Road factory met the same fate at the hands of the Luftwaffe. The serial numbers not being consecutive, the total number made of these Alvises is not known.

© *T. R. Nicholson, 1966*
Post-War Special: A. S. R. Charnock's ex-Chevell car, with 4·3-Litre engine, at Prescott. (Photo: Guy Griffiths)

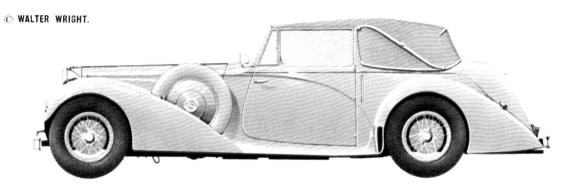

1940 ALVIS SPEED TWENTY-FIVE DROP-HEAD COUPE by Charlesworth. Owner: A. R. Buck, Esquire.

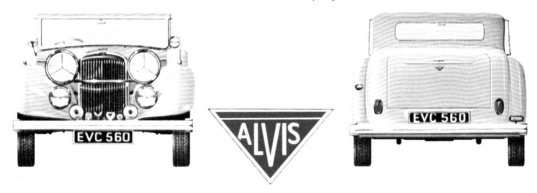

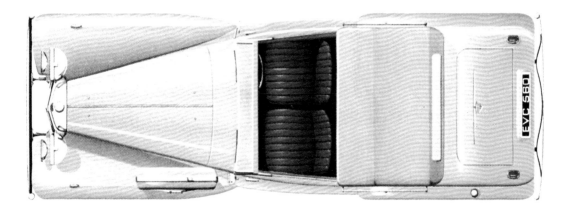

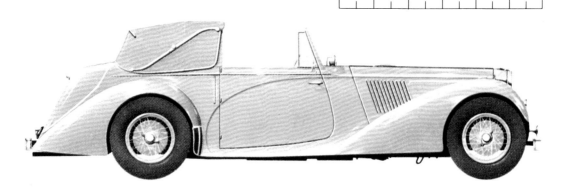

C. G. H. Dunham's Speed Twenty, with its later racing body, about to be overtaken by a Hotchkiss at Brooklands. (Photo: Planet News Ltd.)

SPECIFICATION SPEED TWENTY ALVIS

ENGINE
Six cylinders in line. Bore and stroke (1932–34)
73 × 100 mm., 2,511 c.c. Treasury rating 19·82 h.p. 1935–36:
73 × 110 mm., 2,762 c.c. Camshaft driven from rear of
engine, two overhead valves per cylinder actuated by
pushrods and rockers. Alvis patent multiple valve springs,
1934–36. Detachable head. Four-bearing crankshaft.
Engine rubber-mounted.
Ignition: BTH 12-volt. Combined coil and magneto unit.
Carburation Three SU carburettors. Mechanical fuel
pump (dual electric pumps 1936), 14½-gallon tank at rear
(16 gallons 1935–36).
Cooling: Pump. 1935–36: Pump and fan.
Claimed output: 87 b.h.p. at 4,200 r.p.m.

TRANSMISSION
Clutch: 1932–34: Alvis single dry-plate. 1935–36: Borg &
Beck.
Gearbox: 1932–33: Sliding pinion, in unit with engine.
Four speeds and reverse. Ratios 4.55:1, 6.42:1, 9.3:1, 14.3:1
or 4.77:1, 6.6:1, 10:1, 16.9:1. 1934–1936: All synchromesh,
separate.
Final drive: Fully-floating spiral bevel. Ratios 4.55:1 or
4.77:1.

CHASSIS
Frame: Channel section steel, dropped. 1934–36: cruci-
form central crossmember.
Wheelbase: 10 ft. 4 in. normal. 11 ft. wheelbase also
listed.
Track: 4 ft. 8 in.
Suspension: 1932–33: Half-elliptic (underslung at rear)
with Hartford friction shock absorbers. 1934–36: Inde-
pendent front suspension by single transverse leaf, half-
elliptic at rear. André Telecontrol shock absorbers at
rear. 1935–36: André Telecontrols at front and rear.
Brakes: Mechanical, 14 in. drums.
Lubrication: Luvax-Bijur one-shot chassis lubrication.
Wheels: 19 in.
Price: £600.
DWS permanent jacks 1934–36.

WEIGHT
Complete Vanden Plas Sports Tourer 1932: 26 cwt.
1935: 27 cwt.

SPECIFICATION 3½-LITRE ALVIS

Generally as for 1936 Speed Twenty, with the following
major differences:
ENGINE
Bore and stroke 83 × 100 mm., 3,571 c.c. Treasury

rating 25.63 h.p. Light alloy pistons. Seven-bearing
crankshaft with vibration damper. Fuel tank capacity 17
gallons. Claimed output 110 b.h.p. at 3,800 r.p.m.
TRANSMISSION
Gearbox: Ratios 4.11:1, 5.9:1, 8.34:1, 12.95:1 or 4.33:1,
6.22:1, 8.79:1, 13.65:1.
Final drive: 4.11:1 or 4.33:1.
CHASSIS
Wheelbase: 10 ft. 7 in.
Price: £775
WEIGHT
Complete Freestone & Webb Saloon 1936: 35 cwt.

SPECIFICATION SPEED TWENTY-FIVE ALVIS

Generally as for 3½-litre, with the following major differ-
ences:
ENGINE
1938–40: dual exhaust manifolds and pipes, each with
three silencers.
CHASSIS
Wheelbase: 10 ft. 4 in.
Suspension: Luvax fingertip-control shock absorbers.
Brakes: Dewandre vacuum servo assistance.
Price: 1937: £600. 1938–40: £625.
WEIGHT
Complete saloon 1938: 36¼ cwt.

SPECIFICATION 4.3-LITRE ALVIS

Generally as for Speed Twenty-five, with the following
major differences:
ENGINE
Bore and stroke 92 × 110 mm., 4,387 c.c. Treasury
rating 31.48 h.p. 1939–40: 19-gallon fuel tank. Dual
coil ignition. Claimed output 123 b.h.p. at 3,600 r.p.m.
TRANSMISSION
Gearbox: Ratios 1937: as for 3½-Litre and Speed Twenty-
five. 1938–40: additional option of 3.82:1, 5.46:1, 7.57:1,
12.02:1.
Final Drive: Ratios 1937: as for 3½-Litre and Speed Twenty-
five. 1938–40: additional option of 3.82:1.
CHASSIS
Wheelbase: 1937: 10 ft. 7 in.
          1938–40: 10 ft. 7 in. or 10 ft. 4 in.
Price: £750
WEIGHT
Complete 1937 Long Chassis Saloon 34½ cwt.
Complete 1938 Short Chassis Sports Tourer 32½ cwt.

The Ferrari Tipo 625 & 555

12

© GORDON DAVIES.

THE FERRARI TIPO 625, winner of
the 1955 European (Monaco) Grand
Prix at Monte Carlo. Average speed
65·80 m.p.h. for 195 miles (100 laps).
Driver: Maurice Trintignant.

The Ferrari Tipo 625 & 555

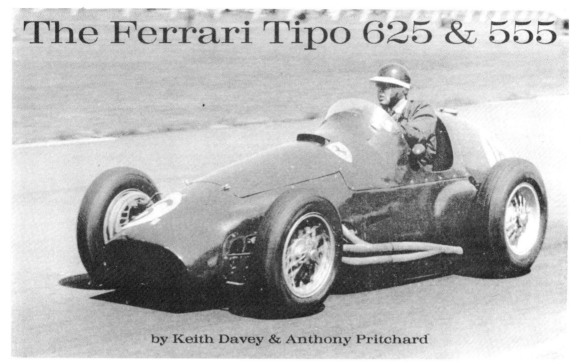

by Keith Davey & Anthony Pritchard

Hawthorn's 625 in the 1955 British Grand Prix at Aintree. (Photo: T. C. March)

By the beginning of 1954, after only five years' participation in Grand Prix racing, Ferrari was already the most prolific, successful and controversial of the ten or so racing car manufacturers building single-seaters at that time. After a determined start with the 1½-litre supercharged and 2-litre unsupercharged V-12 Formula One and Two cars, he had completely dominated Formula 2 racing since its inauguration in 1948 and had challenged and finally vanquished the seemingly invincible Alfa Romeo 158s with the 4½-litre Grand Prix car in 1951.

It was during 1950 that Ferrari first became aware of the effective use which the H.W.M. team were making of their rather under-powered 4-cylinder engines on the slower circuits, where their favourable torque characteristics meant that the Ferraris were being quite hard-pressed. This prompted Ferrari to commission a 4-cylinder Formula 2 engine for racing during 1952–53 and Lampredi had it ready by the Modena G.P. at the end of the 1951 season. Ascari showed the potential of the 4-cylinder car by winning the race by a wide margin from the V-12 2-litre car of Gonzalez. During the two years in which all major events were run to Formula 2 regulations, Ferrari's new cars were beaten only twice—at Rheims in 1952 by the very fast, but equally unreliable Gordini, and in the 1953 Italian G.P. by the A6SSG Maserati of Fangio.

Always looking to the future, however, Ferrari began development work on a 2½-litre car for the 1954 season. Two cars had already been built with V-12 engines, and took 2nd and 3rd places at Syracuse in 1951, but at Bari in the same year there had appeared a 4-cylinder car with a capacity of 2,490 c.c. (94 × 90 mm.), with which Taruffi took 3rd place. This car was not seen again until the Formule Libre Buenos Aires G.P. in 1953, when three were entered for Farina, Villoresi and Hawthorn, and took first three

places in that order. These three cars were virtually identical to the Tipo 625 raced the following year.

Also during 1953, groundwork was being done on what was to become the 555 Squalo of 1954, and prototypes for the 1954 season, designated the 553, appeared in 2-litre form at Monza for the Italian G.P. Because of their unsatisfactory handling, the two cars were relegated to the junior members of the team, Maglioli and Carini.

THE 625

The Tipo 625 was, therefore, a 4-cylinder design with a capacity of 2,490 c.c. (94 × 90 mm.). The light alloy block and crankcase were cast in one unit and the one-piece crankshaft ran in five Thinwall lead indium bearings. The cylinder head was also of light alloy and incorporated the water jackets with the steel cylinder liners screwed into recesses in the combustion chambers which obviated the need for a head gasket. There were two valves per cylinder inclined at an angle of 58 degrees and twin overhead camshafts driven by a train of gears from the nose of the crankshaft actuated the valves via two hair-pin springs with light alloy inverted tappets and double coil springs. The same train of gears drove the oil and water pumps and the twin Marelli magnetos. There were twin plugs per cylinder. Lubrication was on the dry sump principle with a 15-litre oil tank mounted in the tail behind the 38-gallon fuel tank. Twin fuel pumps were fitted, one belt-driven from the prop-shaft and the other on the end of a camshaft. The fuel used was a mixture of 40 per cent methyl alcohol, 30 per cent benzole and 30 per cent 100-octane petrol; to this was added an extra 1 per cent of castor oil. In its original 1954 form, the 625 or Tipo 'Argentina' developed 230 b.h.p. at 7,000 r.p.m., but the later version, as driven by Trintignant in the 1954 German G.P., with a 12·8 : 1 compression ratio and strengthened bottom

Gonzalez (foreground) on the starting grid at Silverstone for the 1954 Daily Express Trophy. The car is the 555 Squalo.
(Photo: T. C. March)

The winner at Barcelona in 1954—Hawthorn's 555 Squalo, fitted with coil spring front suspension. Note the litter collected in the air intake.
(Photo: G. Goddard)

end, developed the following outputs:

B.H.P.	R.P.M.
76·7	2,500
92·1	3,000
145·6	4,000
199·5	5,000
230·8	6,000
244·8	6,800

Transmission was by a multi-plate clutch to a 4-speed gearbox in unit with the rear axle; the driving plates of the clutch were of treated steel and the driven plates of hard aluminium. The gearbox was housed in a light alloy casing split vertically and the final drive incorporated a limited slip differential.

The chassis frame was of the ladder-type, comprising two oval-section tubular members with heavy-section cross-bracing at the front and rear, and light-section cross-bracing at the rear of the engine and in front of the gearbox unit. A tubular superstructure was built up round the cockpit to support the body panels and provide additional rigidity. Front suspension was by a low-mounted transverse leaf spring and double wishbones, the lower ones being connected directly to the spring. A de Dion axle was used at the rear with the tube passing behind the final drive casing and was located on each side by two parallel radius arms; a transverse leaf spring ran below the final drive unit. The steering was of the worm and wheel type and incorporated a two-piece steering column. Hydraulic two-leading shoe brakes were fitted to all four wheels; the shoes were of light alloy as were the finned drums which were 13·8 in. in diameter. 16 in. wheels were used all round, being 5 and 5½ in. wide front and rear.

THE 555 'SQUALO'

Although of very different appearance to the 625, the 'Squalo' was in essence purely a development of this model. The only substantial modifications made to the prototype 553 for the 2½-litre Formula were to increase the bore and stroke from 93 × 73·5 mm. to 100 × 79·5 mm., giving a capacity of 2,497·56 c.c. Just as on the 625 the twin overhead camshafts were driven by a train of gears from the nose of the crankshaft, but the two valves per cylinder were inclined at an included angle of 100 degrees. Generally, the design of the one-piece crankcase and block and cylinder head was similar to the 625, including the operation of the valves and the method of seating the cylinder liners. However, the crankshaft webbing was strengthened and the bearing area enlarged, as on the later versions of the 625. Two Weber type 52 DCOA carburettors were fitted, a type specially designed for this engine and, as on the 625, these were mounted on a framework welded to a longitudinal chassis tube with supplementary rubber mountings to reduce the effects of engine vibration. The power output of the engine on a 12 : 1 compression ratio was initially 250 b.h.p. at 7,500 r.p.m. Although it was a higher revving engine than the 625, piston speed was lower at 19·5 metres per second, compared with 21 m.p.s. for the 625. There were individual exhaust pipes for each cylinder, those from numbers one and four cylinders merging, as did those from the other two cylinders. These pipes joined into a single tail pipe running high up alongside the cockpit.

Hawthorn adjusts his goggles in the 1954 French Grand Prix.

The result of a major engine blow-up–Gonzalez at Rheims, 1954 French Grand Prix.

Transmission was as on the 625 by means of a 4-speed gearbox in unit with the rear axle, and driven through a multi-plate clutch. Drive from the gearbox was taken through a pair of spur gears to the differential. Drive to the wheels was by double universally-jointed half-shafts. Because of the use of side-mounted fuel tanks, there was only a small tank in the tail and this facilitated removal of the final drive, complete with casing, for axle ratio changes.

The chassis had a shorter wheelbase at 7 ft. 0 in. and both front (4 ft. 1 in.) and rear track (3 ft. 11½ in.) were narrower. The multi-tubular space frame tapered towards the rear and had a transverse tubular structure at the front on which the steering box was mounted and which located the front suspension. This was by unequal length wishbones with ball-joint attachment to the hubs and a transverse leaf spring attached to the lower wishbones. At the rear there was a de Dion axle with the tube, which ran in front of the final drive, located by a block sliding on a vertical guide. There were twin radius arms on each side and a transverse leaf spring running above the final drive unit. Houdaille shock-absorbers were again used all round.

Not only was it intended that the 555 engine should be considerably more robust than the 625, but the new car was also lower and, by the use of the side tanks, the better distribution of the fuel load should have improved the handling qualities. The appearance of the 555 led to it becoming known as the 'Squalo' or shark.

THE 1954 SEASON

For the first two races of the season, Ferrari used the 625 model. In the Argentine G.P. the team faced stiff opposition from the new Maserati 250F, also a derivative of the previous year's Formula 2 car. The early laps of the race were led by Gonzalez' Ferrari (running in Argentine colours) followed by the cars of Farina and Hawthorn; but then the first of several heavy showers fell, and after two laps Fangio's Maserati took the lead. When the rain stopped, Gonzalez and Farina overtook Fangio, but Hawthorn spun, was push-started by spectators and disqualified. When the rain again started to fall, Fangio regained the lead with the Maserati, only to stop to fit a set of rain tyres. According to Ugolini, the Ferrari team manager, five instead of the permitted three mechanics worked on the Maserati during the tyre change, so he lodged a protest, and on the assumption that it would be upheld slowed the Ferraris down. Fangio, however, regained the lead, the protest was rejected, and Farina and Gonzalez had to be content with 2nd and 3rd places, with the Ecurie Rosier entry of Trintignant 4th and Maglioli, who had never been in the running, 9th. The Ferraris should have scored an easy victory in the Formule Libre Buenos Aires G.P. after Fangio retired with axle trouble on the 9th lap. However, Farina retired, also with rear axle failure when in the lead, Hawthorn spun on the last lap when the engine seized as the result of a con-rod failure, and Trintignant found himself an unexpected winner. Farina, who had taken over from a rather sick Gonzalez, was 3rd, and Hawthorn was classified 6th.

First event of the European season was the Syracuse G.P., where the 555 made its debut. The race proved a disaster for Ferrari, as on the 5th lap, when Marimon's Maserati was leading Hawthorn and Gonzalez, the 250F driver hit a straw bale. A cloud of straw obscured Hawthorn's vision, and his 625 crashed into a wall and burst into flames. Hawthorn leaped out of his car and Gonzalez stopped to help him extinguish his clothing. The Squalo rolled forward and caught fire too; both cars were completely destroyed and Hawthorn received quite bad burns. After Marimon's retirement, the race was won by Farina with Trintignant, who had been invited to join the team after his South American success, 2nd.

There were four minor events before the first Grande Epreuve in Europe. At Pau, Gonzalez with a 625 was eliminated when in the lead; the crankshaft

Hawthorn, on his way to 2nd place in the 1954 British Grand Prix with a 625, leads Moss' 250F Maserati. (Photo: T. C. March)

Hawthorn's 625 in the pits at the 1954 German Grand Prix.
(Photo: Louis Klemantaski)

*Ascari's only drive for Ferrari in 1954—the Italian Grand Prix,
where he drove a 625 fitted with a 555 engine.*
(Photo: Keystone Press Agency Ltd.)

the wet at 82·79 m.p.h., while the winning time of Trintignant in his heat was 87·37 m.p.h. Between the heats and the final Gonzalez' car broke down, with the result that he took over Trintignant's car and his place on the front row of the grid. Trintignant in turn took over Maglioli's car. Not surprisingly, the Argentinian gained an easy win with the 625, but it was subsequently alleged that the switch was made simply to give Gonzalez a more favourable position on the grid, and that the 555, which was supposed to have seized up, was started up after the event. Final minor race before the Belgian event was the Bari G.P., where Gonzalez and Trintignant were 1st and 2nd with 625s and Maglioli 7th.

For the Belgian G.P. at Spa, two 555 Squalos were entered for Farina and Gonzalez, and Hawthorn and Trintignant drove 625s with 555 engines. Although Gonzalez and Farina were both placed on the front row of the starting grid, with Fangio's Maserati, Gonzalez retired at the end of the first lap with a broken oil pipe and Farina, having led for much of the way, was forced out on lap 14 by ignition trouble. This left Fangio with a considerable lead over Hawthorn and Trintignant in 2nd and 3rd places. Hawthorn then pulled into pits, unable to carry on because of exhaust fumes leaking into the cockpit, whereupon the car was taken over by Gonzalez. Trintignant finally finished 2nd, about 20 sec. behind Fangio, and Gonzalez did well to bring Hawthorn's car up into 4th place.

It was at Rheims that the Mercedes-Benz team re-entered Grand Prix racing and it was obvious that the Ferraris were going to have a very difficult time. Fangio and Kling were the fastest two in practice and Gonzalez (555) and Trintignant (625 with 555 engine) were over 6 sec. slower than Fangio's Mercedes and were placed on the third and fourth rows of the grid respectively. Despite the fact that Gonzalez fully extended the Ferrari in the first few laps, he soon dropped back and the engine finally blew up in a most spectacular manner. The Ferraris of Hawthorn and Trintignant suffered a similar fate and only Manzon with a privately entered 625 managed to finish the race, in a very creditable 3rd place, but well over a lap behind the two Mercedes-Benz.

Before the next Grande Epreuve, Trintignant took a comparatively easy 1st place in the Rouen G.P. with a 625 against Gordini and private Maserati

broke when the car was travelling at high speed, and he only managed to control it with great difficulty. As Farina was slowed by a misfire in the early stages of the race and a pit stop for a wheel change after contact with Marimon's Maserati dropped him to the tail of the field, a surprise win was gained by Behra's Gordini from Trintignant. The more usual Ferrari state of affairs reasserted itself at Bordeaux, where the cars of Gonzalez, Manzon and Trintignant took first three places. The 555 reappeared in the *Daily Express* Trophy at Silverstone. The race was run in two heats and a final, and Gonzalez won his heat in

Herrmann's " Stromlinien-wagen" Mercedes leads Hawthorn in the 1954 German Grand Prix. (Photo: Louis Klemantaski)

The 1954 Squalo Grand Prix car. Note the side-mounted fuel tanks. (Photo: Denis Jenkinson)

opposition. Hawthorn broke a con-rod near the end of the race and was disqualified for receiving a push towards the finish from his team-mate. Trintignant's car was a normal 625, but Hawthorn drove a 625 with an engine which was half 625 and half 555. The bottom end of the 625, which had proved more reliable, was combined with the Squalo cylinder head, which was potentially a more powerful design.

The next clash of the Ferrari and Mercedes teams was in the British G.P. at Silverstone. This comparatively slow circuit was well suited to the torque characteristics of the 4-cylinder Ferrari engines, and as the rather featureless corners made it difficult to line up the fully streamlined German cars, the two teams were now much more closely matched. All the Ferraris were 625s with engines like that first tried at Rouen. On this occasion, despite having the services of Ascari and Villoresi, the works Maseratis were not really in the running, and in any case arrived too late for official practice. The fastest in practice were:

1. FANGIO	1 min. 45 sec. (at the expense of damaged bodywork).
2. GONZALEZ	1 min. 46 sec.
3. HAWTHORN	1 min. 46 sec.
4. Moss (Maserati)	1 min. 47 sec. (private entry).
5. BEHRA (Gordini)	1 min. 48 sec.
6. KLING	1 min. 48 sec.
7. SALVADORI (Maserati)	1 min. 48 sec. (private entry).
8. TRINTIGNANT	1 min. 48 sec.

Gonzalez took the lead at the start and was unchallenged throughout the race. At the beginning, Fangio's Mercedes was in 2nd place, but he was having a difficult race, taking to the grass on innumerable occasions, and was overtaken by both Moss and Hawthorn. When Moss retired with rear axle failure, Hawthorn took 2nd place ahead of the ailing Mercedes. Trintignant finished 5th.

After a win by Trintignant against private owners in the Caen G.P., four 625s were entered in the European G.P. at the Nurburgring. Two were standard 625s for Trintignant and Taruffi, but Gonzalez and Hawthorn drove 625s with engines based on the crankcase of the 735 sports model and the 555 cylinder head. Mercedes fielded four cars, three of which had new bodywork with exposed wheels. The Maserati team, shattered by Marimon's fatal crash in practice, were withdrawn. Fangio took the lead at the start from Gonzalez, but the latter, upset over Marimon's death, gradually fell back and on the 16th lap handed over his car to Hawthorn, who had retired with engine trouble. After Kling's stop for attention to the rear suspension, Hawthorn took 2nd place with Trintignant 3rd and Taruffi 6th.

Four cars were fielded in the Swiss G.P., 625s with 735/555 engines for Gonzalez, Hawthorn and Trintignant and an ordinary 555 for Maglioli. Gonzalez was fastest in practice, but once again the Mercedes, aided by their very low bottom gear, took the lead at the start, Kling heading Fangio. Kling, however, spun off on lap one, giving Gonzalez a 2nd place which he retained at the finish. Maglioli was classified 7th out of 8 finishers.

By now, Ferrari was getting quite desperate. In 1953 he had won all but one Grande Epreuve entered. So far, in 1954, he had only won one out of six entered. In an effort to achieve more satisfactory results, five very varied cars were entered in the Italian G.P. at Monza. As the D.50 Lancia was still not raceworthy, he managed to secure for this race the services of his former champion driver, Alberto Ascari, who had been loaned to Maserati for most of the season. Gonzalez drove a 555, Ascari a 625 with a 555 engine. Hawthorn and Trintignant drove 625s with the 625/555 engine and Maglioli a normal 625. Ascari led the race for a considerable distance, but retired with a broken valve, but Hawthorn finished 2nd and Gonzalez, who had retired, took over Maglioli's car, worked it up to 3rd place and then handed it back to the 'owner'. Trintignant was 5th.

Final event of the season was the Spanish G.P., where only two cars were entered. Hawthorn drove into 1st place a 555, now fitted with front suspension by coil springs and an anti-roll bar. Trintignant retired his 625 with a 555 engine because of gearbox trouble. Hawthorn's victory, although well-deserved, was due largely to the early demise of the new Lancias and the poor performance of Fangio's Mercedes, slowed by engine trouble. Nearly all the cars in this race suffered overheating as a result of the air intakes collecting litter thrown down by the spectators.

1954 had not proved as gratifying a season as Ferrari's past experience with the 4-cylinder cars led him to expect. Nevertheless Gonzalez took 2nd place in the Driver's World Championship with 25¼ points to Fangio's 42.

MODIFICATIONS FOR THE 1955 SEASON

625

A 5-speed gearbox and the 555 engine were used in the main in 1955. The suspension was modified by

Double wishbone and coil spring front suspension of the 1955 625.

Cockpit shot of the 1954 625. (Photo: Louis Klemantaski)

fitting coil springs at the front as used on the Squalo at Barcelona and by transferring the transverse leaf from below to above the final drive. The body was re-styled, so as to give the car a lower nose and slightly more aerodynamic lines.

555

These were much improved and were henceforth known as Super Squalos. A new multi-tubular space frame was used with cross-bracing and a tubular superstructure, locating the rear suspension and providing mountings for the body and fuel tanks. A larger fuel tank was fitted in the tail. Generally the lines of the car were sleeker, the air intake lower and wider.

THE 1955 SEASON

For the Argentine races, Ferrari entered a team of the improved 625s driven by Gonzalez, Farina and Trintignant with Maglioli as spare driver. The race was notable for the tremendous heat which overcame everybody except Fangio, who won with his Mercedes, and Mières. Gonzalez made fastest time in practice and held 2nd place until just after the first hour, when

he was overcome by the heat. This car was subsequently driven by both Farina and Trintignant, and took 2nd place, while Farina's car (shared also by Gonzalez and Maglioli) was 3rd. The same cars ran in the Buenos Aires G.P., but had 3-litre sports engines. Of five cars entered, only Trintignant achieved a respectable placing—3rd. Two similar cars with 3-litre engines had been supplied to Peter Whitehead and Tony Gaze to drive in the New Zealand G.P. also held in January, and they took 2nd and 3rd places to Bira's Maserati.

Turin was a Lancia benefit and of three 625s entered, the sole finisher was Schell in 5th place. First race appearance of the Super Squalo was at Bordeaux. Two cars were entered for Farina and Trintignant, but they retired with gearbox and brake trouble respectively.

The first European Grande Epreuve was at Monaco, where Farina and Trintignant drove 625s and Schell and Taruffi 555s. The Ferraris were completely outclassed, but after the retirement of Moss and Fangio (Mercedes), and Ascari's Lancia had crashed into the harbour after a brake had locked, Trintignant found himself in the lead, and won, with Farina, who had made a long pit stop to sort out dented bodywork, 4th. Frère took over Taruffi's car and finished 8th, 14 laps in arrears.

The Belgian G.P. saw only 555s entered. Not unexpectedly, Fangio and Moss took first two places, but Farina, Frère and Trintignant were 3rd, 4th and

Induction side of the 1954 625 engine. (Photo: Louis Klemantaski)

The 1955 625.

5th. Zandvoort has never seemed a circuit suiting Ferraris, and all three Super Squalos entered were slow. Highest finisher was Castellotti, who had joined the team after Lancia's withdrawal from racing, in 5th place. Hawthorn, who had rejoined the team after a short spell with Vanwall, was 7th after transmission trouble.

Because of the Le Mans disaster, the French, German, Swiss and Spanish events were cancelled. There remained, therefore, only two Grandes Epreuves. In the British event at Aintree, Ferrari fielded the 625s on their last works appearance, but they were so outclassed that the fastest, Castellotti, was on the fourth row of the grid. Only one car finished, that of Hawthorn in 6th place, which he handed over to Castellotti as he was feeling unwell. By the Italian G.P., Ferrari had received the V-8 cars from Lancia who had given up racing after Ascari's death. However, the cars were throwing tyre treads in practice, so the 555s which were to supplement them were run instead. They now had 5-speed gearboxes, and minor suspension modifications. As a result they handled much better than many of their rivals on the bumpy Monza concrete, and Castellotti, whose time with a Lancia had put him on the second row of the grid, finished 3rd. Magioli and Trintignant were 6th and 8th.

POSTSCRIPT

Although this race marked the effective conclusion of the racing careers of both the 625 and 555, in the 1956 Argentine G.P. Olivier Gendebien drove into 5th place a Super Squalo fitted with a Lancia V-8 engine. This handled very badly, and the experiment was not continued further. A sole example has survived. This is said to be the car which won the 1955 Monaco race and is now owned by Ian Sievwright. Although a 1955 625, it has a 4-speed gearbox and an ordinary 625 engine. Furthermore, it has no chassis number.

© Keith Davey and Anthony Pritchard, 1966

An unsuccessful experiment—the Super Squalo with a Lancia V-8 engine, which was driven by Gendebien in the 1956 Argentine Grand Prix.

Farina with Super Squalo at Spa, 1955. (Photo: Louis Klemantaski).

625 ENGINE PERFORMANCE AND MODEL IDENTIFICATION

Power at r.p.m.		Design Features
230	7000	Two twin-choke Weber 50 DCO carburetters; C.R. 11:1. As raced in the Argentine, 1954.
250	7500	Two twin-choke Weber 50 DCOA3 carburetters; C.R. 12:1 A revised version with 555 engine which first appeared at Spa, 1954.
250	7500	Two twin-choke Weber 50 DCOA3 carburetters; C.R. 12:1. A revised version incorporating the bore and stroke of the 555 with the crankcase of the 625 which first appeared at Rouen, 1954.
250	7500	Two twin-choke Weber 50 DCOA3 carburetters; C.R. 12:1. A further revised version using the crankcase of the 735 sports model and 555 cylinder head. First appeared at Nurburgring, 1954.
250	7500	Two Weber twin-choke 52 DCOA3 carburetters; C.R. 12.8:1. 1955 version with double wishbone and coil spring front suspension and leaf spring mounted above instead of below final drive unit; 5-speed gearbox and restyled body.

SPECIFICATION (1955 MODEL):

ENGINE:
Capacity: 2490 c.c. (94 × 90 mm.) *No. of cylinders:* 4 in line. *Valves:* two per cylinder inclined at an included angle of 58 degrees. *Valve actuation:* twin overhead camshafts. *Ignition:* twin Marelli magnetos and twin plugs per cylinder. *Lubrication:* dry sump.

TRANSMISSION:
Clutch: multi-plate type. *Gearbox:* 4 or 5-speed in unit with rear axle; normal ratios for 4-speed box, 1st, 2.338:1, 2nd, 1.455:1, 3rd, 1.135:1 and top, 1:1. *Final Drive:* direct drive from gearbox main and lay shafts and incorporating ZF limited slip differential.

CHASSIS:
Frame: tubular ladder-type with cross-bracing and light tubular superstructure. *Front Suspension:* double wishbones, coil springs, anti-roll bar and Houdaille dampers. *Rear Suspension:* de Dion axle, twin parallel radius arms, lateral leaf spring and Houdaille dampers. *Steering:* worm and wheel, turning circle approx. 33 ft. *Brakes:* hydraulic two-leading shoe, with light alloy shoes and 13.8 in. finned light alloy drums. *Wheel Size:* front: 5.00 x 16, rear: 5.50 x 16. *Tyre Size:* front: 5.50 x 16, rear: 7.00 x 16. *Fuel Capacity:* 38 gallons, tank in tail. *Oil Capacity:* 15 litres. *Exhaust System:* four single pipes emerging low down on left-hand side and merging into twin tail pipes.

DIMENSIONS:
Wheelbase: 7 ft. 2½ in. Front track 4 ft. 3½ in. Rear Track: 4 ft. 1 in. *Dry Weight:* 12½ cwt.

555 ENGINE PERFORMANCE AND MODEL IDENTIFICATION

Power at r.p.m.		Design Features
250	7500	The standard 1954 model which first appeared in tests at Monza in late 1953.

250	7500	A revised version with stronger connecting rods, modified valves and coil spring front suspension which appeared at the 1954 Spanish G.P.
270	7500	A further revised version, the Super Squalo, with new chassis frame, larger rear fuel tanks and modified body which appeared in 1955.
270	7500	Version modified by Massimino, with 5-speed gearbox and detail changes to the chassis which ran in the 1955 Italian G.P.
260	8000	Super Squalo fitted with Lancia V-8 engine which ran in the 1956 Argentine G.P.

The last of the four-cylinder Ferrari racing cars—Hawthorn with the Massimino-modified 555 Super Squalo in the 1955 Italian Grand Prix. (Photo: Motor Sport)

SPECIFICATION (1954 MODEL):

ENGINE:
Capacity: 2497·56 c.c. (100 × 79·5 mm.) *No of Cylinders:* 4 in line. *Valves:* two per cylinder inclined at an included angle of 100 degrees. *Valve actuation:* twin overhead camshafts. *Ignition:* twin Marelli magnetos and twin plugs per cylinder. *Carburetters:* two twin-choke Weber 52 DCOA. *Compression ratio:* 12:1. *Lubrication:* dry sump.

TRANSMISSION:
Clutch: multi-plate type. *Gearbox:* 4-speed in unit with the rear axle. *Final Drive:* through spur gears to crown wheel and pinion; drive to the wheels by double universally jointed half-shafts.

CHASSIS:
Frame: multi-tubular space frame with transverse tubular structure at the front. *Front suspension:* double wishbones, transverse leaf spring and Houdaille dampers. *Rear suspension:* de Dion axle, twin radius arms, transverse leaf spring and Houdaille dampers. *Steering:* worm and wheel. *Fuel tanks:* linked side tanks and small tank in tail. *Exhaust system:* four separate pipes merging into two pipes and then into a single tail pipe.

DIMENSIONS:
Wheelbase: 7 ft. 0 in. Front track 4 ft. 1 in. Rear track 3 ft. 11½ in.

RESULTS
1954

Argentine G.P. Buenos Aires Autodrome 17th January 3 hours GRANDE EPREUVE	2nd G. FARINA 625	3rd F. GONZALEZ 625	4th M. TRINTIGNANT 625 (Ecurie Rosier Entry)	9th U. MAGLIOLI 625
	Retired—M. Hawthorn, 625, spun off and disqualified for receiving push start from spectators.			
Buenos Aires City G.P. Buenos Aires Autodrome 31st January 175 miles FORMULE LIBRE	1st M. TRINTIGNANT 625 (Ecurie Rosier Entry) 8th U. MAGLIOLI 625	3rd GONZALEZ/FARINA 625	6th M. HAWTHORN 625	
	Retired—G. Farina, 625, rear axle failure, but took over from Gonzalez who was unwell.			
Syracuse G.P. Syracuse 11th April 268 miles	1st G. FARINA 625 95·32 m.p.h.	2nd M. TRINTIGNANT 625		
	Retired—M. Hawthorn, 625, crash; F. Gonzalez, 555, car burnt out.			
Pau G.P. Pau 19th April 193 miles	2nd M. TRINTIGNANT 625	5th G. FARINA 625	6th L. ROSIER 625 (Ecurie Rosier Entry)	
	Retired—F. Gonzalez, 625, broken c. ankshaft.			
Bordeaux G.P. Bordeaux 9th May 188 miles	1st F. GONZALEZ 625 60·59 m.p.h.	2nd R. MANZON 625 (private entry)	3rd M. TRINTIGNANT 625	
Daily Express Trophy Silverstone 15th May 102 miles	Heat I 1st F. GONZALEZ 555 Heat 2 1st M. TRINTIGNANT 625 Final I 1st F. GONZALEZ 92·78 m.p.h.	4th U. MAGLIOLI 625 2nd R. PARNELL 625 (private entry) 5th M. TRINTIGNANT	9th L. ROSIER 625 (Ecurie Rosier Entry) 3rd R. MANZON 625 (private entry) 6th L. ROSIER	
	Note: Gonzalez' car seized up between heat and final and he took over Trintignant's car. Retired in the final—Manzon, transmission failure; Parnell, broken prop-shaft.			
Bari G.P. Bari 23rd May 207 miles	1st F. GONZALEZ 625 85·08 m.p.h.	2nd M. TRINTIGNANT 625	7th U. MAGLIOLI 625	
Belgian G.P. Spa 20th June 315 miles GRANDE EPREUVE	2nd M. TRINTIGNANT 625 with 555 engine	4th HAWTHORN/GONZALEZ 625 with 555 engine		
	Retired—Gonzalez, 555, engine failure; Farina, 555, engine failure; J. Swaters, 625 (Ecurie Francorchamps entry), engine failure.			
French G.P. Rheims 4th July 315 miles GRANDE EPREUVE	3rd R. MANZON 625 (private entry)			
	Retired—Hawthorn, 555, engine failure; Gonzalez, 555, engine failure; Trintignant, 625 with 555 engine, engine failure; Rosier, 625, engine failure.			

THE FERRARI TIPO 555, winner of the 1954 Spanish Grand Prix at Pedralbes, Barcelona. Average speed 97·99 m.p.h. for 314 miles (80 laps). Driver: John Michael Hawthorn.

Rouen G.P. Rouen-les-Essarts 11th July 301 miles	1st M. TRINTIGNANT 625 81·87 m.p.h. Retired—Hawthorn, 625 with 625/555 engine, broken connecting rod, disqualified after receiving push from Trintignant.		
British G.P. Silverstone 17th July 263 miles GRANDE EPREUVE	1st F. GONZALEZ All cars 625s with 625/555 engines 89·69 m.p.h. Retired—Rosier, 625 (Ecurie Rosier entry), broken valve; Manzon, 625 (private entry), cracked cylinder head; Parnell, 625 (private entry), engine failure.	2nd M. HAWTHORN	5th M. TRINTIGNANT
Caen G.P. La Prairie 25th July 131 miles	1st M. TRINTIGNANT 625 88·50 m.p.h.		
European G.P. Nurburgring 1st August 312 miles GRANDE EPREUVE	2nd GONZALEZ/HAWTHORN 625 with 555/735 engine 7th L. ROSIER 625 (Ecurie Rosier entry) Retired—Hawthorn, 625 with 555/735 engine, rear axle failure.	3rd M. TRINTIGNANT 625 8th R. MANZON 625 (private entry)	6th P. TARUFFI 625
Swiss G.P. Bremgarten 22nd August 299 miles GRANDE EPREUVE	2nd F. GONZALEZ 625 with 555/735 engine Retired—Hawthorn, 625 with 555/735 engine, oil pump failure; Trintignant, 625 with 555/735 engine, engine failure.	7th U. MAGLIOLI 555	8th J. SWATERS 625 (Ecurie Francorchamps entry)
Italian G.P. Monza 5th September 313 miles GRANDE EPREUVE	2nd M. HAWTHORN 625 with 555/625 engine Retired—Gonzalez, 555, gearbox oil seal failure; Ascari, 625 with 555 engine, broken valve; Manzon, 625 (private entry), engine failure.	3rd MAGLIOLI/GONZALEZ 625	5th M. TRINTIGNANT 625 with 555/625 engine
Spanish G.P. Pedralbes 24th October 314 miles GRANDE EPREUVE	1st M. HAWTHORN 555 with coil spring front suspension Retired—Trintignant, 625 with 555 engine, engine failure; Manzon, 625 (private entry), engine failure; Swaters (Ecurie Francorchamps entry), engine failure.		
1955 Argentine G.P. Buenos Aires Autodrome 16th January 3 hours GRANDE EPREUVE	2nd GONZALEZ/FARINA/TRINTIGNANT 625 with 555 engine Retired—Trintignant, 625 with 555 engine, engine failure.	3rd FARINA/MAGLIOLI/TRINTIGNANT 625 with 555 engine	
Buenos Aires City G.P. Buenos Aires Autodrome 30th January 175 miles FORMULE LIBRE	Heat 1 1st G. FARINA 625 with 3-litre engine Heat 2 3rd M. TRINTIGNANT (all 625s with 3-litre engines) Final 3rd M. TRINTIGNANT Retired—Farina, after collision with Birger's Gordini.	6th C.BUCCI 9th C. BUCCI	5th F. GONZALEZ 625 with 3-litre engine 7th U. MAGLIOLI 10th F. GONZALEZ 11th U. MAGLIOLI
Circuit of Turin Valentino 27th March 235 miles	5th H. SCHELL 625 Retired—Farina, 625, gearbox trouble; Trintignant, 625, engine trouble.		
Bordeaux G.P. Bordeaux 24th April 188 miles	Retired— Farina, 555 Super Squalo, gearbox trouble; Trintignant, 555 Super Squalo, brake trouble; de Portago, 625 (works-supported private entry), overheating.		
European G.P. Monte Carlo 22nd May 195 miles	1st M.TRINTIGNANT 625 65·19 m.p.h. Retired—H. Schell, 555 Super Squalo, broken piston.	4th G. FARINA 625	8th P. TARUFFI/P. FRÈRE 555 Super Squalo
Belgian G.P. Spa 5th June 315	3rd G. FARINA 555 S/S	4th P. FRÈRE 555 S/S	6th M. TRINTIGNANT 555 S/S
Dutch G.P. Zandvoort 19th June 260 miles	5th E. CASTELLOTTI 555 S/S Retired—Trintignant, 555 Super Squalo, gearbox trouble.	7th M. HAWTHORN 555 S/S	11th J. CLAES 625 (Ecurie Francorchamps entry)
British G.P. Aintree 16th July 270 miles	6th HAWTHORN/CASTELLOTTI 625 Retired—Trintignant, 625, engine failure; Castellotti, 625, rear axle failure.		
Italian G.P. Monza 11th September 311 miles	3rd E. CASTELLOTTI All with improved 555 Super Squalos. Retired—Hawthorn, improved 555 S/S, gearbox trouble.	6th U. MAGLIOLI	8th M. TRINTIGNANT

148